MAN IN HIS TIME

Man lives in the allotted span of his present, past and future life. He who was before him and will be after him, and who therefore fixes the boundaries of his being, is the eternal God, his Creator and Covenant-partner. He is the hope in which man may live in his time.

1. JESUS, LORD OF TIME

Man lives in his time. This simple statement denotes the second circle of problems to which we must now turn in our investigation of the constitution of human existence. We first described this constitution by saying that man is the soul of his body as established by God, namely, by the Spirit of God. He is "soul and body totally and simultaneously, in indissoluble differentiation, inseparable unity and indestructible order."

He lives as the soul of his body. But all along, though we have not yet stated it explicitly, this presupposes that he is temporal. If he lives at all, he lives in his time. His life is a series of the acts of his own movement, enterprise and activity. The fact that this is possible both as a whole and in detail presumes that man has the necessary time to accomplish these acts, i.e., that he is in a position to move in a definite way from his own past through his own present to his own future; to be engaged in the fulfilment of these acts and therefore in change, and yet always to retain his own individual identity. Yet this is not self-evident. It is perfectly possible that there should be no road leading from the past through the present to the future. In this case there would either be no acts and no change, or their fulfilment would necessarily entail the loss of individual identity. But on these terms human life would be quite impossible. If man had no time, if his existence were timeless, he would have no life. Of course, time is not an exhaustive basis of his life. This consists in the fact that it is given him by the Spirit of God to be the soul of his body. But time is the *conditio sine qua non*[EN1] of his life. If he is to fulfil his being and nature as the soul of his body, he cannot do without time. He must acquire time and possess it. Even the eternal God does not live without time. He is supremely temporal. For His eternity is authentic temporality, and therefore the source of all time. But in His eternity, in the uncreated self-subsistent time which is one of the perfections of His divine nature, present, past and future, yesterday, to-day and

---

[EN1] necessary condition

[438] to-morrow, are not successive, but simultaneous. It is in this way, in this eternity of His, that God lives to the extent that He lives His own life. But man, who is not God, who is a creature and not the Creator, cannot live like this. If he is to live at all, he needs an inauthentic temporality distinct from eternity. He needs the time created by God, in which past, present and future follow one another in succession, in which he can move from his past through his present to his future, in which these three elements, corresponding to his life-act as a whole and in detail, form a sequence. We speak of "created time," but it would be more accurate to say "co-created." For time is not a something, a creature with other creatures, but a form of all the reality distinct from God, posited with it, and therefore a real form of its being and nature.

When God began to create heaven and earth—according to the first creation-saga of Genesis—then, long before there were any living beings, when this primal history before all history began, time also began. There was a first week culminating in a Sabbath. This was not only the day when God rested, but the first day in the life of the first man. If the created world were also eternal, it would in fact be a second god. And in that case it would not be a suitable field for the free, creative acts of God or the corresponding movements of His creatures. Time is the form of the created world by which the world is ordained to be the field for the acts of God and for the corresponding reactions of His creatures, or, in more general terms, for creaturely life.

Man lives as he has time and is in his time. It is his time to the extent that it is not God's eternity, not the simultaneity of present, past and future, but their succession. And it is his time to the extent that it is given him in a fixed span when he is created the soul of his body to live before God. It is for the sake of this life willed by God, and as its form, that he has time. He has it, therefore, as his lifetime; as the time for each of his individual life-acts and for their connected sequence, his total lifetime. He has no more and no less time than this, and no different time. He is in this time, and this time alone. The constitution of man's being as the soul of his body presupposes his temporality. We must now ask and state what is meant by this form.

Both question and answer must again be those of a theological anthropology. The man whose temporality is the subject of our investigation is the creature whose relation to God is revealed to us in His Word, and whose being is both the history in which, elected and called by God, he is engaged in responsibility before Him, and also a corresponding being in encounter with his fellow-men. When we speak of man in his time we are speaking of the life of this creature and of the presupposition of the constitution of this creature. Human life takes place in the reciprocal relation between God and man on the one hand, and man and his fellow-men on the other. We have no knowledge of what life means generally or apart from this, as the life of plants and animals. We can speak of this only loosely and hypothetically. But we do know what human life means; that it takes place in this twofold relation. We know this [439] because it is revealed to us in the Word of God. And in this knowledge we shall here concern ourselves with man, and therefore with his temporality. Man

2

CHURCH DOGMATICS

For further resources, including the forewords to the original 14-volume edition of the *Church Dogmatics*, log on to our website and sign up for the resources webpage:
http://www.continuumbooks.com/dogmatics/

KARL BARTH
CHURCH DOGMATICS

VOLUME III

THE DOCTRINE
OF CREATION

§ 47

THE CREATURE III

EDITED BY
G. W. BROMILEY
T. F. TORRANCE

t & t clark

Published by T&T Clark

A Continuum Imprint

The Tower Building, 11 York Road, London, SE1 7NX
80 Maiden Lane, Suite 704, New York, NY 10038

www.continuumbooks.com

Translated by G. W. Bromiley, J. W. Edwards, O. Bussey, Harold Knight, J. K. S. Reid, R. H. Fuller,
R. J. Ehrlich, A. T. Mackey, T. H. L. Parker, H. A. Kennedy, J. Marks

British Library Cataloguing-in-Publication Data
A catalogue record for this book is available from the British Library

ISBN13: 978-0-567-53534-4

Typeset by Interactive Sciences Ltd, Gloucester, and Newgen Imaging Systems Pvt Ltd, Chennai
Printed and bound in Great Britain by CPI Antony Rowe, Chippenham, Wiltshire

PUBLISHER'S PREFACE TO THE STUDY EDITION

Since the publication of the first English translation of *Church Dogmatics I.1* by Professor Thomson in 1936, T&T Clark has been closely linked with Karl Barth. An authorised translation of the whole of the *Kirchliche Dogmatik* was begun in the 1950s under the editorship of G. W. Bromiley and T. F. Torrance, a work which eventually replaced Professor Thomson's initial translation of *CD I.1*.

T&T Clark is now happy to present to the academic community this new *Study Edition* of the *Church Dogmatics*. Its aim is mainly to make this major work available to a generation of students and scholars with less familiarity with Latin, Greek, and French. For the first time this edition therefore presents the classic text of the translation edited by G. W. Bromiley and T. F. Torrance incorporating translations of the foreign language passages in Editorial Notes on each page.

The main body of the text remains unchanged. Only minor corrections with regard to grammar or spelling have been introduced. The text is presented in a new reader friendly format. We hope that the breakdown of the *Church Dogmatics* into 31 shorter fascicles will make this edition easier to use than its predecessors.

Completely new indexes of names, subjects and scriptural indexes have been created for the individual volumes of the *Study Edition*.

The publishers would like to thank the Center for Barth Studies at Princeton Theological Seminary for supplying a digital edition of the text of the *Church Dogmatics* and translations of the Greek and Latin quotations in the original T&T Clark edition made by Simon Gathercole and Ian McFarland.

London, April 2010

HOW TO USE THIS
STUDY EDITION

The *Study Edition* follows Barth's original volume structure. Individual paragraphs and sections should be easy to locate. A synopsis of the old and new edition can be found on the back cover of each fascicle.

All secondary literature on the *Church Dogmatics* currently refers to the classic 14-volume set (e.g. II.2 p. 520). In order to avoid confusion, we recommend that this practice should be kept for references to this *Study Edition*. The page numbers of the old edition can be found in the margins of this edition.

CONTENTS

§ 47

needs time, and acquires and possesses it, to live in this twofold relation. What interests us here is that his being is a being in time. It is obvious that the problem of time, too, is a problem of all anthropology. We cannot, therefore, ignore the attempts and conclusions of other non-theological understandings of being. But this should not debar us from approaching the problem from our own particular standpoint, the theological; and therefore from noting what is revealed to us in this respect by the Word of God. At this point too, therefore, we must take our bearings first and decisively from the man Jesus in His time. This will enable us to press forward to propositions in which the general Christian understanding of man will find expression in the light of the problem of time.

Cf. for what follows: Rudolf Bultmann, *Offenbarung und Heilsgeschehen*, 1941; Werner Georg Kümmel, *Verheissung und Erfüllung*, 1945; Oscar Cullmann, *Christus und die Zeit*, 1946 (Eng. Trans. *Christ and Time*, 1951); Marcus Barth, *Der Augenzeuge*, 1946; and Fritz Buri, *Die Bedeutung der neutestamentlichen Eschatologie für die neuere protestantische Theologie*, 1935.

"Jesus, Lord of time"—the title of this Christological and basic sub-section of our investigation indicates the conclusion to which it will lead us. Let me outline it as briefly as possible. Like all other men, the man Jesus is in His time, His lifetime, the time He needs like all other men to be able to live a human life. But in this time of His He lives as the One He is in virtue of His unity with God. That is, He not only lives with God, but *for* Him; not only as His Elect and Called in responsibility before Him, but as His representative to men. And He not only lives with men, but *for* them; not only as a man like themselves in encounter with them, but as their Representative before God. He lives in His time as the Judge by whose Word and work the right of God is vindicated in the sight of men, and therefore that of men is vindicated before God and among themselves; by whom the kingdom of God is thus established among men and His covenant with them fulfilled. It is in this two-fold representation and vindication of right that the man Jesus lives in His time. And it is this content of His life which makes the barrier of His time on every side a gateway. As in His unity with God He lives the life of the supreme Representative and Judge, His life does not belong exclusively to Himself. It is a life lived for God, and therefore for men. And as He lives this life in His time, it ceases to be exclusively His time. His time becomes time for God, and therefore for all men. The question which God addresses to all men, and the question which they address to God, finds its conclusive answer in the life which Jesus lived in the service of God and man. He represents the grace of God, and thus gives man what is right, what is his due. And he represents the gratitude of man, and thus gives God [440] what is right, what is His due. The answer given by the life of Jesus to the questions of God and man makes His time the time which always was when men lived, which always is when they live, and which always will be when they will live. It makes this life at once the centre and the beginning and end of all the times of all the lifetimes of all men. It is the time of man in its whole extent.

3

Wherever men live and have time the decision taken in the life of Jesus holds good; the content of His life affects and embraces them all because it is the answer to the question which God addresses to all men and which they address to God. The two-fold answer which He gives, to God on the one hand and to men on the other, makes Him the Contemporary of all men, whether they have lived, live or will live. The way in which He is their Contemporary varies according to whether they live with Him, lived before Him or will live after Him. Yet He is the Contemporary of them all because He lives for God and for them all. The man Jesus has therefore His time, but He has more than just His own time. He lives in His time, and while it does not cease to be His time, and the times of other men do not cease to be their times, His time acquires in relation to their times the character of God's time, of eternity, in which present, past and future are simultaneous. Thus Jesus not only lives in His own time, but as He lives in His own time, and as there are many other times both before and after Him, He is the Lord of time. This is the insight which must now be established and expounded.

Let us take the simplest and most obvious consideration first. Like all men, the man Jesus has His lifetime: the time bounded at one end by His birth and at the other by His death; a fixed span with a particular duration within the duration of created time as a whole; the time for his being as the soul of His body. The eternal content of His life must not cause us to miss or to forget or to depreciate this form, separating the content from it and discarding the form, as though we could see and have the content without it. For while the content is eternal, it is His human life, the action or series of actions of this human subject, which could not take place unless He had His own particular time. If we abstract Him from His time, we also lose this content of His life. If we retain the content, we must needs retain the form as well, and therefore His temporality. Just because the content is eternal, the presence of God, the unity of Creator and creature, of the life of God with that of man, He has time, the lifetime of this man. Everything we shall say later about the supremely positive and comprehensive relation of fulfilment and promise between His time and the times before and after, rests wholly on the fact that it is always intrinsically and supremely His time. It is as a man of His time, and not otherwise, that He is the Lord of time. We should lose Jesus as the Lord of all time if we ignored [441] Him as a man in His own time. It is in this history—the history which is inseparable from his temporality—that the man Jesus lives and is the eternal salvation of all men in their different times.

The eternal salvation of all men is absolutely dependent on our being able to recount this history: "Once upon a time there was … " Note the "once." "Once" means: "In His time." The New Testament ἅπαξ (1 Pet. 3[18], Heb. 9[26 28]) or ἐφάπαξ (Rom. 6[10]; Heb. 7[27], 9[12]) certainly means "once for all." But the event thus designated—the death of Jesus as the climax of His life—could not have happened once for all if it had not happened once, in its own time. It is in this history, and therefore in time, that the fulness of time is reached, and only so. The Gospels distinguish the life of Jesus from myths proclaiming timeless truth by

4

underlining, though not overstressing, the temporal limitations to which Jesus was subject. Palestine, Galilee and Jerusalem are the indispensable background to His life, giving him a concrete relationship to His contemporary social environment and a definite place in history (Luke 2^{1f}, 3^{1f}). The inclusion of Pontius Pilate in the creed means, *inter alia*^{EN2}, that the Church wished to pinpoint the death of Jesus as an event in time. And it is worth noting that the Synoptists record the precise time of the events of the passion almost to the minute—the cock-crow (Mk. 14^{68} and *par.*), the morning (Mk. 15^1), the third hour (Mk. 15^{25}), the sixth hour, the ninth (Mk. 15^{33} and *par.*) and the evening (Mk. 15^{42} and *par.*). True, the exact year of Jesus' birth cannot be established with any degree of certainty, nor the year of His death, so we cannot be sure exactly how old He was when He died. Yet it would be wrong to boggle at such chronological obscurities. It was enough for the Evangelists to make clear that the history they record was enacted over a particular period of time, and, in the case of the passion, on particular days and at particular hours. To insist on the fact that Jesus Christ "is come in the flesh" (1 Jn. 4^2), that the Logos became flesh and "tabernacled" among men (Jn. 1^{14}), was the best defence against Docetism in its early stages. At bottom Docetism is "the failure to respect the historically unique character of the redemptive deed of Christ" (Cullmann, *Christ and Time*, E.T., 127). The New Testament does not teach any "truth" but that which has its substance in the Johaninne Ἐγώ εἰμι^{EN3}. It proclaims salvation history, and therefore the time of salvation. The lifetime of Jesus is this time of salvation.

But the history of the man Jesus, this salvation history, cannot be recounted unless we remember that the New Testament has something more to say of Him, though still in the form of history, at the very point where the history of any other man would inevitably stop. For Jesus has a further history beginning on the third day after His death and therefore after the time of His first history had clearly come to an end. In temporal sequence, it is a second history—or rather, the fragments of a second history—of Jesus. It is the Easter history, the history of the forty days between His resurrection and ascension. The second stage of our investigation, more difficult, but rewarding, leads us inevitably to this point. For unless we wilfully ignore the clear indication of the New Testament sources, we are bound to recognise that this is a key position for our whole understanding of the man Jesus in His time. It shows us as nothing else can, according to the New Testament, that even as a man in His time Jesus is the Lord of all time. The Jesus whose life and time form the subject matter of [442] the New Testament is the One whom at this time His disciples had heard, and seen with their eyes, and looked upon, and their hands had handled (1 Jn. 1^1); "that eternal life, which was with the Father, and was manifested unto us" (ἐφανερώθη 1 Jn. 1^2). It is impossible to read any text of the New Testament in the sense intended by its authors, by the apostles who stand behind them, or by the first communities, without an awareness that they either explicitly assert or at least tacitly assume that the Jesus of whom they speak and to whom they refer in some way is the One who appeared to His disciples at this particular time as the Resurrected from the dead. All the other things they know of Him, His words and acts, are regarded in the light of this particular event, and are as

---

^{EN2} among other things
^{EN3} I am

5

it were irradiated by its light. Whatever they proclaim in His name, the power of their message, derives from the fact that it was conveyed and entrusted to them by the man Jesus after He was raised from the dead. And to turn to our own particular problem, whatever His being in time means for their being, and for that of all men in their time, derives from the fact that Jesus was among them even in this particular time, the Easter time.

In the first instance, it is essential to grasp that when the New Testament speaks of the event of Easter it really means the Easter history and Easter time. We are here in the sphere of history and time no less than in the case of the words and acts and even the death of Jesus. The event of Easter is as it were their prism through which the apostles and their communities saw the man Jesus in every aspect of His relation to them—as the One who "was, and is, and is to come" (Rev. 4^8). But this prism itself is not just a timeless idea, a kind of *a priori*[EN4], hovering as it were above the relations between Jesus and His followers, above their memory of His life and death, above His presence in their midst or their expectation of His second coming and the final consummation. No, it happened "once upon a time" that He was among them as the Resurrected. This, too, was an event. And it was by this event that the prism was put into their hands. He, the man Jesus, was also in this time, this later time. Not only their faith in Him, or their preaching of Him, but the recollection which concretely created and fashioned this faith and preaching, embraced this time, the time of the forty days. It was by this specific memory, and not by a timeless and non-historical truth, that the apostles and the Churches they founded lived in all the relations between Jesus and them and them and Jesus.

This statement holds good whatever our personal attitude may be to this later history. Its truth does not depend on our own acceptance or rejection of the Easter story, or whether we prefer to accept it differently from the way in which the New Testament describes it, or to interpret it in a different sense. Nor, finally, does it depend on our recognition of its central importance for our own knowledge of Jesus Christ or faith in Him. We may relegate it to the periphery, or regard it as an incidental and dispensable feature in the story. But whatever our own personal attitude to the resurrection may be (and there are many alternatives to choose from), we can at least agree on one point. For the New Testament this later history is not just an appendix or afterthought to the main theme. It is not peripheral to the New Testament, but central; not inessential or dispensable, but essential and indispensable. And it is all this, not in a different sense, but exactly in the sense in which the New Testament takes it. The Easter history is the starting-point for the Evangelists' portraits of the man Jesus. It is the real word with which they approached the outside world, whether Jewish or pagan, whenever they spoke of this man. It is the axiom which controls all their thinking about this man in His time. It is not just a mere reflection of their memory of Jesus or of their present life in communion with Him or of the hopes they set upon His person. It is the original object which is itself reflected in their entire relationship to this man, past, present and future. To put it sharply, while we could imagine a New Testament containing only the history of Easter and its message, we could not possibly imagine a New Testament without it.

[443]

[EN4] unconditionally

1. *Jesus, Lord of Time*

For the history and message of Easter contains everything else, while without it everything else would be left in the air as a mere abstraction. Everything else in the New Testament contains and presupposes the resurrection. It is the key to the whole. We can agree about this quite apart from our own personal attitude to the resurrection. And so we can agree finally that the acceptance or rejection of the Gospel of the New Testament, at any rate as understood by the New Testament itself, depends on our acceptance or rejection of the *evangelium quadraginta dierum*[EN5]. Either we believe with the New Testament in the risen Jesus Christ, or we do not believe in Him at all. This is the statement which believers and non-believers alike can surely accept as a fair assessment of the sources.

R. Bultmann "demythologizes" the event of Easter by interpreting it as "the rise of faith in the risen Lord, since it was this faith which led to the apostolic preaching" (*Kerygma and Myth*, E.T., 42). This will not do. Faith in the risen Lord springs from His historical manifestation, and from this as such, not from the rise of faith in Him. But Bultmann evidently admits that the New Testament witnesses themselves took a different view. And we must at least give him credit for emphasising the central and indispensable function of the event of Easter for all that is thought and said in the New Testament. On the other hand, it is a matter for surprise that W. G. Kümmel never so much as mentions the resurrection in His otherwise excellent book. Can the subject of promise and fulfilment really be treated without mentioning the resurrection passages? Can the general thesis be sustained—legitimate and important though it is in itself—that in the Synoptists the kingdom of God is at once present in the person of Jesus and yet still to come? The same criticism applies to Cullmann's *Christ and Time*, where the resurrection comes in only at the end of the book (*op. cit.*, E.T., p. 231 ff.) and in a special connexion, without any real significance for the author's reconstruction of the New Testament conception of time and history.

We also join issue with Cullmann at another point. It is wrong to suppose that the New Testament authors started with a particular conception of time as an ascending line with a series of aeons, and then inserted into this geometrical figure the event of Christ as the centre of this line. Surely it was a particular memory of particular time filled with a particular history, it was the constraint under which this laid their thinking, which formed and initiated their particular conception of time. What shaped and determined their conception of time was the fact that the God who was the Father of Jesus Christ stood before them as the βασιλεύς τῶν αἰώνων[EN6] (1 Tim. 1[17]), not in the contemplation of a timeless truth, but in the recollection of this particular history. Jesus, revealed in the event of this particular time as the King of the aeons, was the first and proper object upon which the gaze of the primitive community rested. It was from this vantage point that it looked upon the aeons themselves. That is why it is hazardous to dogmatise about the early Christian conception of time, or to try and fit it into a nice geometrical pattern. Does it have such a pattern at all? It may not be impossible to discover one, but it would be wrong to accept as the last word on the subject the picture of an ascending line from infinity to infinity. [444]

But another delimitation which is even more important is demanded by Bultmann's proposed reinterpretation of the resurrection already mentioned. (Cf. for what follows, Walter Claas, *Der moderne Mensch in der Theologie Rudolf Bultmanns*, 1947.) As we have seen, the event of Easter is for Bultmann "the rise of faith in the risen Lord"—this, and no more than this. "Can the resurrection, " he asks, " … be understood simply as an attempt to convey the meaning of the cross? Does the New Testament, in asserting that Jesus is risen from the dead, mean that His death is not just an ordinary human death, but the judgment and salvation of the world, depriving death of its power" (*ibid.*, p. 38). As the revelation of the meaning of the

---

[EN5] gospel of the forty days
[EN6] king of ages

7

cross, it is certainly (with this last act of the Christ-event proper) the "act of God" on which the faith and preaching of the Church are founded. Indeed Bultmann can also speak of "the self-manifestation of the risen Lord" and therefore of "the eschatological event of redemption" (p. 42). But the meaning of the cross, as distinct from the cross itself, is not to be sought in time, but beyond it (p. 36). Apart from the cross and resurrection (understood in this sense) the eschatological event includes "the apostolic preaching which originated in the event of Easter Day" (p. 42), the Church "where the preaching of the word is continued and where believers gather as 'saints,' i.e., those who have been transferred to eschatological existence" (p. 43), and above all the "concrete achievements" of believers, their participation in the cross and resurrection of Christ, in which they die unto sin and the world with Him, and live with Him henceforth in "wrestling freedom" (p. 37f., 40). All these events in time, says Bultmann, are supra-temporal in context and character, both objectively and also subjectively for faith. For by "eschatological" Bultmann means a verifiable event in history and time which also has a supra-temporal significance accessible only to faith. Thus the eschatological event includes the death of Jesus, the faith of the first disciples, their preaching, the Church, the sacraments and the Christian life. But the resurrection, understood as the allegedly objective fact of the restoration of the man Jesus who died on the cross, of His return to life in this world during the forty days (p. 39), is not a part of this eschatological event. It is a "nature-miracle" (p. 8), a "miraculous proof," and as such it must be "demythologized," like so much else in the New Testament. It is a mistaken objectifying of a concept of the Christian understanding of existence which needs be translated back into the reality (p. 10) because it cannot be accepted as an event in time and space and cannot therefore be recognised in its supra-temporal context and character. An "Easter event" in this sense can be regarded only as an objectifying of primitive Christian Easter faith in terms of the mythical world-view of the time, and it is no longer valid for those who have ceased to hold this view. The real Easter event, which belongs to that eschatological occurrence, is the rise of the Easter faith of the first disciples. This was not based on any event in time, but only on the supra-historical, supra-temporal act of God. For the Easter faith of the later Church and for our Easter faith, it has the significance of an "act of God in which the redemptive event of the cross is completed" (p. 42). Here Bultmann is aware that he himself is on the verge of relapsing into mythology, if indeed he has not already done so. But he reassures himself with the thought that this is not "mythology in the traditional sense," since the reference is not to a "miraculous, supernatural event," but to "an historical event wrought out in space and time" (p. 43).

[445]   Our first task is to try to see the implications of this view. If Bultmann is right, there are two ways of taking Jn. 1^{14}, and the even more explicit saying in 1 Jn. 1^1. Either we must deny that these texts have anything whatever to do with the One who manifested His life during the forty days, or we must dis miss these statements (though both of them are fundamental in this context) from the sphere of the relevant content of primitive Christian faith and its preaching, explaining them as the mythological garb for the process in which the original disciples were brought by a direct divine influence to see the redemptive significance of the death of Jesus after it had taken place. On this view, the Easter history is merely the first chapter in the history of faith, and the Easter time the first period in the age of faith. The recollection of this time and history is a genuine memory of Jesus only to the extent that it was in this history and time that the disciples made up their minds about Him and about His death in particular. In so doing, they drew far too heavily on the mythical world-view of their age, and we cannot accept their particular way of expressing it as either obligatory or practical. The point is that Jesus Himself is at work during that history and time only in the faith of His disciples. The "self-declaration" of the "Resurrected" is staged in the minds of the disciples and nowhere else. Nothing happened between Him and them. There was no new,

8

and in its novelty decisive and fundamental, encounter between Him and them to give rise to their faith. They alone were engaged in this history. He was not. They were quite alone. To be sure, they had their faith, which had come into being through an "act of God," whatever that may "signify." They had the insight into the mystery of the cross, which had suddenly become possible and actual. But they were alone. Their faith had no object distinct from itself, no antecedent basis on which to rest as faith. It stood majestically on its own feet. The "act of God" was identical with their faith. And the fact that it took place, that they believed, is the real content of the Easter history and the Easter time, the real burden of the Christian message, the basis of the existence of the Church and sacraments. Jesus Himself had not risen. In its simple and unqualified sense, this statement is quite untenable.

For our part, we maintain the direct opposite. The statement is valid in its simplest sense, and only in that sense is it the central affirmation of the whole of the New Testament. Jesus Himself did rise again and appear to His disciples. This is the content of the Easter history, the Easter time, the Christian faith and Christian proclamation, both then and at all times. This is the basis of the existence of the Church and its sacraments. This—if we may call it so—is the "eschatological event" in its manifest form which it acquired at Easter. This is the act of God—the act in which He appeared objectively in the glory of His incarnate Word, encountering first their unbelief and then, when this was overcome, their faith. Hence they were not alone with their faith. It was established, awakened and created by God in this objective encounter. Only in a secondary sense was their faith the imitation and reflection of the death and resurrection of Jesus in their lives. Primarily it meant that they were able to regard themselves as men for whom Jesus died and rose again. Jesus Himself for them! Hence Jesus and His disciples were not identical in the Easter event. He Himself was with them in time, in this time, beyond the time of His earthly life between His birth and death, in this time of revelation. This is what really took place. In our view, we do violence to the texts of the New Testament if we take a different line, as Bultmann does. But having said that, we must try to explain briefly why we do not find Bultmann's argument convincing.

Bultmann is an exegete. But it is impossible to engage him in exegetical discussion. For he is also a systematic theologian of the type which handles texts in such a way that their exegesis is always controlled by a set of dogmatic presuppositions and is thus wholly dependent upon their validity. In what follows I shall try to come to grips with the most important of these dogmatic presuppositions.

1. Is it true that a theological statement is valid only when it can be proved to be a genuine element in the Christian understanding of human existence? Bultmann rejects the claim that the resurrection of Jesus was an event in time and space on the ground that it does not fulfil this postulate. This, of course, is true enough. For in the resurrection God appears to act in a manner "inextricably involved in a nature-miracle" (p. 8). None of the major affirmations of the creed fulfils this postulate. True, they have a certain bearing on human existence. They provide the possibility and basis for a Christian understanding of this existence, and suitably adjusted they can serve as definitions of human existence. But this is not what they are in the first instance. Primarily, they define the being and action of the God who is different from man and encounters man; the Father, the Son and the Holy Ghost. For this reason alone they cannot be reduced to statements about the inner life of man. And for this reason, too, they are full of "nature," of cosmos. This applies equally to the claim that Jesus rose from the dead. The anthropological strait-jacket into which Bultmann forces his systematic theology, and unfortunately his exegetical theology as well, represents a tradition which goes back to W. Herrmann and even further to Ritschl and Schleiermacher. This tradition can just as easily be exploited in the opposite direction, so as to leave no genuine case against the resurrection of Jesus.

[446]

9

2. Is it true that an event alleged to have happened in time can be accepted as historical only if it can be proved to be a "'historical' fact" in Bultmann's sense?—i.e., when it is open to verification by the methods, and above all the tacit assumption, of modern historical scholarship? This is Bultmann's opinion. It is on this ground that he rejects the account of the forty days. He cannot include its content, in so far as this deals with the living Jesus, and not merely with the disciples who believed in him, among the "'historical' facts" in the restricted sense of the term. He is right enough in this, for it is quite impossible. But he jumps to a false conclusion when he insists that for this reason the facts reported could not have occurred. History of this kind may well have happened. We may well accept as history that which good taste prevents us from calling "'historical' fact," and which the modern historian will call "saga" or "legend" on the ground that it is beyond the reach of his methods, to say nothing of his unavowed assumptions. It belongs to the nature of the biblical material that although it forms a consecutive historical narrative it is full of this kind of history and contains comparatively little "history" in Bultmann's sense. The creation narratives in Gen. 1–2, for example, are history in this higher sense; and so too is the Easter story, except for a tiny "historical" margin. Why should it not have happened? It is sheer superstition to suppose that only things which are open to "historical" verification can have happened in time. There may have been events which happened far more really in time than the kind of things Bultmann's scientific historian can prove. There are good grounds for supposing that the history of the resurrection of Jesus is a pre-eminent instance of such an event. "It is not," he says, "just a phenomenon of secular history, it is a phenomenon of significant history, in the sense that it realized itself in history." He is referring here to the Church (p. 43). And the same is true, *a fortiori*EN7, of the resurrection of Jesus.

3. Is it true that the assertion of the historicity of an event which by its very nature is inaccessible to "historical" verification, of what we may agree to call the history of saga or legend, is merely a blind acceptance of a piece of mythology, an arbitrary act, a descent from faith to works, a dishonest *sacrificium intellectus*EN8? This is Bultmann's complaint (p. 4), and he expressly appeals to the shade of W. Herrmann against those who accept the resurrection of Jesus as an historical fact. Can we let this pass? What grounds have we for accepting the view that the message of Christ's resurrection necessarily has the sinister aspect of a law of faith to which we can subject ourselves, if at all, only in a kind of intellectual contortion? For the New Testament at any rate the resurrection is good news in which we may believe. And this faith, as those who accepted it were gratefully aware, was made possible only by the resurrection itself. They were not able to accept it because the prevailing mythical world-view made it easier to accept then than it is supposed to be to-day. Even in those days the Easter message seems to be utterly "incredible" (p. 9), not only to the educated Areopagites, but even to the original disciples. Hence there is no real reason why it should not be accepted freely and gladly even to-day. If it is not presented as something to be accepted freely and gladly there is something wrong with the presentation. But this is no excuse for rejecting it as something which intellectual honesty forbids us to accept.

4. Is it true that modern thought is "shaped for good or ill by modern science"? Is there a modern world-picture which is incompatible with the mythical world-view and superior to it? Is this modern view so binding as to determine in advance and unconditionally our acceptance or rejection of the biblical message? We are again up against the well-known Marburg tradition with its absolute lack of any sense of humour and its rigorous insistence on the honesty which does not allow any liberties in this respect. "It is impossible to use electric light and the wireless and to avail ourselves of modern medical and surgical discoveries, and at

---

EN7 all the more
EN8 sacrifice of the intellect

the same time to believe in the New Testament world of demons and spirits" (p. 5). Who can read this without a shudder? But what if the modern world-view is not so final as all that? What if modern thought is not so uniform as our Marburg Kantians would have us believe? Is there any criticism of the New Testament which is inescapably posed by the "situation of modern man"? And above all, what if our radio-listeners recognise a duty of honesty which, for all this respect for the discoveries of modern science, is even more compelling than that of accepting without question the promptings of common sense? What if they felt themselves in a position to give a free and glad and quite factual assent not to a *fides implicita*[EN9] in a world of spirits and demons but to faith in the resurrection of Jesus Christ from the dead? What if they have no alternative but to do this?

5. Is it true that we are compelled to reject a statement simply because this statement, or something like it, was compatible with the mythical world-view of the past? Is this enough to make it untenable? Is not Bultmann being a bit too heavy-handed in expecting us to reject this mythical world-view in its entirety? After all, is it our job as Christians to accept or reject world-views? Have not Christians always been eclectic in their world-views—and this for very good reasons? There is absolutely no reason at all why we should really insist on this particular world-view. But we ought not to overlook the fact that this particular world-view contained a number of features which the primitive community used cautiously but quite rightly in its witness to Jesus Christ. But the world-view accepted nowadays has either lost these features, or regrettably allowed them to slip into the background. Consequently we have every reason to make use of "mythical" language in certain connexions. And there is no need for us to have a guilty conscience about it, for if we went to extremes in demythologising, it would be quite impossible to bear witness to Jesus Christ at all. When, for instance, Bultmann (p. 7 f.) dismisses the connexion between sin and death, or the concept of substitution, or the relation between death and resurrection, on the ground that they are particularly offensive and "obsolete" features in this mythical world-view, he is perhaps a warning example of what becomes of a theologian when he all-too-hastily jettisons the mythical world-view lock, stock and barrel. To speak of the "rise of the Easter faith" in the first disciples is a good thing. But we cannot pretend that this is an adequate substitute for what is now rejected as the "mythical" witness to the resurrection of Jesus Christ from the dead.

As I see it, these are the decisive reasons why, in spite of Bultmann, we must still accept the resurrection of Jesus, and His subsequent appearances to His disciples, as genuine history in its own particular time.

This is not the place to develop a complete theology of the resurrection. Let us confine ourselves to one question. What implications has it for the being of [448] Jesus in time that He was in time in this way too, as the Resurrected? What is the implication of the fact that after He had completed the span from birth to death He had this subsequent time? The answer is that the particular content of the particular recollection of this particular time of the apostolic community consisted in the fact that in this time the *man* Jesus was manifested among them in the mode of *God*. It is essential to a true understanding that both his humanity and his deity should be kept in view.

The Resurrected is the man Jesus, who now came and went among them as such, whom they saw and touched and heard, who ate and drank with them, and who, as I believe, was still before them as true man, *vere homo*.

[EN9] implicit faith

We misunderstand the whole matter, and fall into Docetism at the crucial point, if we refuse to see this and even to see it first. Apart from 1 Jn. 1¹, there are two specific texts in which the New Testament emphatically repudiates any docetic interpretation of the resurrection. The first is Lk. 24³⁶ᶠ·, where Jesus appears in the midst of the eleven just as they are about to listen to the story of the disciples on the road to Emmaus. Jesus says: "Why are ye troubled? and why do thoughts (διαλογισμοί) arise in your hearts? Behold my hands and my feet: ὅτι ἐγώ εἰμι αὐτός ᴱᴺ¹⁰: handle me, and see; for a spirit hath not flesh and bones, as ye see me have." And the story continues: "And while they yet believed not for joy, and wondered, he said unto them, Have ye here any meat? And they gave him a piece of a broiled fish. And he took it, and did eat before them." The second is Jn. 20²⁴ᶠ·, the story of "doubting" Thomas. Much injustice has been done to the latter through wrong exegesis. The fact that he wanted to touch Jesus before he came to believe shows only that he had no more doubts than the other disciples had according to the accounts. It is the fact that the risen Christ can be touched which puts it beyond all doubt that He is the man Jesus and no one else. He is not soul or spirit in the abstract, but soul of His body, and therefore body as well. To be an apostle of Jesus Christ means not only to have seen Him with one's eyes and to have heard Him with one's ears, but to have touched Him physically. This is what is meant by Ac. 1²², where we are told that what makes an apostle is the fact that he is a "witness of the resurrection." By beholding His glory, by seeing, hearing and touching the flesh in which this glory is made manifest, those who consorted with Jesus during this time were brought to believe in Him, and thus authorised and consecrated to proclaim the Gospel. "Blessed are they that have not seen, and have believed" (Jn. 20²⁹). This is not a criticism of Thomas, but (cf. 1 Pet. 1⁸) the blessing of all those who, though having no part in the seeing of this particular time, will "believe on me through their word," i.e., through the witness of those who did see (Jn. 17²⁰). It is impossible to erase the bodily character of the resurrection of Jesus and His existence as the Resurrected. Nor may we gloss over this element in the New Testament record of the forty days, as a false dualism between spirit and body has repeatedly tried to do. For unless Christ's resurrection was a resurrection of the body, we have no guarantee that it was the decisively acting Subject Jesus Himself, the *man* Jesus, who rose from the dead.

[449] But it is equally important to note that the man Jesus appeared to them during these days in the mode of God. During this period they came to see that He had always been present among them in His deity, though hitherto this deity had been veiled. They now recalled these preliminary manifestations of glory which they had already witnessed during His earthly life, but with unseeing eyes, and which now, in the light of what took place in these days, acquired for them the particular import which they had always had in themselves, though hidden from them. Now they actually beheld His glory. During these forty days the presence of God in the presence of the man Jesus was no longer a paradox. The dialectic of seeing and believing may be helpful when we try to describe the Christian life and the justification and sanctification of Christians, or the Church and its preaching and sacraments. But when we come to the resurrection it leads us nowhere. "God was in Christ" (2 Cor. 5¹⁹)—this was the truth which dawned upon the disciples during the forty days. He was not both veiled and manifest, both manifest and veiled, in Christ. He had been veiled,

---

ᴱᴺ¹⁰ that it is I myself

but He was now wholly and unequivocally and irrevocably manifest. For the disciples this was not a self-evident truth, nor a discovery of their own, but a conviction that went utterly against the grain. This is made abundantly clear in the resurrection narratives, where the disciples begin by doubting and even disbelieving. But their doubts and disbelief are soon dispelled, never to return. They are definitively overcome and removed in the forty days. "Be not faithless, but believing" (John 20²⁷ᶠ·). This is not just pious exhortation, but a word of power. And to this Thomas gives the appropriate answer: "My Lord and my God." In and with the presence of the man Jesus during this time, in the unique circumstances of the forty days, a decision is taken between the belief and unbelief of His disciples. There takes place for them the total, final, irrevocable and eternal manifestation of God Himself. God Himself, the object and ground of their faith, was present as the man Jesus was present in this way. That this really took place is the specific content of the apostolic recollection of these days.

The fact of faith was created in this history. This faith did not consist in a reassessment and reinterpretation *in meliorem partem*[EN11] of the picture of the Crucified, but in an objective encounter with the Crucified and Risen, who Himself not only made Himself credible to them, but manifested Himself as the ἀρχηγὸς τῆς σωτηρίας αὐτῶν[EN12] (Heb. 2¹⁰) and therefore the ἀρχηγὸς καὶ τελειωτής[EN13] of their πίστις[EN14] (Heb. 12²). This being the case, He was among them as God Himself. "All power is given unto me in heaven and in earth" (Mt. 28¹⁸). The Jesus of the Easter history speaks not only with binding authority, but with effectiveness; not only with validity, but with power. His declarations are able to overcome the fears, griefs, bewilderment, doubts and disbeliefs of His disciples. And the directions He gives them (especially the "missionary charge" of Mt. 28¹⁹) point to an enterprise which will neither depend on the resources or achievements of the disciples themselves nor be thwarted by their inadequacy. "(He) hath begotten us again ... by the resurrection of Jesus Christ from the dead" (1 Pet. 1³). This is true quite apart from any inherent capacity of the disciples or any endowments of their own which they bring to the task. But it is also true quite apart from the obstacles which they might put in the way of this event. When the Bible says that He "hath begotten us again," it can only mean a mighty, creative act of God. That is what those who saw and heard this history remember. They remember it as an event which [450] can never be reversed even when it is behind them as an event of their time and can be only an object of memory and retrospect. But it means something else as well. It means that what they look back upon is the presence of God Himself revealed among them. "God is present"—this is not just an intellectual notion of perception, but it is remembered as a real fact which has taken place before them and which cannot be confessed, but has given them their commission to preach the Gospel to all nations. They live by this recollection; all their thinking and knowledge is grounded in it.

It is this memory which leads them to add the title *Kyrios*[EN15] to the simple human name of Jesus. It is a token of their recognition that God was manifestly present in this man. Whether its origin is to be sought in the Hellenistic Emperor cult, or whether, as would seem more

---

[EN11] in a better sense
[EN12] captain of their salvation
[EN13] author and perfecter
[EN14] faith
[EN15] Lord

13

likely, it is a reproduction of the LXX rendering of Yahweh, it is the name which, according to Phil. 2⁹, "is above every name," signifying absolute deity. This, and the transference of this name to the man Jesus, is borne out by the saying of Thomas in Jn. 20²⁸. We do not have here merely an appraisal and interpretation of the existence of Jesus grounded in the depth and intensity of their contrition. Had it been that, it would have been open to question whether they had not exaggerated His status, and whether we for our part should not content ourselves with a more modest assessment. What we have here is a *Deus dixit*[EN16] spoken in the existence of Jesus during these days. It is a decision which the apostolic Church cannot discuss or revise. For it is He who is responsible for it. He has appeared and acted as *Kyrios*[EN17] among them. It is not they who have given Him this name, but God. And God has given it by exalting Him above all things (ὑπερύψωσεν, Phil. 2⁹) out of and after His death on the cross. Hence this name is inseparable from His person, and His person inseparable from this name. Although they had once known Him, as 2 Cor. 5¹⁶ puts it, "after the flesh," i.e., otherwise than as *Kyrios*[EN18], they now know Him so no more, but henceforth, in retrospect of His resurrection, only as *Kyrios*[EN19]. And in this way, as the only *Kyrios*[EN20] they know, they thus proclaim Him—for how else could they have done so?—and in the certainty given by these days that He was *Kyrios*[EN21] they proceed to interpret and present His life and His words and acts prior to His death. In practice, therefore, the so-called Gospels, if they are taken and read as their authors intended, reveal from start to finish this decision (and therefore indirectly the resurrection of Jesus), and are to be read, understood and accepted or rejected only in face of this decision and therefore in recollection of the resurrection of Jesus. If we try to bypass this decision, concentrating our attention upon a human Jesus who is not the *Kyrios*[EN22] because He is not risen, we simply show that we have failed to take note of what they really say, and intend to say.

But when we go on to ask how all this happened, how the man Jesus was present among His disciples during these forty days as God, we must give the straightforward answer that the Jesus who three days earlier had been rejected by the Jews and put to death by the Gentiles and buried by His disciples was among them again as a living man. He was thus the concrete demonstration of the gracious God, who in the death of this man on the cross did not will that His own right, and that of man, should go by default, but willed to vindicate them, as He did in great triumph. He was then the concrete demonstration of the God who not only has authority over man's life and death, but also wills to deliver him from death. Moreover—and this is what interests us especially in this connexion—He was the concrete demonstration of the God who has not only a different time from that of man, but whose will and resolve it is to give man a share in this time of His, in His eternity. The concrete demonstration of this God, His appearance, is the meaning of the appearance and appearances of this man Jesus, alive again after His death, in the forty days. It may and must be said, not as a postulate but as a legitimate explanation of the facts, that if the

[451]

[EN16] God said
[EN17] Lord
[EN18] Lord
[EN19] Lord
[EN20] Lord
[EN21] Lord
[EN22] Lord

man Jesus was the incarnate Word of this God, if as such he was the Bearer of a hidden glory, of an initially inapprehensible declaration of His nature, and if finally this hidden declaration of His nature was to be effective as well as operative, if it was not to remain hidden but to be disclosed, then everything had to happen as it actually did according to the Easter story in its simple, literal sense. There was no other way. This man, the incarnate Word of God, had not only to be present but to be apprehensible as the triumphant justification of God and man, as the revelation of the divine sovereignty over life and death which delivers man, and finally as the One who exists in the higher, eternal time of God. This, the Revealer of His hidden glory as God's eternal Word incarnate, is what Jesus was in His real and therefore physical resurrection from the dead, in His appearances as the One who was really and therefore physically resurrected. This is the way in which He was "manifested in the mode of God" to His disciples. This is the way in which He was the appearance of God which afterwards formed the object of their particular recollection of this particular time. This is how He was present to their ears and eyes as the Lord, to whom they could not and would not give this title on a spontaneous assessment or interpretation, but were compelled to do so.

Bultmann is splitting hairs when he calls the literal resurrection a "nature-miracle." Far from helping us to understand it, this is merely an attempt to discredit it. It is true enough, for in the appearance of God we necessarily have to do with the whole apprehensible existence of the man Jesus, and therefore nature, i.e., His body, has a part in this event. As a purely mental or psychological event, the appearance would not have been what it was, i.e., that of the Creator of the whole universe and therefore of the whole man. Yet it was not this circumstance, not the fact that the resurrection included nature, and took place as a physical resurrection, which made it what it was. No, it was because God Himself, the Creator, who was first hidden in the lowliness of this creature, in the death of this man, was now manifested in His resurrection, that it was absolutely necessary for this event genuinely and apprehensibly to include nature, and therefore to be physical. This was the mystery before which the apostolic community could adore. It was not interested in any resurrection or actuality of resurrection in general, but in the resurrection of this man, and the resurrection of all men inaugurated by it. In other words, it was interested in something which is beyond the reach of general polemics against the concept of a miracle which embraces nature, and indeed of general apologetics in favour of this concept. The concern of the New Testament was not with this concept but with the contingent fact to which reference is made in the hymn which probably belongs to the most primitive Christian tradition: ὃς ἐφανερώθη ἐν σαρκί, ἐδικαιώθη ἐν πνεύματι, ὤφθη ἀγγέλοις, ἐκηρύχθη ἐν ἔθνεσιν, ἐπιστεύθη ἐν κόσμῳ, ἀνελήμφθη ἐν δόξῃ[EN23] (1 Tim. 3[16]).

When we remember this, we can understand why the evidence for the resurrection can [452] only be fragmentary and contradictory, as is actually the case in the New Testament. Compare, for instance, the Matthean and Lukan accounts, or the Synoptic accounts as a whole, with that of John; or again, all the Gospel accounts with that in 1 Cor. 15. It is clearly impossible to extract from the various accounts a nucleus of genuine history, quite apart from the intelligibility or otherwise of the resurrection itself. The statement in Ac. 1[3] to the effect that

---

[EN23] who was manifest in the flesh, justified in the Spirit, seen of angels, preached unto the Gentiles, believed on in the world, received up into glory

the appearances extended over forty days is obviously connected with the forty days of the flood (Gen. 7⁴; cf. also Ez. 4⁶; Jonah 3⁴), and with the forty days of the temptation at the beginning of Jesus' ministry (Mt. 4²; Lk. 4²). And they may also have some positive connexion with the forty days spent in Canaan by the spies when they went on ahead of the children of Israel (Num. 13²⁵), and with the forty days and nights it took Elijah to get to Horeb, during which he went in the strength of the meat provided by the angel. These parallels are sufficient to show that the forty days are not to be taken literally but typically. They do not offer precise chronological information as to the duration of the appearances. The topography is just as vague. There is no clear dividing line between one scene and another, as a comparison of the various episodes will show. Nor have we any independent sources from which to check the evidence. Hence the harmonisations to which the older commentators resorted in an attempt to supply the deficiencies and clear up the obscurities, are almost amusingly incongruous. The narratives are not meant to be taken as "history" in our sense of the word. Even 1 Cor. 15³⁻⁸ is treated in a strangely abstract way if it is regarded as a citation of witnesses for the purpose of historical proof. True, these accounts read very differently from myths. The Easter story is differentiated from myth, both formally and materially, by the fact that it is all about a real man of flesh and blood. But the stories are couched in the imaginative, poetic style of historical saga, and are therefore marked by the corresponding obscurity. For they are describing an event beyond the reach of historical research or depiction. Hence we have no right to try to analyse or harmonise them. This is to do violence to the whole character of the event in question. There can be no doubt that all these narratives are about the same event, and that they are agreed in substance, intention and interpretation. None of the authors ever even dreamed, for example, of reducing the event to "the rise of the Easter faith of the first disciples." On the other hand, each of the narratives must be read for its own sake just as it stands. Each is a specific witness to the decisive things God said and did in this event. And we can be glad that there is the possibility of adducing one in explanation of the others. Ἐγενόμην νεκρὸς καὶ ἰδοὺ ζῶν EN24 (Rev. 1¹⁸)—it is here that all these very saga-like accounts have their common ground. This, and this alone, is what they have to tell us.

A few words may be said in conclusion about the empty tomb (Mk. 16¹⁻⁸ and *par.*) and the ascension (Lk. 24⁵⁰⁻⁵³; Ac. 1⁹⁻¹²). These stories are indispensable if we are to understand what the New Testament seeks to proclaim as the Easter message. Taken together, they mark the limits of the Easter period, at one end the empty tomb, and at the other the ascension. (It is worth noting that the limits are drawn not only backwards and forwards, but also downwards and upwards.) In the later apostolic preaching both events, like the Virgin Birth at the beginning of the Gospel narrative, seem to be presupposed, and are certainly never questioned, but they are only hinted at occasionally here and there, and never referred to explicitly. Even in the Easter narratives the empty tomb and the ascension are alike in the fact that they are both indicated rather than described; the one as an introduction, the other as a conclusion; the one a little more definitely, though still in very general terms, the other much more vaguely. Indeed, in the strict sense the ascension occurs only in Ac. 1⁹ᶠ. It is not mentioned at all in the genuine Marcan ending (though this is obviously incomplete). In Matthew it is merely implied in the reference of Jesus to the power given Him in heaven and on earth (Mt. 28¹⁸). Luke's Gospel, according to the more probable reading at 24⁵¹, is also very indefinite: διέστη ἀπ᾽ αὐτῶν EN25, while in John it occurs only in the comprehensive

[453]

EN24 I am he that liveth, and was dead
EN25 he was parted from them

16

terms ἀναβαίνειν [EN26] and ὑπάγειν, ὑψωθῆναι [EN27] and δοξασθῆναι [EN28], which are used to embrace the whole ascent to Jerusalem, the crucifixion, the resurrection and the reappearance, and do not refer to the ascension as a concrete event. There are reasons for this. The content of the Easter witness, the Easter event, was not that the disciples found the tomb empty or that they saw Him go up to heaven, but that when they had lost Him through death they were sought and found by Him as the Resurrected. The empty tomb and the ascension are merely signs of the Easter event, just as the Virgin Birth is merely the sign of the nativity, namely, of the human generation and birth of the eternal Son of God. Yet both signs are so important that we can hardly say that they might equally well be omitted.

The function of the empty tomb, with its backward, downward, earthward reference, is to show that the Jesus who died and was buried was delivered from death, and therefore from the grave, by the power of God; that He, the Living, is not to be sought among the dead (Lk. 24⁵). "He is risen; he is not here: behold the place where they laid him" (Mk. 16⁶). "He is not here; for he is risen, even as he said" (Mt. 28⁶; Lk. 24⁶). He is not here! But it is the angels who say this. Since the nativity and temptation the angels have not played any active part. But they now reappear at the tomb. And it is only the angels who say this; who as it were draw the line behind which there can be no going back. They only point to the empty tomb. The empty tomb was obviously a very ambiguous and contestable fact (Mt. 27⁶²ᶠ·; 28¹¹ᶠ·). And what has happened around this sepulchre is a warning against making it a primary focus of attention. The empty tomb is not the same thing as the resurrection. It is not the appearance of the Living; it is only its presupposition. Hence it is only the sign, although an indispensable sign. Christians do not believe in the empty tomb, but in the living Christ. This does not mean, however, that we can believe in the living Christ without believing in the empty tomb. Is it just a "legend"? What matter? It still refers to the phenomenon ensuing the resurrection, to the presupposition of the appearance of Jesus. It is the sign which obviates all possible misunderstanding. It cannot, therefore, but demand our assent, even as a legend. Rejection of the legend of the empty tomb has always been accompanied by rejection of the saga of the living Jesus, and necessarily so. Far better, then, to admit that the empty tomb belongs to the Easter event as its sign.

The same considerations apply to the ascension. It is less directly attested in the New Testament, but unlike the empty tomb it has found a place in the creed, and has its own special feast in the Church Kalender. In contrast to the first sign it points forwards and upwards, thus serving a positive function. Just as the discovery of the empty tomb by the women marks the beginning of the Easter time and history, its end is marked by the meeting of the disciples on the mountain, which in Mt. 28¹⁶ is located in Galilee, but which Ac. 1¹² identifies with the Mount of Olives. The end consists in their θεάσθαι αὐτὸν πορευόμενον εἰς τὸν οὐρανόν [EN29] (Ac. 1¹¹). As the empty tomb looks downwards, the ascension looks upwards. But again the ascension—Jesus' disappearance into heaven—is the sign of the Resurrected, not the Resurrected Himself. "Heaven" in biblical language is the sum of the inaccessible and incomprehensible side of the created world, so that, although it is not God Himself, it is the throne of God, the creaturely correspondence to his glory, which is veiled from man, and cannot be disclosed except on His initiative. There is no sense in trying to visualise the ascension as a literal event, like going up in a balloon. The achievements of Christian art in this field are amongst its worst perpetrations. But of course this is no reason why they should be used to make the whole thing ridiculous. The point of the story is not

---

[EN26] to go up ...
[EN27] to go away, to be lifted up ...
[EN28] glorified
[EN29] in the same manner as you saw him go into heaven

[454] that when Jesus left His disciples He visibly embarked upon a wonderful journey into space, but that when He left them He entered the side of the created world which was provisionally inaccessible and incomprehensible, that before their eyes He ceased to bo before their eyes. This does not mean, however, that He ceased to be a creature, man. What it does mean is that He showed Himself quite unequivocally to be the creature, the man, who in provisional distinction from all other men lives on the God-ward side of the universe, sharing His throne, existing and acting in the mode of God, and therefore to be remembered as such, to be known once for all as this exalted creature, this exalted man, and henceforth to be accepted as the One who exists in this form to all eternity. The most important verse in the ascension story is the one which runs: "A cloud received him out of their sight" (Ac. 1⁹). In biblical language, the cloud does not signify merely the hiddenness of God, but His hidden presence, and the coming revelation which penetrates this hiddenness. It does not signify merely the heaven which is closed for us, but the heaven which from within, on God's side, will not always be closed. The words of the angels—note how they reappear at this point after playing no part in the Easter story proper—are a commentary on this: "Ye men of Galilee, why stand ye gazing up into heaven? this same Jesus, which is taken up from you into heaven, shall so come in like manner as ye have seen him go into heaven" (Ac. 1¹¹). Whatever it is, the cloud which takes Him out of their sight is not a cloud of sorrow. And the view that the ascension is Jesus' "farewell" to His disciples must be treated with caution. The mode of this leavetaking is what matters. He reveals Himself to them not only as the One who according to Mt. 28²⁰ will be with them in this heavenly mode of existence all the days, even to the consummation (συντέλεια) of the age, but also as the One who will come again to usher in this consummation. The ascension is the proleptic sign of the *parousia*, pointing to the Son of Man who will finally and visibly emerge from the concealment of His heavenly existence and come on the clouds of heaven (Mt. 24³⁰). This conclusion to the Easter history gives to the whole retrospective memory of the Resurrected this joyous character. It shows that Jesus did not enter and is not to be sought after the Easter history and the Easter time in any kind of hiddenness, but in the hiddenness of God. And finally it describes the hiddenness of God in such a way as to suggest that it burgeons with the conclusive revelation still awaited in the future. As this sign, the ascension is indispensable, and it would be injudicious as well as ungrateful on any grounds to ignore or reject this upward and forward-looking sign.

For these reasons it was impossible for the apostles to record and depict the history of the man Jesus in His time without adding this post-history, the Easter history. For this particular recollection belonged to their recollection of the man Jesus in His time. And it belonged to it decisively as the recollection of the revelation, of the source of knowledge, of the key to the history previously witnessed by them. The Easter history opened their eyes to the nature of this man and His history, to the previously concealed character of this history as salvation history, and therefore to the fact that what had happened had done so once and once for all, and to the way in which the "once" of this event differed absolutely from that of their own history and all history, and indeed from every other "once." God the Creator had not merely been present to them in the man Jesus, but He had actually appeared in this post-history. This is what illuminated and explained the whole history of this man in His time. This was the light in which this whole history—for it was the history of the [455] same man who had now encountered them as alive from the dead—was revealed as the appearance of God and therefore as incomparable salvation history, as the "once" which is absolutely distinguished from each and every other "once."

It was this fact which gave to the ἅπαξ[EN30] and ἐφάπαξ[EN31] of the New Testament its specific import, so that it could not be confused with any other, but would only acquire necessarily the sense of "once for all." It was this fact which necessarily made the evangelical narration the inalienable presupposition of apostolic proclamation. And again it was this fact which made the apostolic community quite immune from Docetism, from the possibility of a faith in Christ detached from the existence and knowledge of the man Jesus. The glory of the risen Christ was identical with the glory of the Jesus of Nazareth who went up from Galilee to Jerusalem to be crucified. It was identical with the glory of His human person, his human words and works. That this Jesus was the appearance of God, the salvation of the world, was what the disciples remembered as they looked back upon that post-history. He Himself as the Resurrected having indelibly impressed it upon their minds in the course of that history.

The Easter time is simply the time of the revelation of the mystery of the preceding time of the life and death of the man Jesus. The two times are insep-arably linked. They are together the time of the man Jesus to the extent that His person existing in His words and works, His mystery first and then its reve-lation, constitute its content. But this means that this whole time is the time of the appearance and presence of God. At the heart of all other times, both before and after, it is the time in which God Himself was this man, and there-fore had time, a life-time. It is the Creator of all reality distinct from Himself who, taking flesh of our flesh, also took time, at the heart of what we think we know as time. It is the Lord of time who became temporal and had time: His own time at the heart of all the times of the being created by Him; and this time in the same way as He had it in Himself before all created being, as He does not cease to have it above all created being, and as He will have it with all created being when the time of this being is over. Here, in this creature, in this man, who had His own time of life and death, and beyond this His time of revelation, God, the Creator and Lord, had already had time before His time, eternal time. It is the time which He took to Himself, thus granting it as a gift to the men of all time. It is the time which He willed to have for us in order to inaugurate and establish His covenant. It is the time which is the time of all times because what God does in it is the goal of all creation and therefore of all created time. Since God in His Word had time for us, and at the heart of all other times there was this particular time, the eternal time of God, all other times are now controlled by this time, i.e., dominated, limited and determined by their proximity to it. This means positively that they are shown not to be mere illusions. The many philosophical theories of time which deny its reality and regard it as a mere form or abstraction or figment of the imagination can only be finally abandoned when we consider that God Himself once took time and thus treated it as something real. But it also means critically that there is [456]

EN30 once ...
EN31 once for all

19

no such thing as absolute time, no immutable law of time. Not even its irreversibility can be adduced as an inviolable principle in relation to the time which was once real at the heart of time as that of the life and death and revelation of the man Jesus. There is no time in itself, rivalling God and imposing conditions on Him. There is no god called Chronos. And it is better to avoid conceptions of time which might suggest that there is. On the other hand, we need not be surprised if the nature and laws of all other times, and all that we think we know as time, are seen to be illuminated and relativised by this time. Relativised does not mean discarded. Time is real, and will always be so. Even its end—and it will one day come to an end as it once began—will not mean that it is thrown away. Yet even now its meaning does not lie in itself. But as all creation has its goal in what God purposes and will do and does within it for man, for us, so time as its historical form has its meaning in the particular time which God once took for the execution of this purpose, for establishing His covenant with man. This is the hidden meaning of all time, even of all other time. And time in itself has no property, no laws, to preclude the control of all other times by this time, or to prevent this time of *Deus praesens*[EN32] impressing upon them—in varying degrees and in different ways—the stamp of its own nature and law. The fact that all other times have been placed in proximity to this time means that even in them there may be discerned traces of this eternal time, of the true and proper time in which they necessarily have a share because, even though at a different level, they too are real times.

The time in which God revealed His Word is summarily defined in Tit. 1[3] as the καιροὶ ἴδιοι[EN33]. This means the times which God has adopted for His purpose and therefore made His own. There are types of this in the Old Testament, a major and a minor, and both are so eloquent that they call for notice.

The minor is the sabbatical year and the year of jubilee in Lev. 25[1-34]. The sabbatical year (v. 1f.) occurs once every seven years, and while it lasts the land is left fallow. The year of jubilee (v. 8f.)—the *locus classicus*[EN34] for theological opponents of the doctrine of free economy—occurs once every fifty years, being the year after a period of seven times seven years. Its dawn is heralded by the sound of a trumpet through the length and breadth of the land. All agricultural labour must be stopped, and there is a general liberation and restitution. All property is restored to those who have mortgaged it during the previous forty-nine years. The purchase price (only the produce could be bought or sold) varies according to the distance from the year of jubilee, a definite sale of the land being excluded. In this year, which is obviously so important even for relationships in the other forty-nine, the author of Is. 61[1f.] sees a type of the "acceptable year of the Lord," of "the day of vengeance of our God," when all that mourn will be comforted, receiving "beauty for ashes, the oil of joy for mourning, the garment of praise for the spirit of heaviness; that they might be called trees of righteousness, the planting of the Lord, that he might be glorified." I take it that this refers to the Messianic time of redemption. But according to the sermon in the synagogue at Nazareth (Lk. 4[17f.]), this extraordinary year is adopted by Jesus as a type of His own time: "The Spirit of the Lord is upon me, because he hath anointed me to preach good tidings to the

[457]

EN32 God present
EN33 due times
EN34 standard reference

poor; he hath sent me to preach deliverance to the captives, and recovering of sight to the blind, to set at liberty them that are bruised, to preach the acceptable year of the Lord" (v. 18f.). "This day hath this Scripture been fulfilled in your ears" (v. 21). Old Testament scholars tell us that the provisions of Lev. 25 were never actually put into practice, at any rate literally. If that is so, it merely serves to underline the prophetic character of this part of the Old Testament Law. Israel may have failed in this as in other respects, but its failure made no difference to the promise which the Law contained. Its years, the years of its people, of rich and poor alike, were not to drag on indefinitely, but to issue in a year of welcome festivity, liberation and restitution. And this perhaps is the time-consciousness of Old Testament man, not the consciousness of indefinite time, but that of the time of an era destined to culminate in another, and therefore the explanation of a coming time, the end and new beginning by which the present time with its limitation is already illuminated and relativised, being drawn and controlled by it as though by a powerful magnet.

The major Old Testament type, whose connexion with Lev. 25 is sufficiently obvious, is of course the institution of the Sabbath, which is so strongly emphasised in the first creation saga in Gen. 2^{1-3}. "And the heaven and the earth were finished, and all the host of them. And on the seventh day God finished his work which he had made; and he rested on the seventh day from all his work which he had made." In other words, after creating man on the sixth day, God looks back on His whole work of creation and sees that it is good, even very good, i.e., pre-eminently suited for His future purpose. But God does not continue His work on the seventh day in an infinite series of creative acts. He sets a limit to His activity, and thus to His creation as well. The object of His further dealings is this and not another world, the world completed with the creation of man. He now, as it were, ascends His throne and assumes sovereignty over His creation. He has now become its God, co-existing with it, and with man in particular as His last and culminating creation. Without ceasing to be God, He has made Himself a worldly, human, temporal God in relation to this work of His. He is now free to act as that kind of God, and as such He now celebrates and rejoices. Without detriment to His eternal glory, His glory will now be a glory in this distinct realm of heaven and earth and all their hosts, and especially in the existence of man. It is as the Lord of creation and the Lord of man, whose Master He has now become, that He now withdraws and rests. According to the saga, this is the content of the seventh day, of the last of the seven first days of time. This was the day to which time was already moving with its creation, when it became the life-time of other living creatures side by side with the living God. Time was intended for this day, the day in which God thus committed Himself to the world and man. Time was intended for this day as the day of the Lord of the world and of man; as the day of the Lord of the covenant between Himself and His creatures. But the story continues: "And God blessed the seventh day, and hallowed it: because that in it he rested from all his work which God created and made." Here, for the first time, God's sovereignty over His creature is made manifest in the commandment to man to keep holy the seventh day of creation. But it must be remembered that God's seventh day was man's first. Man now has time as well, the time of life. And primarily, and not just conclusively, it is this time, the day of the Lord, and therefore the time to be a witness of God's completion of His work and His rest, sharing in His Sabbath freedom, Sabbath festivity and Sabbath joy; the special time to be with God, the God who in this special time finishes His work and rests from it, no longer being the God who wills to be without the world and man but to be with him. The time of man begins, therefore, on the basis of the work God has done before his time and not with reference to any work still ahead [458] of him. The time of man begins, therefore, with a day of rest and not a day of work; with freedom and not with obligation; with a holiday and not with a task; with joy and not with labour and toil; under the Gospel and not under the Law. These other things will all come, but when they do they will be secondary and additional. The first thing in the time of man is

21

that he belongs to His Creator; just as the last thing in the time of the Creator is that He belongs to His creature.

Basically, then, it was no innovation when the early Christians (1 Cor. 16²; Ac. 20⁷) adopted the first day of the week as a holiday instead of the seventh and called it the κυριακὴ ἡμέρα[EN35] (Rev. 1¹⁰). On the contrary it was a discovery and application of the chronology implicit in Gen. 1–2. For they began the week with a holiday instead of ending it with one. What led to the change was of course the fact that the day after the Sabbath, and therefore the first day of the Jewish week, was the day of Christ's resurrection (Mk. 16² and *par.*). The new chronology surely means that the true meaning of the old is brought to light. When He had created man God saw that everything He had planned and made was good. In the completion of His work, He entered into a free and living fellowship with man, and brought man into fellowship with Himself. Only when this had been achieved could man set off into the week. What looks like his first day, i.e., his first working day, is really his second. His real first day is the Lord's day, the day when God rested from His work and devoted Himself to freedom, festivity and joy. Man is privileged to have a share in this day, descending from its heights to the depths of his first working day. By making God's Sabbath, and the invitation to man to share it, the context of a special day, the first creation saga points clearly and unmistakeably to the fact that the created time series is to include a special time of the salvation planned by God for the whole of His creation; the day of His appearing, His judgment and His mercy, the "great and notable day of the Lord" (Ac. 2²⁰: "And it shall come to pass, that whosoever shall call on the name of the Lord shall be saved" (Ac. 2²¹). This calling upon the name of the Lord in connexion with the special time of His appearance and presence is made possible by the institution of the recurrent Sabbath which concludes the week but also marks a new beginning. Will this offer be accepted or not? Will the Sabbath be kept or broken? Will the Lord's name be invoked or disregarded? This is the challenge of the Sabbath from its first institution. Will man in his own time "enter into God's rest" (Heb. 4¹⁻¹¹) or spurn it? But over and above the human decision of obedience or disobedience the power of this institution, the Sabbath itself (observed or desecrated), is the immutable sign, set up in and with the creation of time, of the particular time of God to which all other times move. Old Testament Israel did not see this day of the Lord. All it saw was the recurrent weekly sign of the Sabbath, and the prophets are full of complaints about its constant failure to keep the Sabbath law and to remember the name of the Lord. Or did it really see this day as it saw the sign, even though it flouted it? However that may be, God remained faithful to Israel and therefore the sign remained. At the end of every week came this seventh day, the only day of the week with a special name (ἄρα ἀπολείπεται σαββατισμὸς τῷ λαῷ τοῦ θεοῦ[EN36], Heb. 4⁹). This was Israel's lack in all its time, but also its promise. The apostolic Church, on the other hand, saw not only the sign, but the actual day of the Lord; and the real dawn of this day; the true Sabbath observed and celebrated with God the Creator through the one man Jesus, in whose day it broke for them too, so that they too may enter into God's rest. And they have to see and understand time, not only with a forward but also and decisively with a backward reference to this day of rest, and must observe the year of the birth of Jesus as the first year of that era, and the day of His resurrection as the first day of their week.

We may now turn our attention to the important New Testament concept of "the fulness of time."

[459]   We naturally begin with Gal. 4¹ᶠ. In this passage Paul suggests that there was a time when the heir, i.e., man elected and created by God to be His son, was still in the position of a

---

[EN35] Lord's day
[EN36] there remaineth therefore a sabbath to the people of God

minor. Although the rightful "Lord of all," he was subjected to "tutors and governors," i.e., the apparently autonomous and omnipotent powers of created being (the στοιχεῖα τοῦ κόσμου[EN37]). Man would thus seem to be no more than a slave among other slaves. "But when the πλήρωμα τοῦ χρόνου[EN38] was come, God sent forth his Son, made of a woman, born under the law, to redeem them that were under the law, that we might receive the adoption of sons." The Son of God "came"; He was sent from God, sent to men. Therefore He was Himself "born of a woman, born under the law." He entered the temporality which is that of each and every man. With Him came the "fulness of time." Note the emphasis laid on the final phrase, at first sight almost as if an independent event had made the mission of the Son possible, as if the time were now ripe, the historical situation favourable, for the mission of the Son. But this is not what Paul meant. The mission of the Son actually brings the fulness of time with it, and not *vice versa*. With the mission of the Son, with His entry into the time process, a new era of time has dawned, so far-reaching in its consequences that it may be justly called the fulness of all time. Man has now reached maturity. He has become God's son and heir, the "Lord of all." He has become a free man. This is the event which gives time its fulness. But the term πλήρωμα τοῦ χρόνου[EN39] has a further meaning. This event does not merely make this particular time fulfilled time. This fulfilled time is before or after all other time. Hence it makes all time, χρόνος as such, in the sequence and succession of which this fulfilment was achieved, fulfilled time. The *raison d'être*[EN40] of all time, both past and future, is that there should be this fulfilment at this particular time. Time may seem to move into the void but it is actually moving towards this event; just as it may seem to move out of the void, but it is actually moving from this event. The fulfilment of time has now "come," epitomising all the coming and going of time. Henceforth all time can be regarded only as time fulfilled in this particular time.

Now let us turn to Eph. 1[9f.], where we read that "before the foundation of the world" it was the good-pleasure (εὐδοκία) of God to achieve a purpose which He had decided and resolved to execute. This purpose was once a mystery, but now it is no longer so, for it has been revealed and executed in the Gospel. The content of this purpose is ἀνακεφαλαιώσασθαι τὰ πάντα ἐν τῷ Χριστῷ[EN41]. That is to say, Christ is to become the Head of all creation. He is to rule it and give it meaning. This is God's plan for the world, and it is the execution of this plan which involves the οἰκονομία τοῦ πληρώματος τῶν καιρῶν[EN42]. Its execution will coincide with the inauguration of the "fulness of time." This is what has happened and has been revealed by the Gospel. For God's plan to sum up all things under Christ as their Head, and therefore the "fulness of time," has actually taken place and may therefore be known by us in terms of this event. Note again how the one depends on the other. The One who wills and accomplishes and reveals the ἀνακεφαλαίωσις[EN43] also wills and accomplishes and reveals the "fulfilment of the times." It is with the summing up of all created being in Christ as its Head that the καιροί—the individual times, of individual created things—are not cancelled or destroyed but fulfilled. None of these times moved into the void. They all moved towards this goal, this event, and therefore this particular time.

These two Pauline texts will help us to understand Mk. 1[14f.], which is so important in this connexion. It gives us first a comprehensive summary of the activity of Jesus. He had been baptised by John and confirmed by the voice from heaven as the beloved Son of God, the

---

[EN37] elements of the world
[EN38] fulness of time
[EN39] fulness of time
[EN40] reason for existence
[EN41] to gather together all things in Christ
[EN42] the dispensation of the fulness of times
[EN43] gathering up

object here too of His εὐδοκία EN44. Then He had been tempted by the devil forty days in the wilderness among the wild beasts, after which angels came and ministered to Him. And now, we are told, He "came" into Galilee, the intermediate territory between Jew and Gentile. He "came," bringing the "glad tidings" of God, saying: "The time is fulfilled, and the kingdom of God is at hand: repent ye, and believe the gospel." We may accept the translation "is at hand," or, "has drawn nigh," for this is the message of John the Baptist in Mt. 3², and the disciples are entrusted with the same declaration in Lk. 10⁹, ¹¹. It implies that the irruption of the kingdom into history is imminent. On the other hand, if we adopt the suggestion that ἤγγικεν EN45 is simply a restrained expression for "has come," the use of this term is quite in accordance with the esoteric character of the pre-Easter history of the man Jesus, being wholly in line, for instance, with His command to the disciples to tell no one that He is the Messiah (Mt. 17⁹). Jesus' Messiahship is His secret, and can be published only when it has been disclosed from within. Similarly, the kingdom of God can be said to have come only when God has revealed it. Until then men must pray for its coming (Mt. 6¹⁰). Indeed, they will still have to pray for its coming even after it has been revealed. Until then the restrained ἤγγικεν EN46 must be used. Yet all the time there is a secretly implied ἐλήλυθεν EN47. This is brought out plainly in the Beelzebub controversy (see Kümmel, *op. cit.*, p. 63f.). "If I by the Spirit of God cast out devils, then is the kingdom of God come upon you" (ἔφθασεν ἐφ' ὑμᾶς, Mt. 12²⁸). The strong man has already been bound, and his house can now be plundered (Mt. 12²⁹). And Jesus' reference to His deeds in the reply to John the Baptist ("the blind receive their sight, and the lame walk … " Mt. 11²ᶠ·) implies that the eschatological salvation is no longer just a future expectation, but a present reality. Lk. 17²¹ puts it beyond all doubt: "The kingdom of God is in your midst." So, too, does the saying: "But blessed are your eyes, for they see: and your ears, for they hear. For verily I say unto you, That many prophets and righteous men have desired to see those things that ye see, and have not seen them; and to hear those things that ye hear, and have not heard them" (Mt. 13¹⁶ᶠ·)—a saying which is in remarkable contrast with Lk. 17²²: "The days will come, when ye shall desire to see one of the days of the son of man, and ye shall not see it (any longer)." We should also notice the reason Jesus gives for the power which even the disciples have over demons: "I beheld Satan as lightning fall from heaven" (Lk. 10¹⁸). How could the kingdom be stormed by violent men (Mt. 11¹²) if it were not already present? And how could a dividing line be drawn between the time before John the Baptist and the time after him, as is done in the continuation of the saying: "For all the prophets and the law prophesied until John. And if ye are willing to receive it, this is Elijah, which is to come. He that hath ears to hear, let him hear" (Mt. 11¹³ᶠ·), if the kingdom had not come after the coming and delivering up of this "Elijah"? And how could Jesus say that He had come to fulfil the law if the kingdom had not already come (Mt. 5¹⁷)? It is not, therefore, surprising to find Mark 1¹⁵ prefacing the statement that the kingdom had drawn nigh with the observation that "the time is fulfilled." There is an undoubted tension between the two phrases. The latter is not esoteric or restrained in this context. It is tolerable and intelligible only if ἤγγικεν EN48 is given an esoteric sense, if it encloses the mystery of an ἐλήλυθεν EN49. For the phrase πεπλήρωται ὁ καιρός EN50 is undoubtedly meant to describe an absolutely unique event marking an end and a new beginning in time. An event of the present gives meaning to the time before it and

EN44 good pleasure
EN45 has drawn near
EN46 has drawn near
EN47 has come
EN48 has drawn near
EN49 has come
EN50 the time is fulfilled

[460]

therefore also to the time after it. "The time is fulfilled" is so emphatic a statement that the one which follows would be quite flat and banal if it really meant no more than that the kingdom had drawn nigh, i.e., if in the ἤγγικεν EN51 we did not read the concealed ἐλήλυθεν EN52. Indeed, in Gal. 4⁴ the parallel to the "fulness of time" is the solemn assertion that God sent His Son into the world, while in Eph. 1¹⁰ the parallel is the ἀνακεφαλαίωσις EN53 of all things in Christ. Moreover, Mk. 1¹⁵ speaks expressly of a coming in a very real sense: ἦλθεν ὁ Ἰησοῦς εἰς τὴν Γαλιλαίαν κηρύσσων τὸ εὐαγγέλιον τοῦ θεοῦ EN54. This is certainly more than a mere announcement. It is an actual irruption rather than mere imminence. If the kingdom could only be announced prior to its manifestation with the coming of Jesus as the Bearer of God's good news, in and with Him there also came, in hidden but very real form, the kingdom and therefore the fulness of time, just as with the [461] coming of Jesus the Law was fulfilled and its whole meaning disclosed. When Jesus came, all the promises and prophecies of the Old Testament were fulfilled. No more was now needed than that this coming should run its course in time. The "year of grace," the "great and glorious day of the Lord," the true Sabbath of which the weekly Sabbath was only a sign, the Sabbath kept by God and man together, was not only at the doors but had actually dawned. If the good news of God was that the time was fulfilled, nothing less could have happened. Anything less would be inadequate to explain the tremendous caesura indicated by the expression "fulness of time," whether we think of the conclusion of the time "until John" on the one hand or the dawning on the other of the new time obviously granted solely for the purpose of enabling men to receive the good news of God, to accept God's immediate presence and rule in time, and therefore to repent and believe, clearly in the form of concrete acts in time. Μετάνοια EN55 means a complete re-orientation, both inward and outward, of the whole man to the God who in a very real sense has turned to him in time. Πίστις EN56 means the unquestioning trust in this God which is the positive side of this re-orientation; the new life which is the only possible life after this event in the time which follows it. In the language of Gal. 4¹ᶠ, it means turning right about and acquiring the confidence of a son who becomes "lord of all" on his coming of age; or, in the language of Eph. 1⁹ᶠ, it means a complete re-appraisal of the human situation in the light of the ἀνακεφαλαίωσις EN57 which has already been achieved. The difference between Mk. 1 and these other passages is that it explicitly calls attention to the consequence of all this for the time which follows. This is of a piece with the fact that it does not speak abstractly about πλήρωμα EN58, but concretely about an event, the event of πληροῦσθαι EN59, the reference being concretely to the coming of Jesus into Galilee, which, unless we are completely mistaken, is identical with His advent, and therefore with the advent of the kingdom. It also explains why the μετανοιεῖτε καὶ πιστεύετε EN60 has so imperatively concrete a reference to the future, and therefore why the beginning of the new time is explicitly indicated with the ending of the old. Mk. 1 makes it clear beyond all doubt that in the life of Jesus we have to do with a real event in time, but with a particular event and therefore a particular time, the time of the centre which dominates all other times. The fact that in His life all time comes to fruition means that all time before it

---

EN51 has drawn near
EN52 has come
EN53 gathering up
EN54 Jesus came into Galilee, preaching the gospel of the kingdom of God
EN55 repentance
EN56 faith
EN57 gathering up
EN58 fulness
EN59 fulfilment
EN60 repent and believe

moved towards it and all time after it moved away from it. In the last resort the only real reason why men had time at all was that—although they did not realise it, apart from the prophets who prophesied "until John"—this day was to come. And the men after Christ have time only in order to orientate their lives in the light of this day which in the series of days has now appeared ἅπαξ [EN61] and ἐφάπαξ [EN62] and is proclaimed with an explicit imperative. A similar idea is expressed in Paul's speech on the Areopagus (Ac. 17[30f.]): "The times of this ignorance (χρόνοι τῆς ἀγνοίας) God winked at; but now commandeth all men every where to repent: because he hath appointed a day (ἔστησεν ἡμέραν), in the which he will judge the world in righteousness by that man whom he hath ordained; whereof he hath given assurance unto all men, in that he hath raised him from the dead."

But behind the application of the concept of the fulfilment to that of time in Gal. 4, Eph. 1 and Mk. 1 there lies a definite view of time. It is pictured as an empty vessel, not yet filled, but waiting to be filled up at a particular time. As all the commandments, promises and prophecies of the prophets and righteous men of the Old Testament, as all its sayings and types, are without content, apart from the coming of the kingdom in the man Jesus, and therefore defective in themselves, yet, being related to this event, and destined all along for this content, they are not for nothing, so too is it with time in itself and as such. It, too, is empty in both the negative and positive sense: empty of this content and empty for this content. It has
[462]   both the defect and the advantage of being time which is hastening toward the time of Jesus and is then destined to move away from His time. Standing as it does in this relation to His time, it is in an indirect, though very real sense, His time. Its fulness resides in His time, in the πληροῦσθαι [EN63], the πλήρωμα [EN64], of the event of His life. In Him, the Son and Head of all things, in the kingdom of God which came to Galilee and was proclaimed in Galilee, all time is brought to an end and begins afresh as full and proper time.

It is important to remember how concrete all this is. The fulfilment of time itself had this particular time which is datable in relation to other times. There is no fulfilment of time without the time of fulfilment. That is why 1 Pet. 1[20], speaking of the time of the revelation of the Lamb chosen before the foundation of the world, calls it the "last" time, the ἔσχατος τῶν χρόνων [EN65]. It is linked with a whole sequence of prevailing times. It forms the term of this sequence, but also marks the beginning of a new sequence of times. It was on the "last" of these days that God, having at sundry times and in divers manners spoken in those days unto the fathers by the prophets, spoke in His Son, whom He had made the heir of all things, and by whom also He created the times (æons, Heb. 1[1f.]). "But last of all (when He had sent one servant after another) he sent unto them his son" (Mt. 21[37]). And it is obviously significant that it was on the last and great day of the feast (Jn. 7[37]) that "Jesus stood and cried, saying, If any man thirst, let him come unto me, and drink." This fulfilment proceeds even during this great day of His until it is completed and lies behind. The day of Jesus lasts, and as long as it lasts He must work the works of Him that sent Him, standing and issuing His summons and invitation. "As long as I am in the world, I am the light of the world" (Jn. 9[4f.]). This text clearly envisages a real day, with a morning and evening; a real time with beginning, duration and end. For it says explicitly: "While it is day," and then continues; "The night cometh when no man can work." Thus the fulfilment of time is itself an event which fulfils time, an event which begins, continues and ends. It is for this reason that Jesus justifies His delay at the marriage of Cana of Galilee with the words: "Mine hour is not yet come" (Jn.

EN61 once
EN62 once for all
EN63 fulfilment
EN64 fullness
EN65 last times

26

2^4), and His initial absence from the feast at Jerusalem with the words: "My time is not yet fulfilled" (Jn. 7^8). The assault of His enemies gathers weight before it reaches its climax and contributes to the fulfilment of time, and it must be held in check until the right moment (Lk. 20^{19}, 22$^{52f.}$). Even the climax is marked by development. First we read: "The hour is at hand, and the Son of man is betrayed into the hands of sinners" (Mt. 26^{45}), and only then: "The hour it come" (Jn. 17^1); "This is your hour and the power of darkness" (Lk. 22^{53}); "Father, save me from this hour" (Jn. 12^{27}). Only then can the clock of Good Friday begin to strike until we reach the $\tau\epsilon\tau\acute{\epsilon}\lambda\epsilon\sigma\tau\alpha\iota$ EN66 which Jesus can say only as He dies on the cross, and which according to Jn. 19^{30} is His very last word. It is for this reason, too, that when Heb. 5$^{7f.}$ comes to speak of what He did "in the days of his flesh," and of the way in which Her brought in the fulness of time, it sums it all up in a reference to the last of His days, the day of the passion. It is as Jesus travels this road to the bitter end that there takes place what the New Testament calls the "fulfilment of time," and His time becomes fulfilled time, and is revealed as such to His disciples in the Easter time.

We have called this time of His at the heart of other times the time of God: eternal time; the time which God has assumed for us, and thus granted to us, the men of all times; the time of His covenant; or, as the Bible sees it, the great Sabbath; the year of salvation; fulfilled time. We must now try to assess the material implications of all this for our understanding of this particular time.

Our previous deliberations should have made it clear that in the first [463] instance the time of Jesus is also a time like all other times; that it occurred once and once for all; that it had beginning, duration and end; that it was contemporary for some, future for others, and for others again, e.g., for us, past. Only a docetic attitude to Jesus can deny that His being in time also means what being in time means for us all. Our recognition of His true humanity depends on our acceptance of this proposition. Even the recognition of His true deity, implying as it does the identity between His time and God's, does not rule out this simple meaning of His being in time. On the contrary, it includes it. Of course there is much more to see and say, but it would all be pointless if we ignored or minimised this simple truth.

It is as well to realise how closely the relevant New Testament formulae support this view. This is the case with the formula which constantly recurs in different forms in the Apocalypse (Rev. 1$^{4\ 8\ 17}$, 4^8, 21^6, 22^{13}), in clear reminiscence of Is. 41^4, 44^6, 48^{12}: I am he that was, and is, and is to come, the beginning and the ending, the first and the last, the Alpha and Omega. Of course these formulae are much too solemn to be taken simply as a description of the being of a man in its temporal limits and in its beginning, duration and end in time, and therefore as a being contemporary, future or past to that of others. The formula says much more than this. But it does include this, as a primary truth within its wider implications. The same holds good of Heb. 13^8: "Jesus Christ the same yesterday, and today, and for ever." This again means more than that the man Jesus lived in a movement from yesterday through to-day to to-morrow. Yet we miss the deeper implications if we overlook the primary and simple meaning of the words.

The three dimensions which play a part in any conception of time are equally important for an understanding of the time of Jesus as the time of God.

EN66 it is finished

But there is a further point to be noticed. The time of Jesus is not only a time like all others; it is also different from them. For all other times are confined to the three dimensions. They begin, they endure, and they come to an end. According to the standpoint of the observer, they are future, contemporary or past.

1. Every other time begins, and therefore from the standpoint of an earlier time it is a future time. This means that it does not yet exist at this earlier time.

2. Every other time has duration, and therefore from the standpoint of the same time it is present. This means that its contemporaneity is limited to its duration, and to that of the contemporary observer.

3. Every other time comes to an end, and therefore from the standpoint of a later time it is already past. This means that it no longer exists at this time.

But these limitations of all other times—the times of all other living creatures—do not apply to the time of the man Jesus.

1. To be sure, the life of the man Jesus has a beginning, and His time was once future. Yet this does not mean that it did not then exist.

[464] 2. The life of Jesus has duration, and therefore it was once contemporary. Yet this does not mean that it was present only in its duration, and from the standpoint of contemporaries.

3. The life of Jesus comes to an end and therefore it became past. Yet this does not mean that it then ceased to be.

The removal of the limitations of its yesterday, to-day and tomorrow, of its once, now and then, is the distinctive feature of the time of the man Jesus. For as such, according to its manifestation in Easter-time, it is also the time of God; eternal time; the time of the covenant; the great Sabbath; the year of salvation; fulfilled time. What is for all other times, the times of all other living creatures, an absolute barrier, is for Him in His time a gateway. We shall now try to formulate positively what we have so far stated only in the form of delimitation.

1. The life of Jesus begins, and therefore it was once future. But the man Jesus already was even before He was. Hence the time before His time, the time when this was still future, because it hastened forward to His future, was also His time, the time of His being.

2. The life of Jesus has duration, and therefore it was once present. But for all its singularity this present reaches back to His past when His time was still future, and forward to His future when His time will be past. The man Jesus is as He was and will be. Even the time of His present, just because it is the time of His present, is also the time before and after His time, and is thus His time, the time of His being.

3. The life of Jesus comes to an end, and therefore there was a moment when His time became past. But its end is such that it is always present and still future. The man Jesus was as He is and will be. Even the time after His time, the time in which His time is already past time, because it is the time of His past,

28

the time which derives from Him, is the time of His renewed presence, the time of His new coming, and therefore again His time.

This means, however, that from the standpoint of the three dimensions of every conception of time, His time is not only the time of a man, but the time of God, eternal time. Thus, as the title of this sub-section suggests, He not only is in time and has time like other men, but He is also Lord of time.

It is clear that—whether as delimitation or positive formulation—this could not be said, or could be said only in abstraction, if to the being of the man Jesus in time there did not belong His being in Easter time. If Christ were not risen from the dead, our treatment of the whole subject would have no basis whatever in the Word and revelation of God. Every assertion beyond the mere fact that Jesus' time was like all other times in that it had beginning, duration and end, would be mere speculation, a house of cards built on our subjective impression of His life in time, and liable to collapse at the slightest touch of justifiable doubts as to the validity of our subjective impression and therefore our competence. Jesus is the Lord of time in the sense expounded because He is the Son of God, and as such the eternal God in person, the Creator of all time and therefore its sovereign Ruler. Either He is this, or He is not the Lord of time at all. But we insist that He is the Lord of time because He has revealed Himself as such, because in the resurrection His appearance has proved to be that of the eternal God. Otherwise we have no grounds for making this claim, and it is better not to pretend that we have. The apostles and the Church of the New Testament can and must say what is said in the formulae of the Epistle to the Hebrews and the Apocalypse—we now turn to their true and explicit sense—because they start at the resurrection of Jesus, because in the light of this event they see the real meaning of Jesus' previous existence in time, and because they regard it as axiomatic that all their thinking and speaking about His whole being in time should start at this point.

[465]

Of all the relevant passages in the Apocalypse, the clearest is Rev. 1[8]: "I am the Alpha and the Omega, saith the Lord, which is, and which was, and which is to come, the Almighty" (παντοκράτωρ). The context leaves us in no doubt that the speaker is not God *in abstracto*[EN67], but God *in concreto*[EN68], God in His identity with the man Jesus. It is equally clear that when the context speaks of His being in time it implies much more than that time has a beginning, duration and end. "I am," says Jesus here, *"the* Alpha and *the* Omega"—ὁ πρῶτος καὶ ὁ ἔσχατος, ἡ ἀρχὴ καὶ τὸ τέλος[EN69], as these letters are interpreted in Rev. 22[13]. Not even this part of the formula speaks of timelessness. For although A and O are the first and last letters, they are part of the Greek alphabet, belonging to the series which includes all the other letters. The first and the last are not outside the series but within it. So, too, it is with Jesus when He calls Himself the Alpha and Omega. He ascribes to Himself a being in time. The same truth emerges unmistakeably from the allusion to the three dimensions, the second dimension being significantly placed first in verse 8: "which is, and which was, and which is to come." His life embraces a present, past and future. Here is no timeless being, but a strictly temporal one, though of course it differs from all other temporal being as that which is divinely temporal. This is made plain, not only by the addition of "the Almighty" at the end of the formula, although this gives verbal support to our title "Lord of Time," but above all by the fact that Ἐγώ εἰμι[EN70] is put at the head of the formula and that

---

EN67 in the abstract
EN68 concretely
EN69 the first and the last, the beginning and the end
EN70 I am

29

ὁ ὤν[EN71] is the first predicate. Ἐγώ εἰμι ὁ ὤν is a quotation from Ex. 3¹⁴: "I AM THAT I AM." This passage speaks of a being in time, but the reference is to the divine being, the being of Yahweh, in time. And the amplification of ὁ ὤν· ὁ ἦν καὶ ὁ ἐρχόμενος[EN72], shows how the author of the Apocalypse understood the "I am" in the predicate: I am (in Rev. 1¹⁷ ὁ ὤν[EN73] is expressly replaced by ὁ ζῶν[EN74]) He who has life in Himself. That is to say, I am sovereign over my own being. Even as present I am He who was and will be. All this is applied to the being of the man Jesus in time. The all-inclusive "I am" rules out any notion that the three dimensions, present, past and future, simply follow one another in succession. The very fact that 1⁸ puts the "I am" and the "which is" first is a plain warning. It means: "I am all this simultaneously. I, the same, am; I was as the same; and I will come again as the same. My time is always simultaneously present, past and future. That is why I am the Alpha and Omega, the beginning and the ending, the first and the last. Since my present includes the past and future it is both the first and last of all other times. All times have their source and end in my time. Of course, all these other times are real times, for at the heart of them I have time. But other times are previous or subsequent to mine. They are overshadowed, dominated and divided into periods by my time. It is my present that makes them either past or future, for my present includes both. I was, and I am to come, as surely as I am and live. This is how the author of the Apocalypse sees the being of Jesus in time. How he came to adopt this view is indicated by Rev. 1¹⁷⁻¹⁸, where the formula: "the first and the last, he that liveth," is immediately followed by the reference: "I was dead, and, behold, I am alive εἰς τοὺς αἰῶνας τῶν αἰώνων[EN75]." There is no doubt that all this is meant to be taken in a concrete sense. It is because He rose from the dead that He liveth. As I am in my time, all time is my time, my before or after.

[466]

Heb. 13⁸ has a very similar meaning and intent: Ἰησοῦς Χριστὸς ἐχθὲς καὶ σήμερον ὁ αὐτὸς καὶ εἰς τοὺς αἰῶνας[EN76]. The context shows that this has a quite practical bearing, for in verse 7 the readers are exhorted to remember their "rulers," those who have preached to them the Word of God. They must take note of their ἔκβασις[EN77], i.e., the outcome, the result, the successful conclusion, of their manner of life, and imitate their faith. The exploits of their faith in the past are thus brought into connexion with the present in which the readers are now living. The readers' faith is to be an "imitation," a continual reproduction, of the faith of their rulers. Their faith is not to be a new or different faith. Why not? Because, says verse 8, Jesus Christ, in whom both the readers and their rulers believed, is the same yesterday, to-day and forever. This saying sounds like a slogan, and can hardly have been coined here for the first time. Probably it is a fragment of one of the early Christian hymns of which traces are to be found elsewhere in the Epistles. But in any case it is of basic importance. "Jesus Christ yesterday" is Jesus in the span of His earthly life, including the Easter period. From the standpoint of the New Testament Church, founded as it was on the testimony and preaching of the apostles, the earthly life of Jesus belongs to yesterday, to the past. Jesus Christ is also in this yesterday. But this Jesus Christ yesterday is the same to-day. Although He has a yesterday, a past, this does not mean that to-day He has become a man of yesterday. On the contrary. He as one and the same is both yesterday and to-day. His time is also the time of His community, and the time of His community is His time. Hence in the time of His community faith can only be faith in Him as He demanded it of His own, and

---

EN71 which is
EN72 which was and which is to come
EN73 which is
EN74 which lives
EN75 for evermore
EN76 Jesus Christ the same yesterday, and to day, and for ever
EN77 end

found it in them, in His time. There can be no earlier or later in the time of the community to cause or permit an alteration of its faith. That is why the faith of the readers of the Epistle can only be a constant reproduction of the faith of those who proclaimed the Word of God to them. But the text goes on to speak of the third dimension of time. To "yesterday and to-day it adds: καὶ εἰς τοὺς αἰῶνας EN78. This may best be translated: "in every conceivable future." Like to-day, every coming day will be His, and the faith then required by Him will be no different from the faith in Him required and found yesterday, and that which is the one possible faith to-day. The sequel in verse 9 should be noticed. "Be not carried about with divers and strange doctrines. For it is a good thing that the heart be stablished with grace." Thus Heb. 13⁸ leads to the same conclusion as Rev. 1⁸ and *par.* Jesus Christ belongs not only to yesterday, or to-day, or an indefinite future. He belongs to all times simultaneously. He is the same Christ in all of them. There is no time which does not belong to Him. He is really the Lord of time. If we ask the author of Hebrews how he came to attribute to Jesus this extraordinary being in time, the only answer which he can give is to refer to the point indicated a few verses later (Heb. 13²⁰). Who is "our Lord Jesus"? He is the great Shepherd of the sheep in the blood of the covenant, whom the God of peace "brought again from the dead." He is the great High Priest who "hath passed through the heavens" (4¹⁴) to sit down on the right hand of the Majesty on high, i.e., God (1³; 8¹; 10¹²; 12²). Unless we are prepared to understand 13⁸ in the light of these other passages, and therefore of the Easter axiom of this New Testament author too, we shall not understand it at all.

We cannot afford to lose sight of the key to the whole matter in the Easter history as we now proceed to a brief exposition of the Christian view of the man Jesus in His time with specific reference to the three dimensions of the concept of time.

1. After Easter and Pentecost, the primary conviction of the New Testament [467] community is that the man Jesus is really but transcendentally present, in a way which could not be said of its contemporary members and other men of their age. His past history, His yesterday, cannot be understood or portrayed as a thing of the past, a thing of yesterday. The yesterday of Jesus is also to-day. The fact that He lives at the right hand of God means that even now He is absolutely present temporally. And to His own on their further journey into time, in and with the witness continually to be proclaimed and heard by them, He has given them His Spirit, the Holy Spirit. But where the Spirit is, there is more than a mere tradition or recollection of Jesus. Of course there is tradition and recollection as well. But the message of His past is proclaimed, heard and believed in order that it should no longer be past but present. Life is lived in contemplation of the kingdom already come, in which everything necessary has been done for the full deliverance and preservation of man, for the fulfilment of the divine covenant. Nor does this rest merely on a retrospective vision, nor on an interpretation and assessment of this past history hazarded at some point and in some way by the men concerned, but on the fact that this history, this time, is not merely past but present, overlapping objectively as it were the present time of the apostles and their communities, pushing beyond its own frontiers to those of this other time and beyond. These men do not

EN78 and for ever

31

make or feel or know themselves the contemporaries of Jesus. It is not they who become or are this. It is Jesus who becomes and is their Contemporary. As a result of this, His past life, death and resurrection can and must and actually do have at all times the significance and force of an event which has taken place in time but is decisive for their present existence. Hence they can and must and actually do understand their present existence as a life of direct discipleship; as their "being in Christ"; as a being done to death with Him at Golgotha, renewed in the garden of Joseph of Arimathea, and on the Mount of Olives (or wherever the ascension took place) entering into the concealment of the heavenly world, or rather, into the concealment of God. Thus its continuation and formation here and now can only be a faithful imitation of their "citizenship in heaven" as it is already actualised proleptically in the man Jesus; an act of faithfulness to the constitution under which they are placed already as God's citizens and members of His household. Their life's work can only be to make known to others who do not know it the lordship of Jesus Christ over the world and men and therefore their time as they themselves know it. Note that if there is anything doubtful for Christians here, it is not His presence but their own. And if there is anything axiomatically certain, it is not their presence but His. There is obviously no baptism or Lord's Supper without His real presence as very God and very Man, both body and soul. But this presence cannot be regarded as restricted to what were later called the "sacra-

[468] ments." For these are only a symbolical expression of the fact that in its worship the community is gathered directly around Jesus Himself, and lives by and with Him, but that through faith He rules over the hearts and lives of all even apart from worship. Hence the gifts of prophecy, teaching, leadership and service, and hence also miracles in the community. Hence, too, the royal freedom of the children of God, but hence also in Christ's stead the apostolic word of witness, the word of knowledge, direction and exhortation. All these are possible because "Christians" have the Spirit and are led by Him.

By way of anticipation we may say that the historical distance, the past, in which Jesus confronts them is not abrogated by His presence. His yesterday is not cancelled by His to-day. The Evangelist does not disappear in favour of the apostle. On the contrary, His presence stimulates interest in the past and in the tradition of Jesus, revealing the unfathomable but clear depths of His prior life on earth. Yet He cannot be regarded merely as a figure of the past. A community interested only in a historical Jesus would be an unspiritual community in the New Testament sense, i.e., a community without the guiding Spirit. The fact that the man Jesus was includes the fact that He is; but the fact that He is excludes that He is no longer.

Again by way of anticipation, the presence of Jesus in His community is full of import for the future. His presence impels and presses to His future, general and definitive revelation, of which there has been a particular and provisional form in the Easter history. Hence even the presence of Jesus in the Spirit, for all its fulness, can only be a pledge or first instalment of what awaits the community as well as the whole universe, His return in glory. But it must never be forgotten that He who comes again in glory, this future Jesus, is identical with the One proclaimed by the history of yesterday and really present to His own to-day. The thorough-going eschatology for which the interim between now and one day necessarily seems to be a time of emptiness, of futility, of lack, of a progressive and barely concealed disillusionment, is not the eschatology of New Testament Christianity. And again it is only an unspiritual community which can tolerate such a view. The fact that the man Jesus will be includes the fact that He is; but the fact that He is does not exclude that He is "not yet."

We may summarise this in the words of Rev. 1⁸, "I am (he that) is." The present in which there is real recollection of the man Jesus and the particular and preliminary revelation accomplished in Him, and real expectation of this man and God's final and general revelation with Him—this present "between the times" is His own time, the time of the man Jesus.

There is such a wealth of exogetical material available on this point that we must confine ourselves to a few concrete indications. "This day," says Jesus in Lk. 4²¹, "is this scripture fulfilled in your ears." The reference is to all that is written about the "acceptable year of the Lord." This "to-day" with its fulfilment, with its intimate connexion with the name and history of the man Jesus, is the content of the apostolic message and the meaning of the life of the apostolic community. The Church's "to-day" is likewise the acceptable year, the great Sabbath, the fulfilled time of the man Jesus. According to Rev. 1¹⁰ it is on "the Lord's day" that the New Testament seer found himself "in the spirit" ($\dot{\epsilon}\gamma\epsilon\nu\acuteo\mu\eta\nu$ $\dot{\epsilon}\nu$ $\pi\nu\epsilon\acute{\upsilon}\mu\alpha\tau\iota$ EN79), and heard behind him the mighty voice: "as of a trumpet," bidding him see and write down what he saw. It is not only right but necessary to recall here the trumpet of the year of jubilee in Lev. 25⁹. The apostolic day is the day of the apostles' Lord, His now, His "to-day." And, in a remarkable manner, the event of that yesterday is the vitality of to-day, the new thing whose perception and propagation is the purpose of the present time. "The times of this ignorance God winked at; but now commandeth all men every where to repent" (Ac. 17³⁰). "And you, that were sometime alienated and enemies in your mind by wicked works, yet now hath he reconciled in the body of his flesh through death ... " (Col. 1²¹ᶠ·). "(You) in time past were not a people, but are now the people of God: which had not obtained mercy, but now have obtained mercy" (1 Pet. 2¹⁰). "For ye were sometimes darkness, but now are ye light in the Lord" (Eph. 5⁸). "The mystery (was once) hid from ages and from generations: but now is made manifest to his saints" (Col. 1²⁶). "Behold, now is the acceptable time; behold, now is the day of salvation" (2. Cor. 6²). "To-day if ye will hear his voice, harden not your hearts" (Heb. 3⁷). "But exhort one another daily, while it is called To-day" (Heb. 3¹³). Why all this emphasis on "to-day"? Because, as Heb. 4¹⁻⁸ explains, the Sabbath day has dawned. Because we now have not only the weekly recurring sign of the seventh day, but the fulfilment of this sign, the reality to which it had pointed so long. The day of rest has arrived for God and His people, and none must neglect to enter into it to-day. The whole of the Old Testament is before them as an awful warning against neglect. This Sabbath has dawned to-day and must be kept, because this day have I begotten thee" (Heb. 1⁵; 5⁵, quoting Ps. 2⁷), and as "a priest for ever after the order of Melchisedec" (Heb. 5⁶, 7¹⁷, ²¹), as "a priest continually" (Heb. 7³), have I appointed Thee; because "unto you is born this day ... a Saviour" (Lk. 2¹¹); because

[469]

EN79 I was in the Spirit

"this day is salvation come to this house" (Lk. 19⁹). All this happened yesterday for the sake of to-day—the birth of Jesus, His visit to the house of Zacchaeus, His death on the cross, His burial and resurrection. And as a consequence we to-day, in our time, have died and been buried and risen with Him in baptism. We can therefore walk in newness of life, as described in Rom 6¹⁻¹¹. The time which Jesus filled up to His death, and revealed in its fulness during the forty days, this last time up to its last day and its last hour, was as such the future day of the apostles and their community. The day of His death was revealed on Easter Day to be the day of their life. And they now stand in the grey twilight before the dawn. They now advance into this day, which will eventually be theirs, but for the moment is only His. All this does not rule out the idea of a recollection or tradition of Jesus. On the contrary, it is εἰς τὴν ἐμὴν ἀνάμνησιν ᴱᴺ⁸⁰ that the bread and cup of the Lord's Supper are to be distributed and received in the community (1 Cor. 11²⁴ᶠ; Lk. 22¹⁹). And Timothy is expressly charged to remember (μνημονεύειν) Jesus Christ risen from the dead (2 Tim. 2⁸). Note, too, the stress laid on remembrance in 2 Pet. 1¹²⁻¹⁵. On this possibility of real recollection and genuine tradition hangs the whole history and temporality of this event, with all that this involves. There is no place for any "Christ-mysticism," or even Christ-ethics of living, dying and rising again in discipleship of Christ, such as would suppress or replace the history of Jesus or render it superfluous. Nor can any spirit which drives men away from the recollection and tradition of Jesus be His Spirit, the Holy and sanctifying Spirit. On the contrary: "the Holy Spirit, whom the Father will send in my name, he shall teach you all things, and bring all things to your remembrance (ὑπομνήσει) whatsoever I have said unto you" (Jn. 14²⁶)." He shall glorify me; for he shall receive of mine, and shall shew it unto you "(Jn. 16¹⁴). Hence also the parable of the vine: the branches must abide in Him, for apart from Him they can do nothing; they cannot bring forth fruit, but only wither and decay (Jn. 15¹⁻⁸). What really happens is that the history of Jesus itself becomes history again; past time becomes the time of His renewed presence. "Heaven and earth shall pass away; but my words shall not pass away" (Mk. 13³¹). "I will not leave you comfortless; I will come to you" (Jn. 14¹⁸)."Lo, I am with you alway, even unto the end of the world" (Mt. 28²⁰). "Where two or three are gathered together in my name, there am I in the midst of them" (Mt. 18²⁰). And in Paul we find the converse. What belongs to the past? Not Jesus, but the life which we have been living to-day in so far as it has not been lived in the Spirit and therefore in Him, but in the flesh as our own independent life (2 Cor. 5¹⁶). Who are Christians? Those who by baptism into Jesus' death have been buried with Him (Rom. 6⁴); who can no longer live unto themselves, but only unto Him who died and rose again for them (2 Cor. 5¹⁵). And who is Paul? The man who lives, yet lives no longer, because Christ lives in him; the man who can live his present life in the flesh only in the faith of the Son of God who loved him and gave Himself for him (Gal. 2²⁰). "If any man be in Christ, he is a new creature: old things are passed away; behold, all things are become new" (2 Cor. 5¹⁷).

[470]

This, then, is how matters stand with the One who is the object of recollection and tradition. The fact that He is this certainly cannot mean that He is to be sought among the dead. In no circumstances is He to be found in that company (Lk. 24⁵). He is "awakened" or "raised" or "brought up" ἐκ τῶν νεκρῶν ᴱᴺ⁸¹. This means that for a brief space He was one of the great host of those who once lived but have now perished and live no longer. But then He was called and taken from this host as ἀπαρχή ᴱᴺ⁸² (1 Cor. 15²⁰) or πρωτότοκος ᴱᴺ⁸³ (Col. 1¹⁸). This shows Him to be the effective appearance of God, which is not only unforget-

---

ᴱᴺ⁸⁰ in remembrance of me
ᴱᴺ⁸¹ from the dead
ᴱᴺ⁸² firstfruits
ᴱᴺ⁸³ firstborn

table but makes itself felt again and again. Thus, while there is recollection and tradition from the standpoint of the action of the community, objectively and in fact He Himself is the acting Subject who lifts the barrier of yesterday and moves into to-day, making Himself present, and entering in as the Lord. This is the inner connexion between Easter and Pentecost. The living One, who is no longer to be sought among the dead, who "died once but ... liveth unto God" (Rom. 6¹⁰), is not only alive Himself, but quickens others too, proffering Himself as the Creator and ground and soul of life. Having risen from the dead. He promises His followers His Spirit who will shortly come down from heaven as depicted in Ac. 1–2. The description in Jn. 20²¹⁻²³ obviously speeds up the time-table, for after the risen Lord has greeted His disciples with peace, and given them the missionary charge: "As my Father hath sent me, even so send I you," there follows immediately: "He breathed on them, and saith unto them, Receive ye the Holy Ghost." And in the remarkable passage 2 Cor. 3¹⁷⁻¹⁸ it seems to be speeded up even more, for here the risen Lord is Himself the Spirit whose presence means liberty. For all the variations, however, it is clear that Pentecost is the result of the resurrection, achieved in the time of the apostles, yet not by the apostles, but in and to them. It is the result of the revelation of the fulfilment of time accomplished in His life and death. It is the bridging of the gulf between His past and their present; the assumption of their time into His.

The most illuminating comment on this point is provided by the story of the conversion of Paul, and the appointment, commissioning and sending forth of this new apostle who now appears in such remarkable circumstances. His conversion is brought about by an event which, like the transfiguration of Jesus before His resurrection, would appear to belong in essence to the forty days. For it consists of nothing less than an appearance of the exalted Jesus in person. Paul himself is quite explicit about this, for in 1 Cor. 15⁸ he numbers it with the appearances of the forty days. Elsewhere he appeals to his conversion as a proof that "the gospel which was preached of me is not after man. For I neither received it of man, neither was I taught it, but by the revelation of Jesus Christ" (Gal. 1¹¹ᶠ). It pleased God "to reveal his Son in me, that I might preach him among the heathen" (Gal. 1¹⁶). Again, it is by an account of his conversion that, according to Ac. 22¹⁻²¹, Paul defends himself before the people of Jerusalem, and later before Agrippa (Ac. 26²⁻²³). It is the story of his conversion which evokes from the Jews the cry: "Away with such a fellow from the earth; for it is not fit that he should live" (Ac. 22²²), and from the Hellenist Agrippa the ingenuous comment: "Paul, thou art beside thyself; much learning (τὰ πολλὰ γράμματα) doth make thee mad" (Ac. 26²⁴). What is it that makes his conversion so important to Paul himself for his mission to Jews and Gentiles, and so scandalous and strange to his non-Christian hearers? Clearly the real reason is that even the time after the life and death of Jesus, and after the forty days, is a time when this man is still a Subject capable of and in fact engaged in action. For this personal appearance of Jesus, this event which changes Saul into Paul, the persecutor into the apostle, this "one born out of due time" (1 Cor. 15⁸) into the executor of the commission laid upon all the apostles, this event so strangely late in time, so long after Jesus had lived and manifested Himself—what does it show? It shows that the Jesus of that earlier time is still at work. The life and work of the apostles is wholly and utterly dependent on His presence. Their whole recollection and tradition concerning Him is not centred on a figure of the past, on a dead man, but on One who even after His earthly time is still an acting Subject, doing new things, creating in history. It is not from within themselves supported by their fragmentary recollection of past days and the corresponding tradition—this would be a real gospel "after man" (Gal. 1¹¹)—that the apostles and the primitive community derive their *raison d'être*ᶠᴺ⁸⁴ and their commission. It is not from within themselves that they derive their consolation and the

[471]

ᶠᴺ⁸⁴ reason for existence

necessary defiance in face of the rage of the Jews and the contempt of the Greeks; their faith, hope and love; the ordering of their common life and direction for the life of individuals. They receive all these things from the Lord who is Himself Spirit, conducting His own cause, and present amongst them in the hiddenness of God but no less really, indeed with supreme reality. It is the first of the two times, that of the life of Jesus, which makes the second, the time of the Church founded upon the apostolic witness, the interim period prior to His general and definitive revelation, not only possible and necessary, but full of meaning and substance.

That is why, in the second time, it is impossible to dismiss the first as merely past and over. We have now to recognise that this view is an incredible error, the product of wilful ignorance and prejudice. The hidden power of the first time, the fact that it is not past but present, is now disclosed. Jesus was not found among the dead, but among the living; the living One and the Lifegiver. Yet He was the self-same Jesus who had previously gone about with His disciples ; thronged by the multitudes and the devout of Galilee and Jerusalem; seen, but not really perceived; heard but not really understood; touched but not apprehended; recognised and yet denied; respected and yet betrayed; the great Prophet, the Messiah of Israel, and yet rejected and cast out by His own people and crucified by the Gentiles.

The story of the walk to Emmaus in Lk. 24$^{13f.}$ is the passage which shows most clearly what view of the earthly life of Jesus was vanquished and removed by the resurrection and the gift of the Holy Spirit in the second time, the time of the apostles and the apostolic community; and also how this came about. As they were walking on the road to Emmaus these two disciples were talking about πάντα τὰ συμβεβηκότα ταῦτα[EN85]. That is to say, they were talking about the enacted life and death of Jesus as though it were a matter of past history. Hence it is not surprising that when Jesus asked them what they were talking about, they

[472] ἐστάθησαν σκυθρωπά[EN86] (v. 17), they stood still, gazing back like Lot's wife, and were gloomy and sullen and sad. The same word occurs in Mt. 6^{16}, where it is applied to the Pharisees when they fast. "Can the sons of the bride-chamber mourn (and disfigure their faces like the Pharisees) as long as the bridegroom is with them? but the days will come, when the bridegroom shall be taken from them, and then shall they fast" (Mt. 9^{15}). Now that Jesus had died it would seem that the time for fasting had arrived. Jesus is no more than a bit of past history: "τὰ περὶ τοῦ Ἰησοῦ τοῦ Ναζαρηνοῦ[EN87], which was a prophet mighty in deed and word before God and all the people: and how the chief priests and our rulers delivered him up to be condemned to death and crucified him." This is how they remember Him now. "But we trusted (ἠλπίζομεν[EN88]—even that has become past history!) that it had been he which should have redeemed Israel: and beside all this, to-day is the third day since these things were done" (v. 21). Even the beginning of the Easter story had found its way into this sad history, and they tell how the women had found the tomb empty and how the angels appeared to them saying that He was alive. But so far from cheering them, this news had merely plunged them into further despondency (vv. 22–24), while v. 11 even goes so far as to say that "their words seemed to them in their sight as idle tales (λῆρος); and they believed them not." "And certain of them which were with us went to the sepulchre and found it even so as the women had said: but him they saw not" (v. 24), Even this does not get them any further. Even the Easter message, or its prelude, the news of the empty tomb, is still the object of mere recollection, and of very dubious recollection at that. Nor was their gloom dispelled when Jesus reproached them (vv. 25–27) for their stubborn incomprehen-

---

[EN85] all these things which had happened
[EN86] they stood there, looking sad
[EN87] the things concerning Jesus of Nazareth
[EN88] we hoped

sion and rebuked them for refusing to believe not only the tales of the women, but even what the prophets had said. Nor did they abandon their sorrow when He expounded τὰ περὶ αὐτοῦ from the Old Testament, thus proving that it was necessary for Christ to suffer these things and (through this suffering) to enter into His glory. Not until He performed a certain action was this state of affairs changed ("And their eyes were opened, and they knew him," v. 31). That action was not something new and special, but the very action He had performed on the night of His passion when He re-interpreted the passover as a prefigurement of His own passion and death in their saving significance, thus showing that the deliverance of Israel from Egypt had now become a reality. "And it came to pass, as he sat at meat with them, he took bread, and blessed it, and brake, and gave to them." This was what dispelled their gloom. "He was known of them in the breaking of the bread." That was the momentous news they brought back to the eleven and their companions when they returned to Jerusalem. Clearly the meaning is that the full power of the earthly life of Jesus, hitherto veiled from their eyes, was now made manifest. It was the same Jesus who had lived and died and was buried, none other, who had appeared to them, as in the meantime (v. 34) He had appeared to Peter. He, the Bridegroom, on whom they had hitherto looked back in retrospect as men who were σκυθρωποί[EN89], had now come to them in a form in which He could never leave them again, in which He could never again be to them a mere figure of the past, in which they could never think of Him as One who was "no longer" with them. The historical Jesus as such had removed the veil of the merely "historical" from their eyes and came to them as the Lord, the same yesterday and to-day. This was the burden of the apostolic account of the resurrection, of their Easter history. The limitation of the past had been burst. The past of Jesus had become a present reality.

It is surely no accident that Luke, the Evangelist who more than any other has the reputation of being a historian, records this story as an indispensable commentary on all the other Easter narratives. If the prologues of the two books addressed to Theophilus (Lk. 1[1-4] and Ac. 1[1-3]) are read in the light of the Emmaus story we shall see how the various elements are interconnected (not without some overlapping, for Luke is no mere pedant): the history of the words and works of Jesus; then, as a link in the chain, the history of the proofs that He was alive during the forty days; and finally the history of the apostles. He does not allow the first history to lose its significance or sink into the mere past in the final history to which he himself belongs. For the latter would be nothing without the former; it is simply its sequel. And the intervening history of the Easter period is simply a revelation of the first history which dispels the errors, prejudice and blindness of the apostles and the community. Hence the New Testament necessarily took the form of "the Gospel and the apostle," as Marcion later put it (Marcion may have been a heretic in detail, but he was undoubtedly a genius in general apprehension). It was the substance of the words and works, the passion and death of Jesus; it was Jesus Himself whose life and ministry and self-offering the disciples and their contemporaries had witnessed—it was this Jesus who encountered them in the Easter time, emerging from the past as a figure of the present, alive for evermore, abiding with them, their Lord and Contemporary for all time. It was He and none other, in the form which belonged to the past, who must now be manifested to them as the content of the Gospel. For the word "Gospel" in the New Testament has the concrete meaning of witness to the Jesus of history. There was no need for uniformity in this testimony. The Early Church never felt the need for a uniform, complete and consistent "life of Jesus." It was possible and even necessary, as Lk. 1[1] suggests, for many "to set forth in order a declaration of those things which are most surely believed among us." It makes no difference that there are several different versions of Christ's resurrection appearances, that they are independent of one another or that

[473]

[EN89] looking sad

37

they vary in detail. Any idea of a harmony of the Gospels is quite foreign to the Early Church. That we should have Gospels "according to St. Matthew," "according to St. Mark," etc., with all their parallels, their overlappings, and contradictions, is supremely in keeping with the theme recorded, with the figure of the past who in the forty days appeared to so many different people in so many different ways. All that matters was that they should all go back directly or indirectly to this source, the revelation of the event of Easter; that they should be presentations of this theme, of this figure of the past whose abiding presence is guaranteed by the event of Easter. A true Evangelist is one who draws upon this source, and in his own particular way hands on this object. To take up this tradition and proclaim this object is the function of the apostle, who in contrast to the Evangelist looks forwards and not backwards. There is, of course, no reason why one man should not fulfil both functions. Indeed, in the last resort they must be one and the same person. An Evangelist is *ipso facto*[EN90] an apostle, for the tradition he records is by its very nature the apostolic *kerygma*. Again, since the apostle is a bearer of the *kerygma*, he is an active bearer of the tradition. There is obviously a sense in which the apostle Paul himself is an Evangelist. He is no less the bearer of a definite tradition, part of which is received directly from the Lord. But the function of the apostle is not that of the Evangelist. As an apostle he does not merely relate the facts about Jesus, but proclaims the meaning behind these facts. He proclaims Jesus as the Lord, the Messiah of Israel and the Saviour of the world. He proclaims this figure of yesterday as alive to-day, and reigning to-day in virtue of what He was yesterday. This is the word of a true apostle, and he derives it from the events of the forty days. These are the source of what the New Testament calls the "Word of God." The apostle knows that Jesus reigns to-day only because He has encountered him as the Resurrected. And the fact that he must proclaim this to Jews and Gentiles rests again on the command he received from the Resurrected. But Jesus the Lord whom he proclaims is identical with that figure of the past who has made Himself eternally present as the Lord in the Easter time. That is why the apostle, too, depends on the tradition of this object, and is responsible for this tradition. Thus the apostle and the Evangelist stand

[474]

back to back. The "Gospel and the apostle," as the two parts of the New Testament, form an indissoluble unity. They look to two different times. But they both come from the Easter time. And in the light of the Easter time the two different times are made one time in which the present is filled by the past of Jesus, because this past has not remained the past but irrupted into the present; because He has made Himself present, and thus made the present His new time.

2. But the being of Jesus is not restricted to the present. It is also a being in the past, a past being; and it must be independently seen and evaluated as such. The temporality of Jesus does not consist merely in the fact that He is, and is again, continually, from day to day and hour to hour. At any rate, this is not how the New Testament saw it after the first Easter, at the beginning of the great intervening time to which we ourselves belong. Jesus not only is; He has also been. As in the preceding discussion, we shall now try to put ourselves in the position of the community at the beginning of this intervening time, looking in this direction, not at random, but self-evidently with reference to the witness of this first community. Our gaze is directed backward from this present (although always in the presence of the man Jesus). What do we see? What is the yesterday of this to-day?

The answer seems at first sight quite simple. What we see is obviously the

---

[EN90] for that very reason

pre-Easter life of Jesus: His death on the cross; His parting from His disciples; His going up to Jerusalem; His journeys in Galilee; His words and deeds during this time; and a few glimpses of His boyhood and infancy. But if we really see Him in all this from the standpoint of the first community, and therefore as the One He already was in all this in the light of the Easter revelation; if we see Him as He really lived in New Testament recollection, and is really shown us in the Gospel tradition, we are irresistibly impressed by the fulness of this yesterday, of this time which was. How could it be of less importance than the time of the apostolic present? What advantage has the latter except that in it the revelation of what is concealed in the former is attested, believed and presented by the Holy Spirit? But does not the former also have the advantage that in it there flow the underground waters which come to the surface in the Easter time as a spring which swells to a great river in the time of the apostles? Does not the apostolic to-day derive its mystery, power and dignity wholly and utterly from this yesterday. Here in this yesterday it takes place first and properly that the kingdom of God comes and is proclaimed in parable, but also by signs and wonders. Here it is that the reconciliation of the world with God is accomplished on the cross. Here it is that the foundations of the community are laid. Here it is that the great dividing line is secretly but very really drawn which marks off the new age from the old. Here there lives and moves and acts and suffers the Lord who reveals Himself as such at the resurrection, and then in the power of this revelation builds, maintains and rules His community until [475] the new age is consummated. Here this Lord, the true Son of God, is also true Man, born of the Virgin Mary and made like one of us. *Et incarnatus est!*[EN91] Above all He is and therefore has been in this perfect. He would not be if He had not previously been.

Yet, surprisingly enough, our consideration of the past being of Jesus cannot stop at the limit which seems to be no less inexorably set by His birth on the date of His entry into human time and history as by His death as the date of His exit. For the appearance of the man Jesus from 1 to 30 A.D. is not to be taken as an arbitrary intervention of God, and therefore as something wholly new in history. Indeed, the New Testament would seem to suggest that the true problem and reality of the past of this man begins at the point where it necessarily disappears out of sight and we can only say of His being that it was "not yet." The yesterday of the New Testament obviously suggests as such a prior yesterday, a time preceding even the time of His way from Bethlehem to Calvary. As the time of the apostles and the whole time of the community has its beginning in the particular time of the appearance of the man Jesus in history, so the latter time is the climax and end of a long time before it, which runs into it and belongs inseparably to it, but to which it also belongs. The particular time to which the New Testament looks back in the first instance belongs to the time when the unique event which forms the content of this particular

---

[EN91] And he became incarnate!

time, the history of the man Jesus, has not actually occurred, but is objectively prefigured and subjected by reason of the action of the same God who later brought it to pass—and with such reality that we cannot say of the man Jesus that He was "not yet" in this time before His time, just as we cannot say of the time after His earthly life, the time of the apostles and the community, that He is "no longer." We refer, of course, to the prophetic time and history of the people of Israel attested in the Old Testament. This is the next stage in our retrospective consideration of the time before. The apostolic community of Jews and Gentiles regarded itself as the people of Abraham, Isaac and Jacob now come to its promised goal. The Lord Christ was for it the Messiah to whom the Old Testament had pointed forward, the Son of Man and Servant of God. His teaching was the authoritative exposition of the Law, the Prophets and the Psalms of Israel. His cross was the confirmation of Israel's faithlessness and the even greater faithfulness with which God had called and led the fathers. The acts of Jesus, and His resurrection as the crown of all His acts, was the disclosure or revelation of the reality, so long concealed, of the covenant between God and this people; the declaration of the election of this lost people. In the end, only a forlorn remnant survived, until finally, with the treachery of Judas, Peter's denial and the flight of all the disciples, even this remnant had apparently disappeared. For at the bitter end only the one man Jesus, rejected by Israel and crucified by the Gentiles, remained as the human partner in this covenant. So concealed was the reality of the divine covenant with Israel in this last and supreme hour of its history—concealed in the tomb of this sole Representative of Israel. But that was not the end. On Easter Day the disciples saw this one man alive: the One who had been judged by all and was now delivered from judgment; the One who was snatched from the host of the dead. And in Him they saw all come to life again. The promise made to the Fathers had not been annulled, but fulfilled. The history of Israel recorded in the Old Testament was not in vain, but destined for this goal. The words of the Law and the Prophets, uttered so long ago, had not faded away, but now rang out as never before. Even the sacrificial system had not been abolished by the destruction of the temple, threatened and then accomplished by the one and once-for-all sacrifice of Calvary. When He who had come opened their eyes to see Him as He really was, they saw in Him, and through Him in the long history of Israel, the reality of the divine covenant. In this magnificent panorama they saw— and this was the first thing to catch their gaze—a single though manifold prefiguration and expectation of the One who had actually come when this history had come to an end and the voice of the Old Testament, and even its repetition and recapitulation in that of the preacher in the wilderness, had been silenced. Who was it, then, who had come? The One who was to come in all that time before. The One who was prefigured and expected in it. Hence, although in and for itself this time was not His time, in virtue of its content, of the history in which He was prefigured and expected, it had also become His

[476]

40

time. He was the Lord of this history too, because He was the goal and meaning of this time before. Hence it is no blasphemy but the sober truth, no allegorical fancy but the assertion of the most proper sense of the Old Testament, if we give Him the name of Him who already in the Old Testament called Himself the One who is and who will be.

Yet the apostolic community looked back even further into this yesterday from the place which we must take up with it if we are to achieve a true understanding. The covenant which God made with Abraham and his seed, and which was fulfilled in Jesus, was not an arbitrary intervention of God and therefore something wholly new in history. It was simply the initial stage in the execution of the purpose God intended when He caused history to commence in and with creation and therefore in and with the beginning of time generally. The apostolic community understood creation itself only as the external basis of the covenant attested in the Old Testament, and therefore the covenant as the internal basis of creation. It thus saw in the man Jesus, prophetically prefigured and expected in Israel, and finally appearing in His own time, the real object of God's foresight and fore ordination in the creation and ordering   [477] of reality distinct from Himself. Hence for the apostolic community the yesterday of Jesus extends beyond the prior yesterday of the Old Testament to the primal history and primal time which are beyond the reach of "historical" investigation, not only in practice, but in principle; to the history and time when being, history and time began as such. Is this just speculation? But surely if creation and covenant are so integral to one another even in the Old Testament that neither can be considered apart from the other; if in the Old Testament the covenant is always eschatological and prophetic in character, and is never actually realised; if finally—and this is the point on which everything else depends—Jesus is the One who was to come as the fulfilled reality of the covenant, is it speculation to say that even the time of creation was His time? To the extent that it was the time when the Creator began to execute His will, it too was His time; the time when He was the primary, proper object of this divine will, foreseen and foreordained in the creation of all things.

And there are a few passages in the New Testament which suggest that the apostolic community no less self-evidently regarded a further unprecedented and yet very obvious step as both possible and necessary. As the man Jesus had been in His appearance on the way, in the prefiguration and expectation of the divine covenant with Israel, and in the divine foresight and foreordination in creation, so He had been in the counsel of God before creation and therefore before all time. If the lesson of Easter is true, if the man Jesus was really the manifestation of God, how can we possibly think of an eternity of God which does not also and primarily include His time, His future, His present, but also His past? How can it be denied that in God's free plan and resolve He was before the beginning of time and all things, and therefore that He was really, supremely and fully, that He divinely was?

But two delimitations are required. On the one side, because He was really, supremely and fully, after the manner of God, the fact that He was, His historicity, cannot conflict with His being in the present. On the contrary, as the One who never was "not yet" he cannot possibly be "no longer," but is the same yesterday, and to-day. From this past He can and must be seen and understood as the One who is always present.

On the other side, His real and supreme and full and divine past cannot conflict with His being in the future. On the contrary, in all prior time right back to the eternity of God Himself, He is the One who comes: coming in the eternal counsel of the Father; coming in the work of creation; coming in the history of the divine covenant with Israel; and coming finally in the hiddenness of His pre-Easter life. It is as the One who comes in this totality that He was

[478] revealed in the forty days. Hence the fact that He is the One who has been divinely and in fulness is the decisive reason why His presence in His community in all its divinity and fulness must always be understood as that of the One who comes, and cannot be understood otherwise.

Again, it is all summed up in Rev. 1[8]: "I am—which was." The past to which we look back from the present of the man Jesus is, like this present and the future which lies before it, His time, the time of this man Jesus.

In illustration we must again confine ourselves to the most salient passages.

The transfiguration as recorded in Mk. 9[2-8] and *par.* is a good example of how the apostles regarded the pre-Easter life of Jesus from the present to their own time. It might almost be said to anticipate the Easter-history as the latter does the return of the Lord. At a first glance it looks like any other miracle story. But it is really unique, for this time the miracle happens to Jesus Himself, and is not something performed by Him. It comes wholly from outside. He does not say or do anything to bring it about. Perhaps it is meant to be taken as a preliminary key to all the other miracles. "He was transfigured before them." Moses and Elijah appear, talking with Jesus (according to Lk. 9[31], it was about "his decease which he should accomplish at Jerusalem"). A cloud, the symbol both of concealment and revelation, overshadows them. A voice speaks from the cloud: "This is my beloved Son: hear him." Everything suggests a theophany. Hence the note in Mk. 9[2] and Mt. 17[1]: "after six days" (Lk. 9[28] says it was eight days), is not to be dismissed as an irrelevant detail. Immediately before the transfiguration comes the famous saying: "Verily I say unto you, that there be some of them that stand here, which shall not taste of death, till they have seen the kingdom of God come with power." The Markan and Matthaean versions are to be read in the light of Luke's express statement that the transfiguration took place eight (six) days "after these, sayings." In other words, the transfiguration, for the Evangelists at least, was a first and provisional fulfilment of the promise contained in that saying. But the six (eight) day interval between promise and fulfilment is no doubt intended to suggest that the transfiguration with its fulfilment of the saying marks the dawn of a special Sabbath. We are obviously in close material proximity to the resurrection story. This is further suggested by the location of the episode on a high mountain; by the statement in Mt. 17[6]: "(They) were sore afraid"; by Lk. 9[32] (cf. Jn. 1[14]): "They saw his glory"; and by Peter's curious proposal, recorded in all the versions, to erect three tents (again cf. Jn. 1[14]). Evidently Peter wanted the vision to stay, if only for a short time. Mark's comment on this is: "He wist not what to say" (9[6]), which implies that he did not really understand what he was saying. But the vision did not stay, as Peter hoped it would. It vanished as quickly as it had come. Jesus is again seen alone, and no longer transfigured

42

before them. He tells them (Mk. 9⁹) to say nothing about it to anyone until He is risen from the dead. This obviously suggests that the transfiguration is the supreme prefigurement of the resurrection, and that its real meaning will not be perceived until the resurrection has taken place. It is surprising that 2 Pet. 1¹⁶ᶠ, speaking of the apostles as eyewitnesses and preachers of the "power and coming of our Lord Jesus Christ," says nothing about the resurrection itself, but seems to regard the preceding transfiguration as more important. The obvious post-Easter parallel to the transfiguration is the conversion of Saul. And its purpose in the pre-Easter period is obviously to demonstrate that even in this time, although in concealment, He was actually and properly the One He was revealed to be in His resurrection. And even this time was not without transitory indications of His true and proper being. In Jn. 2¹¹ the account of the miracle of Cana and Galilee closes with the words: "This beginning of miracles did Jesus ... and manifested forth his glory." This would seem to imply that the miracles of Jesus are to be taken as "signs" in the sense that they point to what He already was, to the hidden presence of the kingdom of God which would later be unveiled during the forty days in an abiding manifestation, in a σκηνοῦν ᴱᴺ⁹² of the Lord in the midst of His disciples—a disclosure which will become definitive and universal at the end of all time in His coming again. That there are such signs, and that in the transfiguration, as in no other miracle, this sign is performed on Himself, shows that the mystery of His being revealed at the resurrection has not been acquired in the meantime but had been present all along and was in fact *revealed* at this later point. [479]

The baptism of Jesus (Mk. 1⁹⁻¹¹ and *par.*; cf. Jn. 1³²⁻³⁴) belongs to the same cycle of tradition as the transfiguration. We must emphasise the meaning of this event only as it concerns our present context. That it is related to the transfiguration is obvious at a glance, for we have a similar voice from heaven and much the same words: "Thou art my beloved Son, in whom I am well pleased," or in the Lukan version (Lk. 3²²): "This day have I begotten thee." The opening of heaven indicates that this is no ordinary miracle, but a divine epiphany. Mt. 3¹⁶ further suggests that it was only Jesus Himself who appreciated its divine significance. In Jn. 1³²ᶠ the Baptist solemnly and explicitly confesses that he is a witness in this matter. The crucial point is that the Holy Spirit visibly came on Jesus "and abode upon him," as Jn. 1³²ᶠ twice records. This addition is textually uncertain in Mk. 1¹⁰, while Matthew and Luke clearly know nothing of it. All the same, taken together with the voice from heaven, it offers the only conceivable explanation of the καταβαίνειν ᴱᴺ⁹³ of the Spirit, which is obviously very different from a mere prophetic calling and illumination. Who is the man who submits to baptism? Who is it who now becomes the central figure of the Gospel story? The divine epiphany gives the answer. It calls Him the beloved Son of God, begotten long before, the object of God's good-pleasure from of old. It marks Him out as the One who, secretly or openly, known or unknown, is this in fact, and always will be on the way which lies ahead of Him. It marks Him out as the One He necessarily must be as the Son of God; the One who is and will always be the Bearer of the Spirit, the immediate Hearer and Preacher of the Word, the accredited Agent of the divine commission. The baptism of Jesus may also be regarded as an anticipation of the resurrection. For like the resurrection it adds nothing to what He already is. He is already the Son of God, the begotten and beloved of God, the object of His good-pleasure. This is what the voice from heaven so clearly shows. And as regards the Holy Spirit, the texts are quite clear that Jesus was not endowed with the Spirit for the first time at the moment of His baptism. Indeed, Mt. 1²⁰ tells us that He was conceived by the Holy Ghost.

ᴱᴺ⁹² dwelling
ᴱᴺ⁹³ descent

What happened at the baptism was that on the basis of divine revelation Jesus (and, according to the Fourth Gospel, John the Baptist as well) saw the $\kappa\alpha\tau\alpha\beta\alpha\acute{\iota}\nu\epsilon\iota\nu$ [EN94] of the Spirit upon Himself; His communication from the Father to the incarnate Son. The hour of baptism is thus an hour of revelation; an early, momentary and unrepeated disclosure of the mystery of this man, which has always been and always will be His mystery.

The infancy narratives must be added to this series as a third, or first, link. We shall confine ourselves to the clearest of these in Lk. 2^{8-14}, where the angels announce to the shepherds the birth of Jesus at Bethlehem. Once again everything has already happened as fully as possible. "And she brought forth her first-born son, and wrapped him in swaddling clothes, and laid him in a manger, because there was no room for them in the inn." This is supreme reality, though wrapped in supreme obscurity. There can be no adding to or enriching of it by what transpired in the fields where the shepherds were keeping watch over their flocks by night. What does happen is that the event in the inn is revealed to them in the fields. An angel of the Lord appears to them. This reminds us already of the divine epiphany at the resurrection—an impression which is confirmed by what follows: "The glory of the Lord ($\delta o\xi\acute{a}$ $\kappa\upsilon\rho\acute{\iota} o\upsilon$) shone round about them, and they were sore afraid." As at the transfiguration and in the resurrection appearances, fear is man's first reaction to a mystery surpassing his understanding. But the fear is always temporary, for "perfect love casteth out fear" (1 Jn. 4^{18}). So the angel says: "Fear not: for, behold, I bring you good tidings of great joy, which shall be to all people"—i.e., when it is revealed to the whole people of Israel. Note that this is a real birth, whether known by few or many, or by these sooner or later. But this birth is made known to the shepherds in the field by God's revelation, and immediately and on the spot it causes them "great joy": "For unto you is born this day in the city of David a Saviour, $\ddot{o}s$ $\dot{\epsilon}\sigma\tau\iota\nu$ $X\rho\iota\sigma\tau\grave{o}s$ $K\acute{\upsilon}\rho\iota os$ [EN95]." This is the revelation of the reality of this birth in the darkness of the night in the field. The Saviour is there, the Christ is there, the Messiah is there—$\dot{\epsilon}\tau\acute{\epsilon}\chi\theta\eta$ [EN96]! And the word of the angel is not left unsupported. A whole choir of revelation joins in, "a multitude of the heavenly host, praising God and saying … "; adoring yet again the reality of this birth; declaring that in the existence of this babe there is irrevocably accomplished the complete triumph of God above and the complete assistance of the men below who are the objects of His goodness: "Glory to God in the highest, and on earth peace among the men of his good pleasure." It is impossible to exaggerate the importance of the perfect reality of this event if it is to be understood aright. This is what is made known to the shepherds in the field. Things will not continue in this strain even in Luke, though we are obviously meant to gather that this is how they began. In this Gospel, too, darkness around the new-born Child is thick enough, and the revelation of His glory isolated until we reach the Easter story. But at any rate this is how Luke wanted his account of the words and deeds of Jesus to begin—in this stream of light. In Luke, as in Matthew, the effect on the reader is to make him realise that from the very outset he is in the presence of a mystery which embraces and motivates the whole story. And thus the way in which the Gospels look back to this beginning shows the height from which the forward-looking apostolic Church descends. It descends indeed from the mount of transfiguration. It has not created its "Christ of to-day." But as He was the same yesterday, revealed by the angels at His birth, confirmed by a voice from heaven on the banks of Jordan, and transfigured on the mount, He Himself has created the Church.

But the man Jesus belongs not only to yesterday, but as such to the day before. He is the Christ of Israel and of Israel's Scriptures. His being is one which is hidden, yet not only hidden but also revealed, in this time before. A few remarks must suffice to clarify what we

[480]

[EN94] descent
[EN95] who is Christ the Lord
[EN96] he has been born

said more generally with reference to this second and higher stage of His past. For further details see, for example, *C.D.* I, 2, pp. 70–101.

It is best to begin with the fact that the earliest Christians, and especially the Evangelists and apostles, always were obviously forced, directly or indirectly, explicitly or implicitly, to connect their accounts and preaching with this time before, i.e., with the history of Israel, in which Jesus had not yet appeared, but was already present as the One prefigured and expected. If we wanted to obliterate these references and to read the New Testament apart from the Old, it would be necessary to delete not only Matthew, the Epistle of James and the Epistle to the Hebrews, but all the New Testament, and especially the Pauline writings. These references may vary in detail, but they agree in substance that the particular time of the man Jesus was as such the fulfilment of this time before, i.e., that what took place in this particular time was the reality to which all the events of this prior time were moving, so that it is only with the final event in this particular time that the events of this prior time form the perfect and meaningful whole which they do in this context. Hence the references to the Old Testament which we find in the New tell us that the history and time of Israel were prophetic, their meaning and perfection consisting in the fact that they moved towards the history and time of the man Jesus. Prefiguring and expecting this history and time of the man Jesus, they belonged to His time. Indeed, no less really than the history and time of the apostles, although inversely, it *was* His time. [481]

That is what the old man Simeon meant when he held the baby Jesus in his arms and said: "Mine eyes have seen thy salvation, which thou hast prepared before the face of all people; a light to lighten the Gentiles, and the glory of thy people Israel" (Lk. $2^{30f.}$). What Simeon perceives is not a new but the old salvation prophetically prefigured and expected in Israel. That is why he can now "depart in peace." His time has reached its goal; his history, having attained this point, has not been in vain. In the same sense Paul is conscious of being ordained by "the God of our fathers" to "know his will, and see that Just One" (Ac. 22^{14}). That is why he lays so much stress on the fact that the death and resurrection of Jesus took place κατὰ τὰς γραφάς EN97 (1 Cor. $15^{3f.}$). That is why he begs the Christians to learn from himself and Apollos the rule μὴ ὑπὲρ ἃ γέγραπται EN98. That is why he calls the Old Testament Law "our schoolmaster to bring us unto Christ" (Gal. 3^{24}), and Christ the "end of the law" (Rom. 10^4), and the purpose of his preaching, not to destroy, but to establish the Law (Rom. 3^{31}). That is why he said to Agrippa (Ac. 26^{22}): "I continue unto this day, witnessing both to small and great, saying none other things than those which the prophets and Moses did say should come." That is why he went so far as to say that the rock from which the fathers drank in the wilderness was Christ (1 Cor. 10^4), and that it was only because of the veil over their hearts that the Jews could not understand their own Scriptures (2 Cor. $3^{14f.}$). The Fourth Evangelist is just as clear about this point, for he attributed to Jesus the saying: "Search the Scriptures; for in them ye think ye have eternal life; and they are they which testfy of me" (Jn. 5^{39}). He also makes Jesus say of Moses: "He wrote of me" (Jn. 5^{46}); and of Abraham: "(He) rejoiced to see my day; and he saw it, and was glad" (Jn. 8^{56}). And the Evangelist himself says of Isaiah: "These things said (he), when he saw his glory, and spake of him" (Jn. 12^{41}). Similarly, faith in Jesus according to Lk. 24^{25}, is simply a matter of believing "all that the prophets have spoken," as conversely: "This day is this Scripture fulfilled in your ears" (Lk. 4^{21}). Finally, it is not just fanciful imagery, but a visible confirmation of the Pauline κατὰ τὰς γραφάς, that in Mk. $9^{4f.}$ and *par.* Moses and Elijah appear with Jesus at the transfiguration. They belong to Him. He belongs to them. They talk with Him, and according to Lk. 9^{31} they talk concretely about His death.

EN97 in accordance with the Scriptures
EN98 not above that which is written

Particularly in the light of this scene, I find it hard to see how the idea of "contemporaneity" between the history of Jesus and the prophetic history of Israel can be flatly rejected (Cullmann, *op. cit.*, E.T., p. 132 f.). Perhaps Cullmann has allowed himself to be too much influenced by the unfortunate precedent of the Epistle of Barnabas, and too much hampered by his conception of "linear time." The truth is that the contemporaneity in question here does not exclude a certain non-contemporaneity as well. After all, Abraham, Moses and the prophets, and all the other figures of the Old Testament, still remain what they are in their own right. They are clearly distinguished from Jesus, and there is no question of their being identical with Him. Unless they all existed in their own right it would be difficult to account for the fact that the Early Church paid particular attention to them and accepted the Old Testament Canon along with the New, or rather the New along with the existing Old. In their relationship to Jesus the fathers have their own word and their own particular time, just as Jesus in turn has His own word and very different time compared with them. Yet it is none the less true that the non-contemporaneity in question does not exclude a certain contemporaneity. Being what they are, the patriarchs point forward to Jesus. In this they resemble John the Baptist, a figure quite distinct from Jesus, in whom the Old Testament seems to be personified at the beginning of the New, and whose special mission is exactly the same, i.e., to point to Jesus. Speaking to their own age, the fathers do in fact speak of Jesus. And what about Israel, the people of the covenant, in whose history Jesus is certainly promised and expected but has not yet come, and yet is not simply absent, since in all its history He is promised and expected? Was not the time of Israel necessarily another time as the time when He was still far off, but also His own time as the time when He was promised and expected? Just as the tradition and recollection of Him makes Him the Contemporary of the Church, so in the time of Israel the promise and expectation of His coming makes Him the Contemporary of Israel. In both cases it is a spiritual contemporaneity, perceptible only through Him, and only in faith. Where there is no revelation on His part or faith on ours, even the Church can see only the place where He is no longer present, and accordingly the history of Israel will become a history in which He has not yet come. The line of time, with its obvious differentiation of distance and proximity, then acquires in both cases an absolute significance. But if we may and must count on a genuine self-declaration and awakening of faith (by the resurrection), and therefore on His spiritual presence in both cases, there is no need to reduce His existence id the history of Israel to the bare fact that He is the clue to its meaning and that it is "permissible" for "believers" to "see" in it the "preparation" for the coming of the crucified and risen Jesus (Cullmann, *ibid.*, p. 131–135)—as though this were not an objective fact. If there is a spiritual presence of Jesus the distance of Israel's time on the regressive line of time makes no difference to the fact that its history was His pre-history, and that He was in it before He was, i.e., before this history reached its consummation, so that when He came, it was not only possible but necessary to recognise Him in this pre-history and its record. If His time is the real divine centre of all time, are we not forced to see it as the time which embraces and controls all time before and after Him? Consider the decisive place occupied by the Old Testament in the early Christian liturgy. Consider the ease with which the Church accepted the Canon of the Synagogue. Above all consider the degree to which the New Testament is impregnated with the Old. Such phenomena cannot be satisfactorily accounted for on secondary motives, or from accidents of history. We have here an intrinsic necessity of the highest order, an insight which the later Church may have done much to obscure, and which may even strike us as strange, but which for the apostles and their communities was a self-evident truth. They were forced to accept it because they looked back to Jesus. It was not a matter of interpretation or construction, but they obviously knew from the very outset that the man Jesus was the fulfilment of the prophetic history of Israel, that its history was the beginning of His, and that its record in the Old Testament was

[482]

the record of Him. The only way to Him was by reading, understanding and expounding Moses and the prophets, and therefore hearing His Word as the fulfilled and final Word of God, but the Word already proclaimed and attested. His figure had not merely a forward dimension, into their own time in which He was in their midst, but also a backward dimension in which He was in the midst of the fathers. Now that He, the Saviour, the Christ and the Lord, had come and was revealed, now that the crown and climax of Old Testament history had appeared, the crowd of witnesses to this history sounded out again with new life and vigour, and had to be heard again and genuinely understood. And the the apostles and their communities, with their own testimony, could be as it were a choir responding antiphonally to the first choir and confirming the fulfilment of the promise. Conscious though they were of the differences, they could only form a single people with the people of the God of Israel, seeing the time of this people and their own time fused into a single time of Jesus. To live in the presence of Jesus and the past of the Old Testament was for them one and the same thing. They were not introducing an alien element into their tradition and recollection of [483] Jesus when they set it in relation to the Old Testament. Nor were they introducing an alien element into the Old Testament when they related it to Jesus. They knew the true nature of both. Each was intelligible only in the light of the other. Had they been faced with the familiar question of our own age, they would probably have answered with the counter-question whether not only the Old Testament but Jesus Himself is not interpreted "allegoric-ally " if this relation, this connected past of Jesus as He that was to come and He that did come, is overlooked and neglected.

But the New Testament does not stop here. In the same direction, and in the name of the same Old Testament witness, it goes further back than the history of Israel which began with Abraham. It tells us that Jesus, as the Word of God, was the real basis of creation whose time thus embraces the beginning of all created time. "In the beginning was the Word," (Jn. 1¹). Hence this word is "from the beginning" (1 Jn. 1¹). "Ye have known him that is from the beginning" (1 Jn. 2¹³ᶠ). He is Himself "the beginning of the creation of God" (Rev. 3¹⁴), "the firstborn of every creature" (Col. 1¹⁵), the "head of all principality and power" (Col. 2¹⁰). Indeed, it was by Him that God established all things (Col. 1¹⁷): "For by him were all things created, that are in heaven, and that are in earth, visible and invisible, ... all things were created by him, and for him" (Col. 1¹⁶). "Thou, Lord, in the beginning hast laid the founda-tion of the earth, and the heavens are the works of thine hands" (Heb. 1¹⁰); "Through whom also he made the ages" (Heb. 1², R.V. margin). And it is put even more concisely in 1 Cor. 8⁶: δι' οὗ τὰ πάντα EN99. The clause in Jn. 1²: "The same was in the beginning with God." would be an unnecessary and confusing repetition from v. 1 if it did not indicate the person who was later to be the subject of the whole Gospel narrative, and of whom we are told in 1¹⁴ that the Word was made flesh and dwelt among us. The Prologue is not speaking of an eternal Son or divine Logos *in abstracto*EN100, but of a Son and Logos who is one with the man Jesus. It is equally impossible to interpret any of the other passages cited above *in abstracto*EN101, as a study of the context will in each case show. What the New Testament says about the being of Jesus Christ in and as the beginning of all being is distinguished from all contemporary speculation on that subject, which it resembles formally but refutes in substance, by the fact that in its adoption and development of the Old Testament wisdom teaching (1) it does not offer any metaphysical explanation of the mutual relation between God the Father and the man Jesus, or of their co-existence, but simply shows what is meant by the statement that

---

EN 99 through whom are all things
EN100 in the abstract
EN101 in the abstract

47

Jesus Christ is *Kyrios*[EN102]; and (2) it does not speculate about a hierarchy of mediators, but simply bears witness to God and man in their co-existence, and therefore to Jesus Christ as very God but also as very man, the meaning and ground of all creation. In other words, it offers us an ultimate—or penultimate—word about the sense in which the man Jesus is called Lord, i.e., that He has revealed Himself and is to be accepted as He was, in the eternal counsel and purpose of the Father, and as its most specific content, when all things began to be. It also teaches us that the whole wisdom and power of the Creator at the beginning of all being were concretely the power and wisdom which appeared and were revealed in the man Jesus: that He was the purpose and ground of the divine creative action at the beginning of all times. It was in this way, not abstractly in His Son, but concretely in the giving of His only begotten Son, in the unity of His Son with the Son of Man Jesus of Nazareth (Jn. 3¹⁶), that God willed to demonstrate His love to the world, having already loved it in creating it. *Mundi factor vere Verbum Dei est: hic autem est Dominus noster, qui in novissimis temporibus homo faetus est*[EN103]. (Irenaeus *Adv. Haer.* V, 18, 3). Just as from an external point of view the creation makes possible and provides the basis for God's covenant, its history, its promise and finally its fulfilment, so from an internal point of view the covenant makes possible and provides the basis for creation. If the man Jesus, whose incarnation, crucifixion and resurrection took place in the days of Augustus and Tiberius, is this fulfilment of the covenant and the meaning and purpose of creation, it follows that He was also its ground, and therefore that He was already at the beginning of time as the One who was to come in the plan of God. Time in its beginning was enclosed by His time, and to that extent was itself His time.

[484]

But the New Testament takes a further and higher step still. At a few points it has even more to say about "Jesus Christ yesterday." This is obvious at once from the second and third clauses of Jn. 1¹: "The Word was with God, and the Word was God." It would be inadvisable to take the ἦν[EN104] in these clauses as implying a timeless existence. Nor should we overlook the immediate continuation: "The same was in the beginning with God." The οὗτος[EN105] here refers to the incarnate Logos. It is He who was "in the beginning." And not only that, but even before this beginning He was with God and was Himself God, participating in the divine being and nature, before created time began, in the eternity of God. This eternity includes not only the present and future, but also the past. God's eternity does not invalidate past, present and future, and therefore time; it legitimates them. In it they have their origin and true character. In it yesterday, to-day and to-morrow are one, and in their unity genuine and real. The man Jesus is in this genuine and real yesterday of God's eternity, which is anterior to all other yesterdays, including the yesterday of creation. This is the claim made by the Jesus of the Fourth Gospel (Jn. 17²⁴): "Thou lovedst me before the foundation of the world." We are reminded of the εὐδόκησα[EN106] and γεγέννηκα[EN107] of the baptism narrative, and of the designation of Jesus as the "beloved" or "elect" Son of God in this story and in the account of the transfiguration. These terms probably refer to this antecedent past. Again, we read in 1 Pet. 1²⁰ that the "lamb without blemish and without spot" was not only "foreordained before the foundation of the world, but was manifest in these last times for you." As the context shows, this means that in human history, and beyond all history, human or otherwise, there is no other or higher law than that of the divine mercy, now revealed, established and applied in the oblation of the Lamb of God. This is no positive law, to be

---

[EN102] Lord

[EN103] The creator of the world is truly the Word of God: He is, moreover, our Lord, who in these last times was made man

[EN104] was

[EN105] this

[EN106] I have begotten

[EN107] I am well pleased

restricted or repealed by another of the same kind. There is no place from which it can be relativised. It is the true "natural law" which necessarily limits and relativises all positive law. For the Lamb of God foreordained before the foundation of the world is the person and work in which this law had been revealed. In similar vein Eph. 1^4 asserts that God chose us in Jesus Christ "before the foundation of the world, that we should be holy and without blame before him." Once again, this means that every choice and decision made in human history, and indeed in the whole course of created time, is subordinated to the choice and decision made in God's eternity before all created being and its time, i.e., that Jesus Christ was elected by God, and we in Him. A similar idea is expressed in Rev. 13^8 which tells us that there is a "book of life of the Lamb slain," to be included in which "from the foundation of the world" signifies the great decision which alone can offer deliverance in the great tribulation caused by the beast from the abyss. In short, we may say that wherever the verbs προορίζειν, προτίθεσθαι, προετιμάζειν, προγινώσκειν [EN108] and the substantives πρόγνωσις and πρόθεσις [EN109], occur, there is a reference to this day before yesterday, the pluperfect of God's time, in which the event of the particular time of Jesus, and in and with it the ensuing time of the community, the calling and sanctification of those who belong to Jesus in and with His own history, their justification in judgment, their deliverance from death and their glorification, were all foreseen and resolved, and to that extent had already taken place. It would be a complete misunderstanding if we were to object that the singularity of this event and its eternity as attested in these passages are mutually exclusive. On the contrary, these passages accentuate its absolute singularity by insisting on its predetermination from all eternity. A thing which is resolved from all eternity necessarily has the character of absolute singularity. At this last and highest stage, the pre-existence of the man Jesus coincides with [485] His eternal predestination and election, which includes the election of Israel, of the Church, and of every individual member of His body.

3. The being of Jesus in time is not merely a being in the present or the past. It is also—and this brings us to our third and final point—a being in the future, a coming being. From the standpoint of the apostles and their communities it has also to be said, and with no less reality and truth, that He comes.

With no less reality and truth!—we must lay primary emphasis on this point. There is no difference of degree between the being of Jesus in the three dimensions, whether in substantiality, importance or urgency, in dignity or value. Regarded from the normative standpoint of the time of the apostles, He is as much He who comes as He who has come and is present. Christians live no less in expectation than in recollection or simply in His presence. Hence the Church's proclamation of Him is no less eschatological than soteriological and pneumatological. It is no less proclamation of His future and the approaching end of time than of His past in which time has found its beginning and centre, or of His present in which we move from that beginning and centre to the end of time.

It is no less so, but, as we must add at once, no more. The apostles did not wait for the Lord, or live in hope in Him, in such a way that the Jesus of Nazareth of yesterday, who was promised in the Old Testament, who was at the

---

[EN108] to foreordain, to intend, to prepare beforehand, to foreknow
[EN109] foreknowledge ... purpose

beginning of all things, and who was in the counsel of God before the beginning of all things, faded into the background and became colourless and unimportant. And even less was this the case with His living presence, lordship and grace among them, His being in the Spirit in the life, upbuilding and mission of His community, their present life in His Spirit. It is not the case that only in the coming of the Lord do we have to do with His proper being, and with an improper in His first coming and presence. There is no justification for trying to systematise the being of Jesus from this standpoint. The New Testament always thinks and speaks eschatologically, but never with full logical consistence. Its only logical consistence is to think and speak on all sides and in all dimensions and relationships Christologically. And it is for this reason that with equal emphasis and seriousness it can always think and speak eschatologically as well.

As, in the New Testament sense, the being of Jesus yesterday and to-day can finally be understood and explained only in the light of the resurrection, so it is with His being εἰς τοὺς αἰῶνας EN110, and therefore with His general and definitive manifestation as Judge, Consummator and new Creator as this is promised and therefore expected in the near if indefinite future. Clearly, it would not be inconceivable *rebus aliter stantibus* EN111, i.e., if there had been no resurrection, for our knowledge of Jesus Christ to have been restricted to His past and present, the past somehow prolonged into and determining the present. In this case the apostles and their communities would have contemplated the future in terms of the propagation, intensification and practical realisation of the Christianity which they championed. Hope would then have meant confidence in the power of the Gospel to cleanse and sanctify the individual and to permeate society. The apostles would have looked forward to a progressive immanent development of the new life opened up by the resurrection, and then of the state of human and creaturely things generally, in the direction of an ideal of good and happy humanity corresponding to the beginning, to be attained approximately in this world and perfectly in a better hereafter, and identifiable with the kingdom of God. Indeed, there have been whole periods in the history of the Church when this version of the Christian hope has been regarded as necessary both in theory and in practice. The New Testament does not contain a single shred of evidence to support this view. Compared with what the New Testament calls hope, this Utopian version can only be described as a fabrication, however well-meaning and attractive. The salient feature about it is that in the last resort it can do without Jesus. It may know Him as the Jesus of yesterday and to-day, but it knows nothing of Him as the One who is εἰς τοὺς αἰῶνας EN112, as the One who comes. Its knowledge of the man Jesus and His time obviously lacks this third dimension. And this raises

[486]

EN110 in eternity
EN111 if things stood differently
EN112 in eternity

50

the question whether there is any real understanding of His yesterday and to-day. In the New Testament, neither the inner life of the community nor its missionary proclamation suggests the initial stages of a growth leading to a better future either here or hereafter. Not even the parables of the mustard seed, the leaven and the seed growing secretly really inculcate this doctrine. No, the New Testament looks forward, not merely to a better future, but to a future which sets a term to the whole time process, and in its perfection includes and surpasses absolutely all the contents of time. This future will be a wholly new order, quite independent of all creaturely and even Christian development. Nor is it a distant prospect, but a sure and immediate hope. It is for this reason that according to the New Testament the community purifies and sanctifies itself; and for this reason that it proclaims the Gospel to the world in this last time. Not is this future merely the result of what Jesus Christ was yesterday and is to-day. It is again He Himself, His own person and work, in a new mode and form. The last time which dawned with His appearance, and in which the community has its mission and task; and the conclusion of time, the judgment and the consummation which, corresponding to the time of creation, will form the content of this concluding time and of the ensuing time of the being of all things in God—this time too, as the New Testament sees it, is wholly and utterly His time, the time of Jesus, the time of His being. The New Testament does not look for an amelioration of present conditions or for an ideal state, but for the coming of the Lord—*Maranatha* (1 Cor. 16^{22})—in a definitive and general revelation; and therefore for the justification and redemption of individuals in judgment; for the end and new beginning of the cosmos; for the kingdom as the last thing corresponding to the first which was in the counsel of God before all times. We obviously neglect or forget or deny the Easter revelation of the man Jesus, and therefore the substance of the whole witness of the New Testament, if we misunderstand the Christian hope in this way, ignoring so completely the third dimension of the being of Jesus in time. For the Easter revelation was the permission and command which placed the apostles and their communities in a position to believe in Him as the One to whom they owed absolutely everything, to love Him as the One in whom they had everything, and to hope in Him as the One from whom they had to expect everything. For everything was really to be expected from the risen Jesus. He could not possibly be known only as the One who had come and was present. As the One who had come and was present He had necessarily to be known also as the One who comes. We have to take into account what it meant and means to look back to the fact of the resurrection of Jesus, to come from this fact. We say that this relationship could not consist in a mere recollection, although it was also a relationship of recollection. It could not possibly be the view of the apostles and their community that now that His past had reached its goal and fruition in the event of the forty days a kind of past had begun when the Bridegroom was taken from them, and could now live on only in their hearts and minds, so that they had to do without Him in reality and in

[487]

51

truth, managing without His help. To think of the Resurrected, even when He was no longer seen, was to think of the living Lord, not absent but present to-day and every day to His own. It was to live in faith in Him, and therefore in love for Him, and therefore, even when the forty days were over, in His time, fulfilled time. But this living Lord Jesus yesterday and to-day could not be believed and loved as such without being expected in hope as the One who is εἰς τοὺς αἰῶνας EN113, as the One who comes.

His glory could still be known only as His own: both backwards from the event of the forty days to His life and passion and death, to His existence as the promised One of Israel, as the Agent of creation and as the object of the eternal counsel of God; and forwards from this event in His being as the Lord of His community, in His imperishable words, in His Holy Spirit and the gifts of His Spirit, in baptism and the Lord's Supper, in the very fact that He can be the object of faith and love, and that His name can be proclaimed to Jews and Gentiles. But His glory, although it was His own, was also His glory for them; His glory as the inheritance of eternal life ordained for them; His glory as the promise of a new heaven and a new earth. This is what encountered the participants in the forty days in His Easter revelation. This is what they were privileged to see and hear and touch, to behold as well as to believe, during this period. It was in this recollection that Jesus was present to them. They were already witnesses of His full, conclusive, definitive and general revelation. For this revelation is His visibility for and to the creatures as the Saviour of whom He came and was crucified and raised in the whole existence of His own in the community and also in the world of which the community is ordained to be the salt and the light. What the participants in the forty days saw in the Easter revelation in His person was already the great *consummatum est*EN114—in its fulfilment, in its effectiveness in and to His own, and even in and to the lost for whose sin and salvation He died, and for whose enlightenment concerning His death He was raised again. The first disciples received this enlightenment already. They saw that it had all been done for them and for the whole world. They were granted at this point a foretaste of their inheritance and a glimpse of the new creation.

At this point! It is as the witnesses of what happened at this point, as the witnesses of Jesus' resurrection, that they are apostles, the foundation of His community. It is on the basis of their witness, and of the fact to which they bore witness, that there is faith in Jesus and love for Him within the community. All this was resolved and included in what happened at this point, in the resurrection. The forty days, although they became a thing of the past for those who participated in them and especially for the community gathered by their word, were a strong, irrefutable and sure, but isolated promise, which as such formed the beginning and starting point of the whole time which followed. In

[488]

EN113 in eternity
EN114 it has been accomplished

this promise there was enclosed the glory of Jesus for His own, the inheritance which was to be theirs, the new creation. This promise entitled them to believe and love, but for the time being they could not see or hear or feel anything more. What was now before the eyes and ears of the apostles and their communities was the fact that they not only had faith and love, but that even they too, not to speak of the world outside, were subject to sin and error, sighing and tears, suffering and death. What they now saw and heard and felt was certainly the word of proclamation, the sacraments of baptism and the Lord's Supper, the fellowship and gifts of the Spirit between brothers and sisters, but also the great "not yet," the almost overwhelming difficulties and tasks arising from their witness to Jesus in the world, the convulsions of the Roman Empire moving to its climax and its fall, the frailty of Christian flesh requiring constant exhortation and comfort and warning and punishment, much weakness and tribulation in which even the voice of the Spirit could only be a sigh and a stammering, a cry of yearning.

Yearning for what? This is where the Christian hope comes in: not as a *Deus ex machina* or a piece of wishful thinking; but as a grasping of the promise which was the basis of the community and which stood firm in the face of all [489] human weakness and tribulation. For the revelation of Easter was the origin of the community and therefore the beginning, actualised already and therefore past, of the full, conclusive, general revelation of the man Jesus, and therefore of His direct and comprehensive visibility for and to all those for whom as the Son of God He became man, the beginning of the visibility of their participation in His glory. Hence it was no mere escape, but the most natural and basic thing in the world, when in the staggering contrast between their faith and love on the one hand, and their experience of the great "not yet" on the other, the apostles and their communities grasped the promise implicit in the origin of their existence, from this beginning living with a view to its continuation and completion. In recollection of the forty days their only option was expectation of this continuation and completion, and therefore of the return of Jesus. If the event of the forty days was only an indication and a promise of the general revelation of glory still to come, as a genuine temporal event it was real beginning of the justification which abolishes sin, of life victorious over death. To look back to this event is necessarily in this recollection to look forward to the same event, which, having begun at this point, could only be interrupted, but is destined to be consummated when this interim period has run its course and the existence and mission of the community have served their purpose. The Christian community has necessarily to be a gathering in this hope. The Christian has necessarily, then, to be the man who seizes this hope and lives in it. There is no other possibility either for the community or for the individual. The origin of both in the resurrection of Jesus makes it necessary that there should be not only faith in Him who was, and love for Him who is, but also hope in Him who comes.

He who comes is the same as He who was and who is. The Resurrected Himself, therefore, is already He who comes, who restricts His coming to the circle of His then followers, and then interrupts it, to resume and complete it at a later point. For what took place in the resurrection of Jesus was already in the concealment and temporal isolation of this event the revelation of the kingdom of God, of the gracious Judge of all men, and of the life of all the dead. Nothing which will be has not already taken place on Easter Day—included and anticipated in the person of the one man Jesus. And so Jesus in His coming is simply the risen Jesus resuming and completing His coming and thus vindicating that beginning and promise. For what will take place at His return is just that the arch of His time which began with the revelation of His first coming, and then vaulted over the interim time of the community, of the Gospel and the Spirit, of faith and love, the time given for the conversion of the world, will then be completed. It vaults over the interim time as well. Jesus is [490] the Lord in this time too, the Lord of the cosmos no less than the Lord of His community. Hence even this interim time is His time and therefore fulfilled time. But as His time it needs to be completed as it was begun by Him as an interim time, a time of His invisibility. As the One He has shown Himself to be He must again appear in confirmation of the fulfilment of time, in a glory which is no longer particular and transitory, but universal and permanent, embracing the whole of creation both in heaven and earth. The unity of His glory and our glorification already achieved in His resurrection has again become the future, His future, for us. For us, therefore, the resurrection and the *parousia* are two separate events. But for Him they are a single event. The resurrection is the anticipation of His *parousia* as His *parousia* is the completion and fulfilment of the resurrection.

The hope of the apostles and the community could only be hope in Jesus. It could only be a looking to His being in this third dimension. After all that has been said, this hardly needs to be proved in detail. The first community hoped because it owed its existence to the promise vouchsafed in the resurrection of Jesus: "begotten again unto a lively hope by the resurrection of Jesus Christ from the dead" (1 Pet. 1³). Hence it could hope only in Him, in His coming in glory commenced in the resurrection and to be completed in the *parousia*. Even materially it could not expect any future which was not as such the expectation of His coming. The New Testament community does not hope for the attainment merely of abstract blessings, as for example the resurrection of the dead, or justification in the day of judgment, or a life of eternal bliss. Nor does it hope for crowns or palms or white robes or the glory of a new heaven and new earth or any other spiritual, moral or material blessings in a future kingdom of God. Or rather, it hopes for all these things in and with the fact that it hopes for Jesus Himself. All these things are simply the glorification of the creature which is latent and implicit in His glory, initially revealed in His resurrection, and finally to be revealed in His return. These are merely predicates, appendices and concomitant phenomena of His manifestation. He is and was and will be the kingdom, and in Him will be all the restoration, salvation, perfection and joy of the kingdom. Strictly speaking, there are no "last things," i.e., no abstract and autonomous last things apart from and alongside Him, the last One. Consequently there is no diffused hope, but only the one hope concentrated upon Him, and therefore full and perfect. Hope detached from Him, independent longing and desire, would merely be idle dreaming.

Once this is realised, it is easy to see why New Testament hope could only be hope for the imminent coming of the kingdom, and why this expectation could never give way to disillusionment, but only be constantly renewed. The apostles and their communities lived in faith and love; in the recollection of the Jesus of yesterday and the consciousness of His to-day; in the remembrance of the Gospel history (and the history of the covenant with Israel, and cre- [491] ation, and the eternal counsel of God), and therefore in the one great remembrance of His past coming, but also in His direct presence as created by the fellowship of the Holy Spirit. This being the case, how could His future be remote? After all, He Himself as the Resurrected was the sole but convincing ground of their hope, and its exclusive but all-embracing object. He Himself was the Judge, He the resurrection and the life, the kingdom in all its fulness. This being the case, how could He whom they trusted and loved be other than close at hand as He whom they expected? "Behold, I stand at the door, and knock" (Rev. 3^{20}). Would He be the One who has come, and is already present, and is trusted and loved, if He did not stand immediately at the door and knock as the One who comes and is expected? If this is the One whom we expect, we cannot expect Him the day after to-morrow, but to-morrow. The termination of His coming cannot be distant, but imminent. And no dawn and progress of a new day without His coming, no continuation of time apart from the events of His new revelation, can alter this expectation in the very slightest, let alone menace or destroy it. That which necessarily gives rise to this hope and makes it an imminent hope also makes it a constant hope, renewing it every day, and protecting it against disappointment, frustration and scepticism. In His past and present form, as the One who rose again from the dead and is now by His Spirit the living Lord, Jesus accompanies His followers even through the interim time with its great "not yet." How then can any further division of time prior to His coming be other than a part of His time, and therefore fulfilled time? If His yesterday and to-day in their fulness compel us to look forward to His near coming in the future, the fulness of this yesterday and to-day is great enough to make this forward look a patient expectation. Patience does not mean torpor or somnolence or resignation or indifference. Patience in the New Testament sense is perseverance. To persevere is not to give up expecting the Lord, and expecting Him soon. It is to refrain from grumbling and complaining at having continually to expect Him. It is not to wait for someone and something but for Jesus Himself, who yesterday and to-day does not allow us to wait in poverty and despair, but fills each new portion of time with His fulness, so that there is no worse waste of time than to grumble and complain at His absence instead of continually giving thanks for what He was and rejoicing in what He is. To persevere then, means to continue expecting the Lord and expecting Him soon. It is to live in hope, in glad but patient hope, no less surely than to live in faith and love. For the object of hope is identical with that faith and love. It is the man Jesus, the Lord Himself, who is the Lord of all times, who fulfils all times, and who does not leave His followers empty at any time, but in every time makes them rich, and even very rich.

[492]   To understand this, we have only to recall the power of the resurrection, which enabled the apostles and their communities to believe and love and therefore hope. We have only to see that their path was a path from grace to grace, from one revelation to another, and therefore from faith to new faith: ἐκ πίστεως εἰς πίστιν EN115. We must disabuse our minds of the notion that the New Testament community has only darkness or twilight behind it and only the brilliant light of the *parousia* before it. It is not floundering in a slough in which its further progress seems impossible as the great light before it seems to recede into the distance, and it grows tired and perplexed, and is tempted to halt and seek a more solid path. Its consciousness of time is no more dominated by the future being of Jesus in time than His past or present. As we must never forget, its gaze is always on Him. It may look backwards to His past even as far as the eternal counsel of God. It may look to His present at the right hand of God, from which He rules to-day by His Spirit. Or it may look to the future and His general and conclusive revelation. But in every case it looks only to Him. And in Him it sees the fulness of everything for which those enlightened by Him are thankful, whether present or expected. Hence we must not range ourselves with those who according to 2 Peter had grown weary of hope even in New Testament days, because they had grown weary of faith and love, and lost their awareness of the yesterday and to-day of the Lord Jesus. Once they did this, it was inevitable that they should regard an imminent expectation as suspect. But surely not expectation and hope as such? Surely not the resurrection of Jesus? Surely not the *consummatum est* EN116 revealed by the resurrection? All the same, we should be foolish to range ourselves with such people, or to regard them as honest witnesses to the truth in face of an early Christian hope which has long since proved to be illusory. If we do, we implicate ourselves in questions, anxieties and problems which would never have occurred to the apostles and their communities from which these people were on the point of separating, because they could not arise on the presupposition of their time-consciousness, i.e., of their knowledge of the man Jesus. To argue as these others do is to create very different premises which are in fact negated by the New Testament. It is to take up a different position from that on which the Christian Church can honestly call itself by this name.

     It was obviously wrong to try to ignore or weaken or reinterpret the New

---

EN115 from faith to faith
EN116 it has been accomplished

Testament hope, the looking to the man Jesus in the third dimension, the concrete form of this hope as imminent expectation, and the patient joy and joyful patience of the early Christian attitude. When this third dimension is no longer considered, and the movement towards the day of the Lord, and therefore expectation and holy impatience and holy patience are forgotten, the very worst has happened at these decisive points, and at earlier points too. If we can really be satisfied with a Jesus of yesterday and to-day, and therefore [493] with an ideal and goal visible only at a distance and to be attained in an indefinite future, it is a clear sign that we have already lost the living Jesus of yesterday and to-day. We are understanding His past only in a "historical sense." We are expunging the true Son of God, the Messiah, Saviour and Lord, and therefore the witness of the Old Testament to Christ, to say nothing of the man Jesus pre-existent in creation, and eternally before creation in God. We are understanding His presence only psychologically and sociologically. The Holy Spirit has vanished into thin air. The heavenly session and rule of Jesus have become the mythological and highly exaggerated expression of a value judgment in which we may still confront Him independently. There is no real reason why we should not dispense with Him altogether as a historical and present figure. If we still confess Him, there is no constraining power of knowledge behind the word of confession. There is no telling where the trouble first began. Perhaps faith grew feeble, or love cold, or hope empty. But in any case, the collapse of one means the collapse of all. And our only point at the moment is that everything depends also on hope, on expectation, and indeed on the imminent expectation of the man Jesus which is both fervent and placid, impatient and patient. Christian knowledge, the Christian community, Christian existence itself, as the resurrection and the message of the resurrection show, is this whole which is equally necessarily faith, love and hope, and equally necessarily directed to the beginning, centre and end, the end no less than the beginning and centre, the object of faith, love and hope being necessarily identical with Jesus.

"I am ... which is to come." The consciousness of time inherent in this whole is to be summed up in this phrase of Rev. 1[8]. The future to which we look forward from the present of the man Jesus is, like this present itself, and the past which lies behind it, His time, the time of the man Jesus.

Here, too, we shall conclude with some detailed references to New Testament texts.

If we are to understand the New Testament consciousness of time in this third component, it is perhaps best to start with the fact that the apostles and their communities always had before them the witness of the Old Testament to Christ, and therefore the coming Jesus, promised and prefigured, but only prefigured, and according to the Word of God to be expected in the near and certain future. According to the Gospel records before them, however, He had already come, and with Him the kingdom. And on the basis of the climax and crown of these records, of the Easter message, they were privileged to live in His presence. Hence their hope was a hope already fulfilled. It was thus radically distinguished from the ordinary hope or longing in which they might well have been disappointed. Yet they still

went on waiting, or began to wait as never before, together with the fathers of the old covenant, hoping and living wholly and utterly in Advent. Clearly, there was a genuine tension in
their consciousness of time, a tension between the preliminary glory of the resurrection and

[494] its consummation in the future *parousia*. It was in this tension that they believed in Him and
proclaimed Him as the Deliverer of those "who through fear of death were all their lifetime
subject to bondage" (Heb. 2[15]). This, though already accomplished, was not yet realised and
experienced even in themselves, let alone in creation as a whole. They walked by faith and
not by sight (2 Cor. 5[7]). They were indeed saved, but only in hope (Rom. 8[24]). They had
indeed received the Holy Spirit, but only as an $ἀπαρχή$[EN117] (2 Cor. 1[22], 5[5]; Eph. 1[14]), i.e., as
a first instalment of the final gift. The instalment was of a piece with the final gift and a
pledge and guarantee of it, yet it was no more than the deposit on an account, an
$ἀπαρχή$[EN118] (Rom. 8[23]), i.e., the first fruits consecrated to the Deity, but not yet the full
harvest distributed among all the people. They knew of their hidden life with Christ in God,
but only when Christ their life was made manifest would they be manifested with Him in
glory (Col. 3[3f.]). "Behold, what manner of love the Father hath bestowed upon us, that we
should be called (and be) the sons of God … Beloved, now are we the sons of God, and it
doth not yet appear what we shall be: but we know that, when he shall appear, we shall be like
him: for we shall see him as he is" (1 Jn. 3[1f.]). What has still to be realised, as Paul sees it, is
the manifestation of the life of Jesus in His body (2 Cor. 4[10]), the general "manifestation of
the sons of God" (Rom. 8[19]), the making of their "body of humiliation" conformable to His
"body of glory" (Phil. 3[21]), and the liberation of all creatures from the bondage of corruption to the glorious liberty of the children of God (Rom. 8[21]). When Jesus had been
obedient even to the death of the cross, He was exalted by God to be the Bearer of the name
which as the name of the Lord is above every other name. This was clear to the proclaimers
and recipients of the Easter message, and they believed and responded with their confession
and a life of love for Him and for the brethren. But they did not yet see the knees of all things
in heaven and earth bow to Him as the only Lord, nor did they yet hear the song of praise
with which every tongue must willingly or unwillingly confess Him as the Lord (Phil. 2[9f.]).
This was the supremely visible and real tension in their consciousness of time between the
times. But it must be seen and understood that this tension—with the need and yearning
and sighing inevitably entailed—could not have a negative accent, because they saw themselves set in fellowship with the Old Testament fathers, in the time, not to be evaluated
negatively, of their expectation of the coming Lord and His salvation; because they were
privileged to stand with these ancient witnesses of truth in Advent.

2 Pet. 1[16–21] is particularly noteworthy in this connexion. The author is talking about his
proclamation of the "power and coming of our Lord Jesus Christ." He maintains that it is
different from any "cunningly devised fables" ($σεσοφισμένοις μύθοις$). To begin with, he
points out that he had been an eye-witness ($ἐπόπτης$) of the transfiguration. He then continues in v. 19: "Hence we have the word of prophecy the more surely ($βεβαιότερον$);
whereunto ye do well that ye take heed, as unto light that shineth in a dark place, until the
day dawn, and the day star arise in your hearts." According to the Gospel record, Moses and
Elijah had actually stood by the side of Jesus when He was transfigured before their eyes, and
had spoken with Him. This prophetic word was not therefore outmoded, but acquired genuine relevance for those who had their origin in the appearance of Jesus. It was confirmed in
its character as a prophetic word pointing to the future and became an indispensable light
on their path. The disciples did not come down from the mount alone, or as eschatological
innovators, but in company with the ancient witnesses, accredited by the fulfilment of the

---

EN117 firstfruits
EN118 firstfruits

long-prepared history of the covenant and salvation. It was in this company that they moved afresh to meet the coming Lord. The visible and palpable unity of prophecy and fulfilment, of fulfilment and prophecy, is what factually distinguishes their proclamation of the "power and coming of our Lord Jesus Christ" from all "cunningly devised fables."

The same line is taken in Peter's second speech in Ac. 3[19f.] He summons men to repent- [495] ance and conversion and the remission of sins on the ground that "seasons of refreshing" are coming; the sending of Jesus, Israel's destined Messiah, "whom the heaven must receive until the times of restoration of all things (ἀποκατάστασις πάντων), which God hath spoken by the mouth of all his holy prophets since the world began." The implication is that the prophets foretold not only the first advent of Christ, but implicitly His second advent as well, to which the Church now looks and the whole world actually moves. Far from being obsolete, the witness of the prophets has acquired a vital relevance and admonitory significance for the people of Israel to whom the apostles in the first instance addressed their message. Whatever happens, Israel must not miss a second time, and to its final judgment, the chance to experience the fulfilment of this message, as it did the first time to its detriment.

Even more illuminating is 1 Pet. 1[10-12], which merits particularly close attention. In 1[5] the author had stated that those who had been begotten again unto a living hope by the resurrection of Jesus Christ from the dead were being kept by the power of God through faith unto salvation ready to be revealed at the last time. In vv. 6–9 he had spoken of the "joy unspeakable and full of glory" awaiting those who were now suffering persecution. Although these had not seen Jesus they loved Him, and believed on Him without beholding Him. That joy would be theirs in His final revelation. He now continues in v. 1of.: "Of which salvation the prophets have inquired and searched diligently, who prophesied of the grace that should come unto you: searching what, or what manner of time the Spirit of Christ which was in them did signify, when it testified beforehand the sufferings of Christ, and the glory that should follow. Unto whom it was revealed, that not unto themselves, but unto us they did minister the things, which are now reported unto you by them that have preached the gospel unto you with the Holy Ghost sent down from heaven, which things the angels desire to look into." The meaning of this is that they have been translated into the state of faith, hope and love by the fact that the prophets, taught by the Spirit of Christ, have done and are still doing them the same service as the messengers of the Gospel now do them as they are sent by the same Holy Spirit. The prophets preached and still preach to them the sufferings and glory of Jesus Christ, and in so doing they preach their salvation already accomplished in Jesus Christ but still to be revealed to them. The fulfilment of Old Testament prophecy has become a reality among them, and they have thus come to participate in the resurrection of Christ. They are born again to a living hope. Therefore, in spite of the sufferings of the present time, they have been translated into the state of love and faith in One whom nevertheless they cannot see or behold. We may note in particular that the enquiries and declarations of the prophets belong formally and subjectively to their own time and history. But in this historical particularity they were materially and objectively inspired and moved and impelled by the Spirit of Christ, by the truth of His coming person and history, by His sufferings and glory. What makes their enquiries and declarations prophetic is that objectively and materially they are witnesses of Him who was still to come, i.e., of the grace now vouchsafed to Christians. It is for their sake that Jesus Christ suffered, and for their sake that He is glorified. Thus the prophets can be of service to Christians because they are prophets, and their testimony is a προμαρτύρεσθαι[EN119] (v. 11). They too, like the messengers of the Gospel (v. 12), are wholly dependent on the Holy Spirit of Jesus Christ. Like them, they are

---

[EN119] advance testimony

unable to make the object of their proclamation visible or perceptible to their hearers. For them too the salvation wrought in Jesus Christ is a hidden mystery, only to be revealed later. Hence in a way they really minister to Christians "the things which are now reported unto you." But because their testimony takes the form of a προμαρτύρεσθαι [EN120], and their existence that of prophets, unlike the evangelists, and perhaps to their advantage, they are witnesses to the truth that what they attest with the evangelists is not just an ordinary event in the flux of history, and that the God proclaimed by the evangelists as the Father of Jesus Christ is not a new God. *Certitudinem salutis confirmat ab ipsius vetustate: quoniam ab initio mundi legitimum a Spiritu sancto testimonium habuerit* [EN121] (Calvin). Unlike the evangelists, however, and perhaps to their disadvantage, the prophets are witnesses of the Jesus Christ whom they do not yet know as come, and can attest therefore only as One who is still to come. "What or what manner of time" will be His, is all that they can investigate. They cannot bear witness to His actual manifestation. The sufferings and glory of Jesus may form the object of their message objectively and materially, but they cannot be its content subjectively and formally. Since they think and speak only of their own time, the actual occurrence of the event which they foretell can only be for them a matter of research and investigation. Yet this is no fortuitous limitation. Indeed, it is not really a limitation at all. It makes no difference to their testimony or status. As the sufferings and glory of Christ are revealed to the prophets by His Spirit, it is also revealed to them that with the later evangelists, the heralds of the accomplished event of salvation, even in this apparently disadvantageous distinction they have a very real and special service to render to Christians instructed by the latter. The rigorously future orientation of the prophetic message only becomes vital in Christianity. For Christians living in time the enacted salvation has become past. But in its general revelation it is still future. And in this futurity it is the event which leads Christians forward in time, urging them ahead, drawing them on like a magnet, out of the sufferings of the present time, out of the darkness of the present and into the light. The present status of Christians, with its tribulation, is related to that of the future deliverance to which they move as the sufferings of Christ are related to His subsequent glory. The two together, and in this order, are the Messianic reality: the first being subordinate and transitory, the second real and permanent; the first being the way and the other the goal. In virtue of this order and structure of the one event commonly attested by the prophets and evangelists, the evangelical and apostolic message can be no less prophetic, no less a message of Advent, than that of the prophets. It proclaims not only the Crucified, but also the Resurrected; not only the faith and love which Christians are to maintain in their present tribulation as they look back to the completed Messianic event, but, as in vv. 3–9, and in agreement with the structure of this event, the future revelation of the deliverance of those who believe and love (corresponding to the glory of Christ), and therefore Christian hope. Christians could not really come from this event if they were not moving towards it again. Thus it is Christianity which first does justice to prophecy even in its particularity, even in the strict futurity of its message. In fact, this passage seems almost to reduce the apostles and evangelists to the level of subordinates. All that they have to do is to take up the Old Testament message of the future and give it the honour which it could not enjoy prior to the events, in its distinctive character as prophecy. The message of the Messiah already come gives a new edge to the message of the coming Messiah, of the salvation which is not only future, but demonstrated to be future. Now that grace and salvation have become present and future and not just future, the ministry of the prophets really begins, as by the word of the apostles and evangelists the Holy Spirit speaks

---

[EN120] advance testimony

[EN121] The certainty of salvation is confirmed by its antiquity: for from the beginning of the world it has been supported by trustworthy testimony from the Holy Spirit

to Christians in this twofold way, making them Christians, and translating them into the state of living hope in which even in the sufferings of time they move towards the glory of the future revelation. Only here, within the Christian community, does the prophetic word come into its own. Christians have to see themselves standing as it were between two choirs singing antiphonally—the apostles on one side and the prophets on the other. And the passage closes at v. 12 with the statement that even the angels are amongst those who look forward to the future revelation of the salvation already accomplished. They, too, desire to see and look into the mystery of the things, the grace and salva tion, in the proclamation of [497] which the prophets and apostles have ministered to them and do so still. Like the apostles and prophets, like Christians themselves, the angels wait for the consummation of the process inaugurated by the resurrection—a consummation which according to 1 Pet. 4^7 will also be "the end of all things." The word used to denote the "looking into" of the angels ($\pi\alpha\rho\alpha\kappa\acute{\upsilon}\psi\alpha\iota$) is the same as that which in Jn. 20^5 is used of Peter when he looks into the empty tomb. Thus Christians are surrounded by a cloud of witnesses, some eloquent and others silent, some on earth and others in heaven, but all looking into the future. This is sufficient to warn them to hold fast to the state of salvation to which they have been called. "Wherefore gird up the loins of your mind, be sober, and hope to the end for the grace that is to be brought unto you at the revelation of Jesus Christ" (v. 13).

Remarkably enough therefore, but also instructively, it was primarily the Old Testament background to the New Testament message which gave to the first Christian consciousness of time its forward direction and eschatological orientation, and to Christian life the form of a "looking for and hasting unto the coming of the day of God" (2 Pet. 3^{12}). The Gospels would be very different from what they are, i.e., accounts of the historical existence, fulfilled in His crucifixion and revealed in His resurrection, of the man Jesus who was the Lord, Messiah and Saviour, if in telling of Him who was, they were not everywhere full of Advent, of the One who comes and will be in His revelation.

As is well known, the Fourth Gospel takes its own particular line in this matter. In fulfilment of the promise: "I will not leave you comfortless; I will come to you" (Jn. 14^{18}), Easter, Ascension, Pentecost and *parousia* are here seen as a single event, with much the same foreshortening of perspective as when we view the whole range of the Alps from the Jura. This perspective is legitimate and necessary side by side with the other. The Fourth Gospel shows us that it is necessary to understand the event of Easter and that of the *parousia*, with the intervening history of the community under the present power of the Holy Spirit, as different moments of one and the same act. The theses of those who advocate a thoroughgoing eschatology are quite superfluous once this has been realised. There is no need to suppose that there was unforeseen delay in the *parousia*, or that hope in the *parousia* was repeatedly deferred, or that the primitive Church and even Jesus Himself were disillusioned or mistaken on the subject in consequence of an exaggerated enthusiasm—a view which is so clumsy that it is surely condemned from the very outset.

For there is a unity of eschatological outlook even behind and above the different approach which we find in the Synoptists. As we have seen already, the latter start with the initial assumption that the kingdom of God promised in the Old Testament has already entered history as an effective reality in the person and words and acts of the man Jesus. The time is fulfilled as He is present, embarking on a way which will end in His death as the decisive event of salvation, but which is from the very first this way, on the higher stages of which this end is already the meaning not only of the being of Jesus as such, but of all His words and acts. The Synoptists would agree with the view which the Evangelist attributes to John the Baptist in 1^{29}—that from the very outset Jesus is "the Lamb of God, which taketh away the sin of the world." But He is still concealed as the One He is and shows Himself to be in His words and acts. At first, it is only the demons who recognise Him with any certainty in this way: "What have we to do with thee, thou Jesus of Nazareth? art thou come to destroy us? We know thee who thou art, the Holy One of God" (Mk. 1²⁴). The crowds are amazed and dumbfounded, but they only call Him a great prophet (Lk. 7¹⁶). Their spiritual leaders are offended at His claim to be the coming One, and dismiss it as a piece of arrogant self-assertion. But this only shows how blind and deaf they are, how far they have abandoned the hope of Israel, whose first and most discerning and willing advocates they ought to have [498] been in face of this fulfilment. John the Baptist surmises His true status, but according to Mt. 11² he is not sure whether Jesus is He that should come or whether they should look for another. Indeed, He is hidden even from His disciples apart from preliminary illuminations like Peter's confession and the transfiguration. They will forsake Him and flee when He stands at the end of His way. Peter will even deny Him, and Judas will be the first and decisive agent in Israel's last act of unfaithfulness and disobedience to its promise, initiating the handing over of its Messiah to the Gentiles. As the One He is Jesus is thus both present and not present. The kingdom of God is real but not operative. It has come, but not come. It has still to be prayed for. It is present in reality, but not in revelation. To the extent that the New Testament contains good news, but not yet Easter news, the prophetic history of the Old Testament is continued in the New. The New Testament witness to the Messianic "now" is unmistakeable, yet it is shot through with the "not yet," with more expectation, as though the Messiah were still only promised. In the very centre of the picture Jesus Himself waits, looking forward to things to come, to His own future.

This is the second reason—the Advent witness of the Old Testament was the first—why the apostolic community would not concentrate exclusively on the past or present, but when it thought of Jesus had to look forward to this future. Throughout the tradition—in the New Testament even more clearly than in the Old—we see at the heart of the actuality of salvation a people always blind and deaf, obstinate and determined enemies of God, a Church which always runs away and denies and even betrays Him, and above all Jesus Himself still waiting and looking forward to His own future. How could anyone who remembered this Jesus do other than follow Him, looking with His eyes and according to His express command to the future, His future? But to look to His future is to look to the revelation of His actuality, to the irresistible, invincible and triumphant visibility of His kingdom as it has already come.

The reader of the Gospels is bound to look to the future, if only because the Jesus attested by them was not waiting for nothing but positively living and speaking and acting towards His future revelation. For His goal is not just death, although this is the saving event to which His whole life was in the first instance directed. His goal is the subsequent revelation of the meaning of His death, and therefore the putting into effect of the salvation won in Him for men, for the community, for the whole world, for which He had come as the Fulfiller of time. It is the kingdom with the veil removed, manifest, and visible in glory. Everything Jesus said revolved implicitly, and in the parables explicitly, around the coming kingdom in this sense. And the acts of Jesus, His signs and wonders, are in this sense effective anticipations and therefore real indications of the coming kingdom to which Jesus moves through His provisional concealment and finally His passion, crucifixion, death and burial: not of the reality of the kingdom, for the kingdom was already a reality in His person from the very outset and could not be more real than in His self-offering to death, in which the saving event of His whole existence, His Messianic reality is perfected; but certainly of its revelation, by which the kingdom acquires form and becomes saving and effective for men, for the community, and for the world.

This also explains why New Testament expectation is always characterised as imminent expectation. It is primarily the expectation of the man Jesus Himself (in the subjective sense): the expectation in which He Himself lived and went to His death; the expectation of what He saw before Him as the goal of His life and death. It is the expectation of His own resurrection from the dead. All three predictions of the passion in the Synoptics expressly mention this expectation: "On the third day he will rise again." Yet the Gospels obviously rule out the imminent expectation which is expectation of a definite date. Jesus Himself admitted that He shared the human uncertainty understandable in this respect: "That day and that hour knoweth no man, no, not the angels which are in heaven, neither the Son, but the Father" (Mk. 13^{32}). Even after the resurrection He can still say: "It is not for you to know [499] the times or the seasons, which the Father hath set in his own power," i.e., which He has appointed for the manifestation of His kingdom (Ac. 1^7). The revelation of the kingdom is linked with the consummation of the life of Jesus in His death. It is its revelation. And this fulfilment of His life in His death, which will be followed by His revelation, is accomplished by the incarnate Son in obedience to the will of His Father and therefore in acceptance of the right point of time appointed not by Himself but by the Father. What He does know and teach, because His disciples are always to know it too, is that the kingdom of God, the revelation of its hidden reality, will come soon and suddenly like a thief in the night, as He Himself puts it (Mt. 24^{43}), in a simile repeated in 1 Thess. 5^2; 2 Pet. 3^{10}; Rev. 16^{15}. Its coming will be soon because it is the goal of the limited life in time of Jesus of Nazareth and will follow hard on His death and therefore in the foreseeable future. And it will come suddenly because it is foreordained and foreknown by God alone, and will occur when men are least expecting it, beneficially if terrifyingly upsetting all their expectations and plans, and thus their anxieties and hopes, as actually happened in the first instance with the resurrection of Jesus.

These considerations throw light on Mk. 9^1: "Verily I say unto you, that there be some of them that stand here, which shall not taste of death, till they have seen ($\dddot{\epsilon}\omega\varsigma$ $\ddot{\alpha}\nu$ $\ddot{\iota}\delta\omega\sigma\iota\nu$) the kingdom of God come with power ($\dot{\epsilon}\lambda\eta\lambda\upsilon\theta\upsilon\hat{\iota}\alpha\nu$ $\dot{\epsilon}\nu$ $\delta\upsilon\nu\acute{\alpha}\mu\epsilon\iota$)." This passage assumes that the kingdom of God has already come. What has still to happen is that it should be seen. Some of those standing around Jesus are to see it. It follows, therefore, that this "coming of the king-dom," this revelation of the fact that it has come, must occur within the foreseeable future. The context in which the three Synoptists placed the saying shows that they connected it with the transfiguration, which is its immediate sequel. The indefinite $\tau\acute{\iota}\nu\epsilon\varsigma$ EN122, which is used to indicate those who are to see the kingdom in their lifetime, is probably meant to confirm this. Only "some" (Peter, James and John) witness the transfiguration. But this event is only a proleptic anticipation of the resurrection, as the latter is only a proleptic antici-pation of the *parousia*. This being the case, it is best to see the fulfilment of Mk. 9^1 in all three events, transfiguration, resurrection and *parousia*. In the transfiguration they see and know Him already, though only transitively, as the Resurrected. And in His resurrection they finally see the kingdom come with power, and therefore, *in parte pro toto*EN123, as $\dot{\alpha}\rho\rho\alpha\beta\acute{\omega}\nu$ EN124 and $\dot{\alpha}\pi\alpha\rho\chi\acute{\eta}$ EN125 that which in the *parousia*, as His general revelation, will be comprehensively and conclusively knowable and known as His glory. Not all, but only a few even of His disciples at the transfiguration, and only the disciples at the resurrection, will in their own lifetime see the kingdom of God come in the person of Jesus, and therefore the end of all time. This is the meaning of Mk. 9^1. Calvin's comment is thus correct: *Antequam vobis moriendum sit, regnum illud Dei, a cuius spe vos pendere iubeo, conspicuum erit oculis vestris. ... Adventum vero regni Dei intellige gloriae coelestis manifestationem, quam a resurrectione auspicatus est Christus et plenius deinde spiritum sanctum mittendo et mirificas edendo virtutes exhibuit; nam in illis*

EN122 some
EN123 as a part for the whole
EN124 pledge
EN125 firstfruits

primitiis gustandum suis praebuit coelestis vitae novitatem, quam veris et certis experimentis ipsum ad patris dexteram sedere agnoscerent[EN126]. (*C.R.* 45, 483).

In similar vein Jesus says in Mt. 10[23]: "Ye shall not have gone over the cities of Israel, till the Son of man be come." The disciples' mission to Israel will be overtaken by the coming of the Son of Man; their proclamation of the Messiah among the Messianic people will be forestalled by His own revelation. This saying, which is peculiar to Matthew, occurs in the missionary charge, where it is placed just after the prediction of persecution and sufferings for the disciples in the course of their mission. There are, of course, more encouraging and consoling features in the charge. When the disciples are brought to trial they are not to be anxious what answer to make because the Spirit of the Father will speak in them (v. 19f.). And then "he that endureth to the end shall be saved" (v. 22). This encouragement and consolation is not relative but absolute. A new and wonderful source of help will become available. God will intervene and rescue them from their tribulation. And then we come to v. 23, which obviously takes up the catchword τέλος[EN127] (v. 22). Their own τελειοῦν[EN128] of their task in the cities of Israel, where all that they can really do is to flee from one city to another, will be suddenly cut short by God's τέλος. The Son of Man will come and put a stop to the activities of their persecutors. But it will also mean the end of their own mission. Clearly, this is the supreme form of the promise of help which Jesus gave to His disciples. This is how the special Matthean source means us to take it. He will come in person and judge between them and their persecutors, between the new Israel and the old. The great transition of Jesus Himself, accomplished in His death and according to Mt. 28[16f.] manifested in His resurrection, from His mission to His own people to His mission to the world; the exaltation of His office as the Christ of Israel to His office as the σωτὴρ κόσμου[EN129], is reflected in this saying to the disciples and offers the real clue to its meaning. In the words which immediately follow (vv. 24–25), Jesus predicts the same fate for His disciples as for Himself. It is in this transition, in this exaltation, that the Son of Man "comes" and reveals Himself, but also changes completely the mission and office of His disciples. "Go ye therefore, and make disciples of all nations" (Mt. 28[19]). This mission will be both possible and necessary even before they have finished with the cities of Israel. These cities are only the starting-point of the apostolic mission. They are this still. But the apostles cannot wait any longer for their conversion. "Your blood be upon your own heads; I am clean: from henceforth I will go unto the Gentiles" (Ac. 18[6]). This is what is in store for the disciples according to this saying. They will witness the resurrection of Jesus, which will not only mark the transition and exaltation of Jesus Himself, but their own transition and exaltation to a new and, according to Mt. 24[14], eschatological ministry of proclaiming the Gospel to the ends of the earth. The coming of Jesus is again spoken of as imminent and the saying had the advantage, the practical significance of showing what the promise must have meant for the "little flock" at the pre-Easter period.

There is another saying of Jesus in Mk. 13[30] and *par.*: "Verily I say unto you that this generation shall not pass, until all these things be done." In this case the exegetical situation differs from that of Mk. 9 and Mt. 10. The things which are so imminent that the existing

[500]

[EN126] Before it is appointed for you to die, the kingdom of God, in the hope of which I command you to live, will be visible to your eyes .... Now understand that the coming of the kingdom of God means the manifestation of heavenly glory, which Christ inaugurated by the resurrection, and showed forth more fully by sending the Holy Spirit and displaying wondrous powers; for in those first fruits of his, he furnished a taste of the newness of heavenly life, so that they might know that he sat at the Father's right hand by sure and certain experience

[EN127] telos

[EN128] completion

[EN129] saviour of the world

generation will experience them art not identified directly with the coming of the Son of God as the Gospels see it. For they agree in placing it immediately before the parable of the fig tree. When the sap rises, the branches sprout and the leaves grow, it is a sign that summer is nigh at hand. "So, in like manner, when ye shall see these things coming to pass, know that he is nigh, even at the doors." He is at the doors, not yet present, but near, very near. Since the second half of v. 29 asserts this, the ταῦτα[EN130] of the first half cannot be referred to the days *after* that tribulation, or to the coming of the Son of Man (vv. 25–26), but only to the immediate prelude. And the ταῦτα πάντα[EN131] of v. 30 must have a similar reference, at any rate as understood by the Evangelists. The present generation will witness the immediate prelude to the coming of the Son of Man. This clearly means that they will actually witness His coming. But the emphasis here is on the fact that they will be witnesses of the three groups of events described in vv. 7–20 as the immediate prelude to His coming: of world-wide disasters (vv. 7–8); of the tribulation of the Church (vv. 9–12); and as a climax, the fall of Jerusalem, which the surviving elect must escape by headlong flight (vv. 14–20). The complex in vv. 7–20 is enframed at either end by warnings against the seductions of false messiahs and prophets with their fictitious claim: Ἐγώ εἰμι[EN132] (vv. 5–6 and 21–23). But the point of the whole discourse emerges in vv. 24–27 and 33–37. The light of the sun, moon and stars will be extinguished, i.e., the light of the bodies by which, according to Gen. 1[14], [501] created time is measured. And then (v. 26) God will send forth His angels to gather in the elect from the four winds. But, because the tribulation immediately precedes the final event which is also the end of time, it follows that the Church contemporary with the events of the tribulation—perhaps the Church of to-day!—must (vv. 33f.) watch. Although it does not know—nobody knows according to v. 32—when the καιρός[EN133] of the great καὶ τότε[EN134] of vv. 26 and 27 will occur, yet the Lord of the house will suddenly come at an hour chosen by Himself during the night which begins with these events. The whole point and purpose of the existence of the Church in this night is to watch. This is the point and purpose of the existence of the whole generation which will be overtaken by this night: "And what I say unto you I say unto all, Watch" (v. 37). Be ready for the Messiah, who cannot possibly be mistaken for any other. He will come when all this has taken place. While it is taking place, He is "at the doors" (v. 29)—just as summer is nigh when the sap rises in the fig tree and the branches begin to put forth their leaves. The discourse of Mk. 13 is a repetition of the three prophecies of the passion and resurrection of Jesus elevated to a cosmic scale. It must be remembered that the whole discourse is occasioned by the question of the disciples when Jesus predicted the destruction of the temple (v. 2): "Tell us, when shall these things be? and what shall be the sign when all these things shall be fulfilled?" As Mk. 14[58] suggests, the Synoptists too know something of a saying of Jesus about the rebuilding of the temple after three days, and they are clearly aware that this whole complex is susceptible of various interpretations. Jn. 2[19–22] is illuminative in this respect. The destruction of the temple is a reflection of the death of Jesus Himself, and its rebuilding a reflection of His resurrection. The prophecy of what the present generation will experience supremely in the destruction of the temple will begin to be fulfilled at once with the story of the passion (Mk. 14[1ff.]) with which the life story of Jesus reaches its climax. All the disasters of world history, all the persecutions and trials of the community, and above all the judgment on Israel which culminates in the destruction of Jerusalem, are only the great shadow of the cross falling on the cosmos, the Messianic woes

---

[EN130] these things
[EN131] all these things
[EN132] I am He
[EN133] time
[EN134] and then

which not even the cosmos can evade, the participation in the divine judgment, effected in the death of Jesus, to which even the cosmos is subject, though this judgment is to its salvation, to the salvation of Israel, the salvation of the community, the salvation of all men, and indeed of the whole cosmos. In the cosmos in which and for which Jesus will and must be crucified, things can only turn out as predicted in vv. 7–20. Hence Jesus is primarily foretelling His own impending death when He speaks of these imminent events, and His resurrection when to the comprehensive picture of man tormented by war, division, earthquake and famine, of the persecuted and tormented community, of Jerusalem standing under moral threat, He opposes the imminent end of time, the great καὶ τότε EN135, the coming of the Son of Man to gather His elect, and therefore His triumphant life as the Lord of His community. The disciples can and should look vigilantly to this future in the deep shadows lying across the world, in the afflictions by which it is threatened, in the judgments which must fall on it, and primarily in face of the judgment of which all the other judgments are only the accompaniment, the judgment of His passion, now about to commence. When all this has taken place He will come, He who now goes to destruction. He will then be revealed. He who is now shrouded in the deepest obscurity. He will triumph in judgment upon the cosmos, He who is now vanquished by the cosmos. "Heaven and earth shall pass away: but my words shall not pass away" (v. 31). And according to v. 30 even the present generation shall not "pass away" either until all this has come to pass. Even now, as it begins to experience the passion of Jesus, it is about to take part in the opening of the series of events which will be immediately followed by the coming of the Son of Man. Hence the urgency of the demand that it should look forwards, watching and waiting for Him, and not waiting for any other, nor confounding His coming with that of any other. It thus receives the law which will be normative for every subsequent generation which in its own time and in its own way will witness these events; the law of hope in the One who has already come and will come again in His glory.

[502]

A further case in point is the eschatological saying at the Last Supper recorded by all three Synoptists (Cf. Markus Barth, *Das Abendmahl*, 1945). The clearest version of this is to be found in Mt. 26[29]: "But I say unto you, I will not drink henceforth of this fruit of the vine, until that day when I drink it new with you in my Father's kingdom." The negative form in which this saying is couched recalls the Nazarite vow. Jesus is consecrating Himself to be the sacrificial victim. How he kept this oath will be recorded in Mt. 27[34]. But more important than the negative aspect is the positive—that His next meal, which is the *terminus ad quem* EN136 of the oath, will take place in the kingdom of God, and will therefore be the Messianic banquet. This saying is another expression of urgent expectation. In the brief interval in which a man can go without food and drink Jesus will be with His disciples in the kingdom of God. Next time He sits at meat with them they will see and know that the kingdom of God has come. This is exactly what happened according to Lk. 24[31–35]. There is also emphatic mention of a meal of the Resurrected with His disciples in Jn. 21[5 12 15]. Jesus' intercourse with His disciples during the forty days is comprehensively described as a συναλίζεσθαι ("to take salt with") in Ac. 1[4]. And it is said of the apostles in Peter's speech in Ac. 10[41]: "(We) did eat and drink with him after he rose from the dead." This not only proves the reality of the resurrection (Lk. 24[41f.]), but also its tremendous import and far-reaching consequence. No longer, as at the Last Supper, will they sit at meat with Him in anticipation of His sacrifice, but in retrospect of its completion; not in a re-presentation and repetition, as in the Romanist doctrine of the Mass, but in a simple and full enjoyment of its benefits, of the eternal life won for us in Him, within the revelation of the completion and benefits of

---

EN135 and then
EN136 ending point

this sacrifice, and therefore with open eyes and ears, and even open mouths, within the kingdom of God. For this reason the κυριακὸν δεῖπνον[EN137] of the primitive Church, formally celebrated in repetition of the pre-Easter passover in "remembrance" of the Lord (1 Cor. 11²⁰), is materially a continuation of these festive meals in the personal presence of the Resurrected. While in the Lord's Supper the Church looks back upon the "night in which he was betrayed," it cannot confine the memory to this night. On the contrary, "the death of the Lord" is "proclaimed" (1 Cor. 11²⁶) through the action of the community. It is continually made known to the community and the world, on the basis of His self-revelation at Easter as a saving event. Thus the passover meal becomes an Easter meal: not kept in sorrow but in joy (ἐν ἀγαλλιάσει); not with complicated arguments as to the precise nature of the bread and wine, but in "singleness of heart" (καὶ ἀφελότητι καρδίας, Ac. 2⁴⁶). Each occasion is the Messianic banquet of the revealed kingdom of God. Each is the most pregnant form of the fellowship of Christians with the Lord now revealed to them. Each is an anticipation of His final and general revelation, inaugurated, but no more, in His resurrection. The resurrection was the ἀρραβών[EN138] and ἀπαρχή[EN139] of this final revelation, but the totality is still to come, so that every celebration of the Lord's Supper can only look forward to it. For that reason and to that extent it is celebrated "till he come" (1 Cor. 11²⁶)—and His own general and visible presence renders the Church's human proclamation of His death superfluous. For that reason and to that extent it is particularly appropriate at the Lord's Supper to use the grace: "Come, Lord Jesus, be our Guest." Hence the Gospel accounts of the Last Supper and the institution of the Lord's Supper are to be numbered with the many passages which in the first instance point to the resurrection, which find in the resurrection their initial yet very real fulfilment, but which in the light of this fulfilment point all ages in imminent expectation to the *parousia* as the last event consummating that of Easter.

Our final example is Jesus' reply to the Sanhedrin when He was asked whether He was the [503] Christ, the Son of God. According to Mt. 26⁶⁴ this is as follows: "Thou hast said: nevertheless I say unto you, Henceforth ye shall see the Son of man sitting on the right hand of power, and coming in the clouds of heaven." The Markan version has (14⁶²): "I am" (Ἐγώ εἰμι), but lacks the pregnant "henceforth." The Lukan version (22⁶⁷ᶠ) puts the question with greater reserve: "Art thou the Christ? tell us," and Jesus first answers: "If I tell you, ye will not believe: and if I ask you, ye will not answer me," and only then adds: "Hereafter shall the Son of man sit on the right hand of the power of God,"—with no mention of the coming on the clouds. Only then is the direct question put by the Sanhedrin: "Art thou then the Son of God?" and the reply is a combination of the Markan and Matthean versions: "Ye say that I am." All three Gospels agree that Jesus makes a public declaration of His Messiahship just before the end of His life on earth. It is this admission, together with the prediction of His impending exaltation and second coming, that seals His fate in the eyes of His enemies. The high priest rends his clothes. There is no need of further evidence against Him, for this is blasphemy. The death sentence is pronounced forthwith, and the mocking and scourging follow. We will now confine ourselves to the Matthean version. It is at this point that the passion story proper begins. The Messiah is arraigned by the supreme authority on earth— the high court of the Messianic people. For centuries they have been without a king. Political power has been in the hands of the priestly caste. Now their promised King stands before them, accused before the bar of the priestly aristocracy. Until now He has never publicly claimed to be this King. Indeed, He has prevented His disciples from spreading it abroad. According to Jn. 6¹⁵, He withdrew to the mountains when the crowd wanted to make Him a

---

[EN137] Lord's supper
[EN138] pledge
[EN139] firstfruits

King by force. He deliberately staged His entry into Jerusalem in such a way as to make it clear that, as far as He is concerned, there is no question of any royal claim. True, He is their King, but He must keep this a secret. Now, however, the whole position has changed at a single stroke. He now stands before a body which can rightfully claim to be "anointed." It has a right to ask whether He is the Christ. There is no telling what happy results might How flom the question. Here is Israel's great opportunity. Never before has it had such a chance to affirm and accept its King through the mouth of its supreme representatives. At last the covenant, so faithfully kept on God's side since the days of the patriarchs and now fulfilled, must be ratified by a practical decision on the part of His people. If it is, the kingdom of God will come on earth in all its glory. Thus Jesus' answer: "Thou sayest it," is not to be regarded as ironical. We should remember that Jn. 11^{51} expressly ascribes to the high priest in his official capacity the power to speak as a prophet. Jesus nails him to his own saying: σὺ εἶ ὁ Χριστὸς ὁ υἱὸς τοῦ θεοῦ[EN140], which is identical with Peter's confession at Caesarea Philippi: (Mt. 16^{16}), and which might be taken as indicative, and might even have been meant as such. He is, as it were, making a last offer through the high priest to the whole people of Israel: You say yourself who and what I am. What follows—the *sessio ad dexteram*[EN141] and the *parousia*—can and must in the first instance be seen in connexion with this final offer. The King of Israel who stands before them will "henceforth," i.e., now that Israel has decided its attitude to Him, disclose and reveal Himself. It will now see Him as the One He is, the Son of Man enthroned in the glory of God and coming from His glory. But what will He see in His people when He comes? Will He find it obedient, ready and willing? And what will His coming mean for it? Redemption as a reward for its proven loyalty? We are at the supreme crisis in salvation history, and world history. Did the high priest really mean what He said? Jesus at any rate took him at his word, and affirmed in all seriousness that he had spoken the truth. And by way of confirmation He elaborates it further. He promises to the high priest, to the Sanhedrin, and through them to the whole people, what hitherto He has confined to His disciples. The kingdom will come immediately, and in the full glory of its revelation. "Ye shall see … " No conditions are attached to this offer. It holds good even if the high priest has not really meant what he said, even if Israel, at the supreme moment of its destiny, has not decided for Him but against Him. Jesus is still Israel's King whatever happens, even if it rejects Him. He is who He is and will manifest Himself as such. And the very next moment, of course, they do reject Him. Is. 29^{13} is repeated once more. "This people draw near me with their mouths, and with their lips do honour me, but have removed their heart far from me." It is made clear at once that the high priest's words were not uttered in knowledge, and therefore as a confession of faith. He was the one who was really guilty of blasphemy. For he spoke in blackest unbelief, in malice and guile. The opportunity is there, but it is scorned and thrown away. The decision is still awaited, but it has already been given *in malam partem*[EN142]. So things take their inevitable course. The high priest rends his garments and accuses Jesus of blasphemy. The trial is broken off when it has hardly begun, and the death sentence is pronounced. This means, however, that Israel denies and rejects its king, the King of the last times, who now stands before it as its King, who has confessed and declared Himself as such, and who is the Accuser rather than the accused in virtue of His rejection. For He is who He is, and will manifest Himself as such. They will see Him sitting on the right hand of power and coming on the clouds of heaven—the self-same Jesus whom they have rejected and delivered to death. Against their will He will be victorious, overcoming the death of which they make themselves guilty. They will see Him in this state of the fulfilment

[504]

[EN140] you are the Christ, the Son of God
[EN141] session at the right hand
[EN142] in a bad sense

of all the promises as the Revealer of God's faithfulness in the teeth of all the faithlessness of His people (Jesus Himself excepted); as the righteous Judge, announcing the merited condemnation which would fall on it were it not that He was on the point of taking it upon Himself and suffering in its place what it ought to suffer, were it not that His righteousness is therefore righteousness of His grace. But since this is the meaning of the *sessio ad dexteram*[EN143], since His coming on the clouds of heaven will be the coming of this righteous Judge, it is clear that everything had to happen as it did. It was foreseen and determined, not only in the counsels of wicked man in time, but in the eternal counsel of the righteous God, that the decision made at this point had to be made, that Jesus' last offer had to be rejected, that He "*must* suffer many things of the elders and chief priests and scribes, and be killed" (Mt. 16^{21}). It is not He who is in their hands, but they in His. But what interests us here is that this last offer (destined from all eternity to be rejected, as we have seen) also includes the promise of the irresistibly approaching revelation of the glory of the One who is already and immutably the Lord, and that this promise is actually addressed to His accusers, who themselves stand at this point under the gravest accusation. The passion of Jesus, and therefore the last and decisive act of Israel's unfaithfulness, cannot begin before it has been declared that henceforth—behind the decision first made by God and then by them, and executed in His actual death on the cross—He will be seen only in glory. His resurrection, the outpouring of the Holy Spirit on His community, and His *parousia* as His final appearance to every creature as the Judge, are all to be understood as a unity, as a single fulfilment of this last prediction of His future destiny.

We learn from these illustrative passages (selected as such from the theology of the Synoptists) that when our retrospect of the life and death of Jesus is related to the imminent expectation commanded in the Synoptic Gospels, it cannot possibly remain retrospective, because in these Gospels Jesus Himself continually looks and moves forward to the revelation of His glory which, inaugurated in the resurrection, will be consummated in the parousia.

In conclusion, again adopting the position of the community schooled by the Old Testament and the Gospel accounts of the words and acts of the man Jesus, we maintain as the third ground of its hope the simple fact that it is the community which, after the life and death of Jesus, and the commencement of the final revelation in the forty days, exhibits and experiences the lordship of Jesus in the form of the lordship of His Spirit. We refer to the lordship of Jesus in the time between the resurrection and the *parousia* and therefore between the commencement and the completion of His final revelation. That it has the form of the Spirit means that the community not only derives temporally from this commencement and moves towards this consummation, but that it is effectively established and gathered by the One who was and who comes, being not only ruled but continually nourished and quickened by Him. That is why it lives always in expectation, and even in imminent expectation. That is why its prayer is *Maranatha* (1 Cor. 16^{22}; Rev. 22^{20}). That is why it finds its consolation in His promise: "Behold, I come quickly" (Rev. 22^7, ^{20}). That is why it receives the encouragement: "Behold, I stand at the door, and knock" (Rev. 3^{20}). That is why it is given the consolation: "The Lord is at hand" (Phil. 4^5; Jas. 5^8). That is why it also receives the daily admonition: "And that, knowing the time, that now it is high time to awake out of sleep: for now is our salvation nearer than when we believed" (Rom. 13^{11}).

[505]

In this respect Mt. 25 is of particular relevance for the present existence of the community, for it is asked in this chapter whether it understands and takes seriously and turns to good account its present existence under the lordship of Jesus in the form of the Spirit as considered in relation to the future. Does it realise that the end before it is the consummating

---

[EN143] session at the right hand

coming of the Lord, the glory, the liberation, but also the judgment of the final revelation to which it now moves, so that its present life and action is weighed in the balances of His future?

This is the challenge of the parable of the ten virgins (Mt. 25^{1-13}). It asks the community whether it is active in relation to the new coming of the Lord, or whether it is merely passive. The ten virgins are supposed to go out and meet the bridegroom. This is the meaning of ὑπάντησις EN144 (v. 1), or ἀπάντησις EN145 (v. 6), and it is implied by the description in v. 10 of their going out to escort the bridegroom and accompany him to the marriage feast with their lamps alight. Exactly the same picture is given in 1 Thess. 4^{13-18}, where Paul states that the community, both living and departed, will be "caught up ... in the clouds, to meet the Lord in the air" (εἰς ἀπάντησιν κυρίου EN146). With Jesus Himself, His community as such, in His service, will come and be revealed in the world in glory, and will even assist its Lord in the judgment of Israel (Mt. 19^{26}), in the judgment of the world and angels (1 Cor. $6^{2f.}$), and in His kingly rule (1 Tim. 2^{12}, 1 Cor. 4^8, Rev. 5^{10}), so that it can be called a "royal priesthood" (1 Pet. 2^9), and it can be said that the whole creation is waiting for this revelation of the sons of God (Rom. 8^{19}). The picture of the virgins escorting the bridegroom with their lamps in Mt. 25 is reminiscent of a similar eschatological saying in Dan 12^3: "And they that be wise shall shine as the brightness of the firmament; and they that turn many to righteousness as the stars for ever and ever"—to which allusion is also made in Mt. 13^{43}. When Jesus is finally revealed, the Church of the interim will stand at His side, with its testimony to the whole world. This is the promise of the parable. But it also contains a challenge. Five virgins are wise and five foolish. The wise ones, having kept their lamps alight for a long time, and apparently to no purpose, had themselves fallen asleep from weariness (v. 5). Fortunately, however, they had replenished their lamps with oil and could thus fulfil their function at the decisive moment. The foolish virgins were also to hand with their lamps burning and shining, but unfortunately they had no reserves of oil and could not therefore meet and escort the bridegroom. The available oil could not be divided, and their rush to the shops to buy some could only seal the fact that their lamps were not burning and shining at the decisive moment, and therefore that they would have no share in the entry of the bridegroom. The parable is thus controlled by the question whether oil is available to replenish the lamps at the critical moment. If the lamps stand for the witness of the community, with which it can and should stand at the side of the returning Lord at the end of time, the oil represents something which makes this witness vital and strong not only now but then, something which is essential if it is to render this supreme service in the final revelation, because, if it does not have it, it cannot acquire it, and it will be unable to render this supreme service. The parable asks the community of the interim between the resurrection and the *parousia*, which might stand at any moment before the goal of creation which is the goal of its very existence, whether it will have this absolutely indispensable something. It is a matter of that which will make its witness equal to the revelation of its Lord in this decisive test, even though it may have failed a thousand times in the interval. It is a matter of the harmony in which it must find itself with Him for all its human frailty and perversity if it is to stand at His side in face of the world. What is meant is clearly the self-witness of Jesus by the Holy Spirit apprehended in faith and love. This is what founded the community of the intervening time. That is the content of its witness. This alone can give its witness vitality and strength. That is the only pledge of its hope, constant in all its inconstancy. That is the vital element in virtue of which the community can be equal to its returning Lord for all its lowliness, associating

[506]

EN144 meeting
EN145 meeting
EN146 being led of the Spirit

70

itself with Him and having a place at its side in His final revelation. The parable does not ask the community concerning its witness as such. It presupposes that it will finally be there with its lamps burning and shining. And it asks concerning the oil to furnish these lamps of witness at the decisive moment when its mission reaches its goal; and therefore, since the goal may be reached any moment, concerning that which makes its witness possible here and now, in the interim period. What is its attitude to the source which alone can preserve it? What is its attitude to the self-witness of Jesus now given to it by the Holy Spirit? How about its faith in Him and love to Him? If it lacks that which is necessary enough now but absolutely indispensable at the end, its hope will prove to be its judgment, its witness will be lacking at the very moment when its hope is on the brink of fulfilment, and it will be incapacitated at the very moment of its supreme service. Let the community see to it that it is wise and not foolish. Let it see to it that its relation to the Jesus Christ who was yesterday and is to-day is such that it can only encounter and serve as His community the One who will live and reign for ever.

The parable of the talents (Mt. 25^{14-30}) deals with the same theme, though from rather a different angle. The question is now directed more definitely to the community's present action, for the meaning and results of which it will have to account when the Lord returns. Its Lord has "(gone) into a far country" (v. 14). This is how the interim period is now described. Before His departure, however, He has given His community the care and control of His goods. In this case one is given more and another less: "to every man according to his several ability" (v. 15). But however small or great the amount entrusted, each represents the Lord in the handling of what is no less genuinely His own property and no less valuable. In all its manifold tasks, the Church has the duty of turning this property to profitable use. What is entrusted is His Gospel, and His Spirit. The interval between the resurrection and the *parousia* is the time of Jesus because it is the time of the community and its service. His final revelation will therefore be critical for His community because it will reveal that, entrusted with His Gospel and Spirit, it has really served Him. It will be admitted to the marriage feast only if it has increased in good and loyal service the comparatively few goods entrusted to it. The Word which belongs to it seeks new hearers; it must not cease to pass it on to others. The Spirit given to it seeks new dwelling-places and new witnesses; it must so obey the Spirit that its witness makes new dwelling-places and evolves new witnesses. This is the whole purpose of the witnessing time, the time of the Church. It is not a time when it can be content to guard and keep what it has received. Naturally it must do this too. It can hardly render its service if it fritters away its heritage. The New Testament speaks very plainly at other points about the duty of maintaining what is given in relation to the last time: "I come [507] quickly: hold that fast which thou hast, that no man take thy crown" (Rev. 3^{11}). But the parable of the talents shows us that this cannot be an end in itself. The servant who buried his talent made it safe, but did not put it to use. His conduct was not merely unprofitable, but positively lazy and wicked. It was not merely a refusal of service, but rebellion against the Lord. Thus the community which in the interim period is not a missionary community, winning others by its witness according to the measure of its power, will be banished, at the return and final revelation of the Lord, into outer darkness, where there can be only weeping and gnashing of teeth instead of the promised banquet. At the end of the time between the community will be justified before the Lord, and will stand and have a share in His glory, only if in the time between it has understood and realised that all its faith and love, all its confession and works, are nothing at all without daring and aggression, without sowing in hope; only if it has understood and practised its witness as a commission. For the time between is not the time of an empty absence of the Lord, nor is it the time of a bewildering delay in His return, in which it is enough for the community to maintain and help itself as best it can. On the contrary, it is the time of God's patience and purpose, and it is the business of the community to recognise the character of this time, and therefore never to think that it has plenty of time in this time, but to "buy up" this time in relation to those who are "without" (Col. 4⁵; Eph. 5¹⁶) It can never have enough time here and now for the fulfilment of its task. For it knows what the world does not know, and it owes it to its Lord to make it known to the world. It has the light which cannot be placed under a bushel (Mt. 5¹⁵) but must be put in a candlestick. Note that in the series of historical signs listed in Mt. 24⁶⁻¹¹, the last and culminating sign is the work of the community: "And this gospel of the kingdom shall be preached in all the world for a witness unto all nations; and then shall the end come." Whether this sign is set up or not, is the question of its present existence, addressed to it in this parable in relation to the end of time which will decide concerning it too.

The discourse on the last judgment (Mt. 25³¹⁻⁴⁶) presses home the same question in a third form. It is the Son of Man, the Messianic King, who according to v. 31 f. will come in glory with His angels, take His seat upon His throne, gather the nations around Him, and divide them as a shepherd divides the sheep from the goats. In the centre of the picture, among all the nations, stands the community. It is asked concerning its being and conduct in this present age, again in the light of the approaching end. This community hopes for this Judge, and rightly so. As surely as it is His community, and has received His Word and His Spirit, and bears witness to Him, it expects to be identical with the flock on the right hand, and to be invited to enter the kingdom prepared for it from the foundation of the world (v. 34). How else can the community live but in this expectation? Who but the community can do so? But what is the community that it may enjoy this expectation? This has not yet been decided. It will be decided when Jesus comes again: "We must *all* be made manifest before the judgment seat of Christ" (2 Cor. 5¹⁰). And it is from this future that the parable looks back so strikingly to the present time when Jesus is still hidden. The issue will be decided by the attitude and conduct of the community to Him while He is still hidden. Then it will be known what the community will be which will stand at His right hand in this future. But where is He hidden now? With God, at the right hand of the Father? in His Word and sacraments? in the mystery of His Spirit, which bloweth where it listeth? All this is true enough, but it is presupposed in this parable, and the further point is made, on which everything depends, that He is no less present, though hidden, in all who are now hungry, thirsty, strangers, naked, sick and in prison. Wherever in this present time between the resurrection and the *parousia* one of these is waiting for help (for food, drink, lodging, clothes, a visit, assistance), Jesus Himself is waiting. Wherever help is granted or denied, it is granted or denied to Jesus Himself. For these are the least of His brethren. They represent the world for which He died and rose again, with which He has made Himself supremely one, and declared Himself in solidarity. It is for them that He sits at the right hand of the Father, so that no one can know Him in His majesty, or honour and love Him as the Son of God, unless he shows concern for these least of His brethren. No one can call God his Father in Christ's name unless he treats these least as his brethren. This is the test which at the last judgment will decide concerning the true community which will inherit the kingdom: whether in this time of God's mercy and patience, this time of its mission, it has been the community which has succoured its Lord by giving unqualified succour to them in this needy world. It will be well with it if it has obviously done this, if it has been affected by the concrete miseries of the world, not passing by on the other side with haughty disdain, but being simply and directly human, with no excuses for the contrary. It will then be shown to be the community devoted to God in the person of Jesus. It will then be found righteous at the last judgment and be able stand on the right hand as the community which participates in the work of its Master. It is to be noted, however, that the righteous and therefore the justified at the last judgment do not know with whom they really have to do when they act with simple humanity (v. 37 f.): "When saw we thee an hungred, and fed thee …?" They had helped the least of His breth-

[508]

72

ren, they had helped the world in its misery for its own sake. They had no ulterior motive. As the true community of Jesus, they saw the need and did what they could without any further design or after-thoughts. They could not do their duty or fulfil their mission without realising their solidarity with those in affliction and standing at their side. They found themselves referred quite simply to their neighbours in the world and that wholly "secular" affliction. They had no spiritual strategy. They obeyed without explanations. They thus carried their lamps like the wise virgins or the faithful stewards of the other parables. They were not occupied with metaphysical considerations. They were simply concerned with men as men, and therefore treated them as brothers. If they had not done so, they could not have claimed Jesus as their Brother or God as their Father. It is because they knew Jesus as their Brother and God as their Father that they fed the needy, gave them drink, clothed and visited them. But did they do this? This is what will be revealed when Jesus returns. So will everything they have left undone. The false community will also be revealed and rejected and condemned for its inhumanity. Such is the question addressed to the community of the present by the approaching *parousia*. It is posed to all its members, to its orders and cultus and preaching and theology. What has all this had to do with the afflicted who as such are Jesus' brethren? Has the community been first and foremost human in all that it has done? The question may be comforting or disconcerting, but there can be no doubt that it is crucial, and where it is heard it can hardly fail to be incisive and therefore admonitory. This is the *Magna Carta* of Christian humanitarianism and Christian politics, established not only as a promise but as a warning in view of the approaching end—not so much because it will be the end of all things, but because it bears the name of Jesus, who has come, and will come again.

The situation of the community in the time between, as presented in Mt. 25, may be summed up by saying that it is really the community of the last time. That is to say, it has the completion inaugurated with the resurrection of Jesus as a driving force behind it and the consummation in His *parousia* as a drawing force before it. It comes from the revelation of the man Jesus as it moves towards it, and it moves towards it as it comes from it. "This same Jesus, which is taken up from you into heaven, shall so come in like manner as ye have seen him go into heaven" (Ac. 1[11]). This is what determines the whole logic and ethic of the community of the end. If we are to understand what is meant by ἄγεσθαι πνεύματι[EN147] [509] (Gal. 5[18]; Rom. 8[14]), by περιπατεῖν or στοιχεῖν πνεύματι[EN148] (2 Cor. 12[18]; Gal. 5[16 25]), it is essential that we keep in mind this double motivation of Christian existence in this intervening time. The Christ who comes again in glory is as near to His community as the Christ of the resurrection. As the risen Christ cannot fall behind it and become merely historical, so the Christ of the *parousia* cannot yield before it, so that it has only a profane and empty future not determined by Him, and its situation between the two comings can only repeat and renew itself at every moment of the continuing interim. The community lives under the lordship of Jesus in the form of the Spirit. In the Spirit that double proximity is actual presence. In the Spirit Jesus at every moment of the interim is not only at the right hand of the Father, but also here on earth. Hence the community at every moment is really His and under His lordship. "Lo, I am with you alway, even unto the completion of time" (ἕως τῆς συντελείας τοῦ αἰῶνος, Mt. 28[20]). Two opposite but closely connected errors must be noted at this point and avoided.

The first consists in an underestimation of the majesty of Jesus in this intervening time in consequence of an underestimation of the origin of the community in His resurrection, or, as we may also say, of a failure to recognise the consolation of the Holy Spirit in whose work

---

[EN147] walking in the Spirit
[EN148] to walk by or to live in the spirit

73

the community may find full satisfaction at every moment in its time of waiting. If this is not perceived, the imminent expectation in which it lives is bound to be an enigma and the "delay," the constant "non-arrival," of the *parousia* an offence. The view is thus adopted that early hopes quickly gave way to disappointment and disillusion; that a lofty but impractical expectation was replaced by a clever adaptation to realities ; that a new and more subtle interpretation was given of the original attitude. This movement is thought to be the true secret of the New Testament consciousness of the present. And it may be recalled that there were some who thought along these lines even in the New Testament itself: "Where is the promise of his coming? for since the fathers fell asleep, all things continue as they were from the beginning of the creation" (2 Pet. 3⁴). But the adoption of this conclusion entails the hazardous assumption that this opinion, naturally repudiated in 2 Peter, expresses the painful, laboriously suppressed, but clear and objective truth of the witness of the New Testament. If this is so, the whole of the New Testament must be expounded accordingly, as though it were really wrestling at every point with this opinion, or occupied rather feebly with this objective truth. The real witness of the Evangelists and apostles, and in the last resort Jesus Himself, is to the delay of the *parousia*, though they will not admit it. Any exposition of the New Testament running counter to this opinion (or objective truth), from the days of the apostolic fathers right down to the present, must be denounced as a dishonest and unsuccessful evasion. The one question to be asked of New Testament and theological research is whether and how far it has voluntarily or involuntarily helped to support this opinion and further exposed the insincerity of all attempts to deal with the question which are not consistently eschatological. A kind of monomania develops. Everything thought and said and written is demagogic. Pride is found in being to the whole cosmos a great and maliciously ignored source of unsettlement, and the tedium thereby caused to more usefully employed angels, men and animals is not perceived. The mistake in all this is to be found in its failure to take account of the Holy Spirit as the driving and drawing force behind the community in the time between the resurrection and the *parousia*. For through the Spirit the lordship of Jesus is never merely past or merely future. It is always present, but in such a way that we must expect His coming, indeed, His imminent coming, and yet may wait for it with patience. If this eager expectation of the *parousia* is a genuine problem in the New Testament, of crucial importance for the present, the same cannot be said of anxiety over its supposed delay or non occurence. Regarded in the light of the New Testament teaching about the situation of the community in the last time, this anxiety bears all the marks of a pseudo problem. The answer given in 2 Pet. 3 is just as true to-day as it was then. It is that the question comes from "mockers with mockery" (ἐν ἐμπαιγμονῇ ἐμπαῖκται v. 3). There will be plenty of them in the "last days." But they are people who do not realise (vv. 5–7) that the created world as we know it is only temporary, as the story of the flood once proved. It is moving, indeed, towards total dissolution—"reserved unto fire." The question is that of those who, for all that they are so critical when it would be better to be uncritical, are far too uncritical about their own existence and existentialist philosophy. And when Christians hear their question, they are not ignorant (v. 8) that "one day is with the Lord as a thousand years, and a thousand years as one day" (Ps. 90⁴). In God's sight—and after all they live in His sight—not only is nearness distance, but distance nearness. What are thousands and thousands of years when it is a matter of the longsuffering of God, giving us time right up to the end of time (v. 9), "not willing that any should perish, but that all should come to repentance"? It is to be noted in passing that in 1 Tim. 2⁴ the existence of the state is attributed to the same divine purpose. For Christians who remember this, can even a single day be wasted in thousands and thousands of years? Is there any cause to complain, then, at the delay of the final denouement ? Have they time to worry their fellow creatures with a theology of self-satisfied complacency? No, the objective truth is very different from this theory: "The Lord is

[510]

not slack concerning his promise, as some count slackness " (v. 9). The theory has to be read *into* the New Testament, for the New Testament itself contradicts it both implicitly and explicitly. Only if it is read in can it have any importance for an understanding of the New Testament awareness of the present. And it needs only little experience of the consolation of the Holy Spirit to make this understanding completely impossible.

The opposite error consists in an exaggerated estimate of the greatness of the community in consequence of an equally exaggerated estimate of its present existence in relation to the *parousia*, or, as we may also say, of a failure to recognise the criticism of the Holy Spirit, whose work keeps the community moving towards its Lord in dissatisfaction with its present condition, preventing it from regarding its condition as absolute. When this is not perceived, the community—or the "Church" as it loves to call itself—forgets that it is on the march, and that though the inauguration of Jesus' revelation of His glory is behind it, the consummation is still to come. It secretly anticipates the change of front foretold in Mt. 25 and 1 Thess., when at the end of time it will stand at the side of its Lord before the world. It is not content to be a handmaid like the virgins at the marriage feast, but obviously behaves as if the *causa Dei*[EN149] were in its own hands. Instead of bearing witness to the authority of Jesus, it invests itself with His authority, attributing absolute perfection to its order and ministry and cultus and dogma, and interpreting historical evolution as the automatic development of the divine truth incarnate in itself. Thus at each successive stage of its development it acts and speaks as if it were itself permitted and commanded to blow the last trumpet now. Its doctrine at any given moment is the normative voice of Jesus and His apostles. Its tradition perpetuates the original apostolic witness, claiming equal dignity and attention. Its particular interpretation of the original witness is the authentic interpretation. Its divine commission is the basis of a claim made in its own favour. But in these circumstances, what place is there for Christian hope? In what sense are we still in an intervening time, still waiting for the consummated revelation? Has it not been realised already in the being and activity of the Church? Is there any need for the risen Lord to come again? Is there any more embracing form of His presence and power than that taken already by the Church itself? In 1944 the Congregation of the Sacred Office passed a remarkable resolution to the effect that belief in a visible second coming could "not be taught as a certainty"—the very thing which for the New Testament is the greatest certainty of all on the basis of the resurrection. On this view, all we have left to hope for is the golden lining of a future heavenly glory. And even this is [511] under the control and apparently belongs to the sphere of the Church on earth, with its indulgences, its merited assurances and guarantees, its purchased rights, its express beatifications and canonisations. Certainly there can be no place for a Judge who will confront the Church itself in sovereignty and whom it is bound to fear. If He comes at all, it will be to judge the world for persecuting and oppressing the poor Church in time, for resisting and ignoring it. The Church itself will stand triumphant at His right hand, self-evidently before the judgments have even begun. The future at the end of time will simply be the confirmation of its own present and distinctive perfection. The true and divine safeguard against the real threat of Christian arrogance and pride and sloth and obstinacy has been abandoned. The Church on earth, with its power to change bread and wine into the body of Christ, and to effect this in daily sacrifice, with its infallible teaching office, its Virgin Mary already ascended into heaven, is itself already on the throne with the returning Lord. What need is there then for His return? And how can it take place in this time that judgment begins at the house of God (1 Pet. 4[17])? It is obviously treason even to contemplate the mere possibility. The Church has completely forgotten Mt. 25, and the Seven Letters of the Apocalypse. Yet in these Letters it is not just fallible Christian men but the very angels of the

---

[EN149] cause of God

75

churches who are summoned to judgment at the *parousia*. And what about the prophetic word of the Old Testament, which as such, in its reference to the Lord coming to judgment, is addressed with unparalleled severity, not to the world but typically to the elect people of God with its temples and priests and authorised sacrifices? This is the "de-eschatologising" of Christianity with a vengeance! This is real obstinacy in face of the critical power of the lordship of Jesus Christ in the form of the Holy Spirit. The Church of Rome is the typical form of this de-eschatologised Christianity. But there are also Protestant, Anglican and other versions. Wherever the Church entertains an exaggerated estimate of itself, the same error is at work in its opposite form. For in both cases it is Jesus Himself who is absent, the Lord of the Church who as such is the Lord of time. In the first case He is absent because there is no recognition of the consoling power of His resurrection for the present life of the community. In the second He is absent because no serious account is taken of His future and its critical power for the present life of the community. And as His future is also denied in the one, His presence is also missed in the other, being identified with that of the community. The one error leads to the other. If the community of the last time is already seated on the throne of Christ, it is high time to say that His return is not to be expected. And if that is not to be expected, it is quite in order to look for a self-sufficient community which can dispense with this expectation. But if we are to follow the New Testament, we must resist both errors with the same determination.

2. GIVEN TIME

The subject of our enquiry is the being of man in his time. In order to see man in his time correctly, we have investigated the being of the man Jesus in His time. To do this, we had to start with the revelation of the being of this man in His resurrection from the dead. This enabled us to see His being as that of the Lord of time, and His time as the fulfilment of all time, which, as His own time, extends backwards and embraces all prior time as its beginning, the beginning of all time, and extends forwards and embraces all subsequent time as its end, the end of all time.

[512]

We cannot expect to say the same of man in his time; of man in himself and in general. For his being in time is certainly not that of the Lord of time, nor is his time the fulfilment of time. This can be said neither of the human species as a whole, nor of any of its social groups, nor of any individual man. Our anthropology can and must be based on Christology, but it cannot be deduced from it directly. What is to be predicated of the being of the man Jesus in time is true because this man is also God. But while He is this for us and for the world, it can be said only of Him. It is because the Word was made flesh, the Eternal entered time, that the man Jesus is the Lord of time, and His time is the fulfilment of time, embracing all time, the first and last time which in every present is His own time. As there can be no repetition of the being of this man, there can be no repetition of this human being in time.

It is immediately apparent how differently man in himself and in general, the man who is not Jesus Christ, is in time, has time and is temporal. What, then, is the significance of our own movement from the past through the present to the future, of the fact that we were yesterday and are to-day and will be to-morrow? We may begin by sketching the phenomenon as it presents itself to us, i.e., in its contrasts to the picture of the Lord of time which we have just delineated.

For us the past is the time which we leave and are in no longer. It was once ours. We had our life in it years ago or yesterday or even this morning. In it we made our contribution to history. In it we were then ourselves. But we are so no longer. For, with all that filled or did not fill it, it has now eluded us and been taken from us. It has remained behind, never to be restored. With all its achievements, with ourselves as we then were and cannot be again, it may be partially or completely forgotten. It may almost be thought of as though it had never been. And this is what seems to happen to most of our own past, though it was once ours. The past of the individual and the race and the nations and other social groupings is a great flood of forgotten reality which once had its time but now has it no longer, which has now gone as though it has never had it. Of course there is in the ocean of oblivion an island or two of memory. A few names, figures, events and circumstances are not entirely forgotten. Some of them are shadowy and insubstantial. Some are more clearly defined. Given the means and the skill, it may be possible to reconstruct and recall them plastic- ally. As well as forgetting, there is also memory—abiding or fleeting, direct or indirect, weak or vivid, natural or artificial. There is the voluntary or involun- tary evocation of the past and its contents. In fact, much of our life is made up of memories. But it is a sign of life drawing to its close, of old age and decay, [513] when individuals, nations and other historical societies begin to be absorbed in memory, to live mainly in the past, to be interested chiefly in history and antiquities. And even at best memory is limited. We can recall only a few scraps of the vanished and forgotten past and its contents, its life and history. And even what we recall soon sinks back to oblivion. And in its limited sphere mem- ory is not the present reality. It is simply the subjective accident or skill by which we conjure up the shades of what was once present but is so no more. Thus in the last resort memory, like oblivion, merely demonstrates the gulf which lies between what was and what is. The past has ceased to belong to us. We are no longer the people we were years ago, yesterday, or even this morn- ing. Of course we should like to cling to what was, but the present and the future are already beckoning us. We must press on. The past is already slipping away, never to return. It is a mere conjecture, and a highly dubious one at that, to suppose that we are still what we were and still have what we had.

Similarly, the future is the time which we do not yet have but perhaps will have. We can at least look back at the past as it slips away—both our own past and that of the world at large. But it may well be pure illusion to suppose that we can look to our own being of the future or the world of the future. We do not even know whether we will have a future. We do not know whether the time to come will be ours at all. But even if it will be, it is not ours now. We are only moving towards it. We do not know and cannot conceive its contents, its nature and happenings. We may anticipate it in expectation, but it is only in expectation that we can anticipate it, filling it with definite conceptions, hopes and fears, desires, intentions and plans. And even this anticipatory filling of the future is very restricted, for only the future itself can teach us what is really desirable or dangerous, necessary or superfluous, possible or impossible. Anticipation is no substitute for the reality anticipated. And the future when it comes may partially or totally confound our expectations. It is almost a law of nature that this should be the case. We are always poor prophets even of what is to happen within the next hour or so, to say nothing of a year or two hence, or centuries to come. The future—if we have one at all, and in whatever form we have it—is even more obscure than the past. In relation to it, even our identity with ourselves is only a guess, and a doubtful one at that.

[514] The real nature of our being in time is most obscure of all, however, at the very point where it ought to be clearest, namely, at the moment which we regard as our present. Here, where midway between the vanished past, which we have largely forgotten or only dimly remember, and the unknown future which awaits us (or perhaps does not await us!), we think we can take our ease and enjoy in impregnable security our being and having, and our identity with ourselves, we find that we are wholly and utterly insecure. For what is our present but a step from darkness to darkness, from the "no longer" to the "not yet," and therefore a continual deprivation of what we were and had in favour of a continual grasping of what we will (perhaps) be and have? Our past and future do at least have a real if limited content, but the fulness of our present is obviously only the remarkable act of existence itself in which we have already been deprived of our past, but have not yet been able to grasp the future, everything being wholly behind us and everything (or nothing) wholly before us. What are we now? And what do we have? The past had at least duration; the definite duration of our own and all human days and years which, whether remembered or forgotten, did actually come and go in their sequence. Similarly the future, if it comes at all, can at least have duration, consisting in a further sequence of hours and days. But what is Now? What is the present? It is the time between the times. And this, strictly speaking and as we actually experience it, is no time at all, no duration, no series of moments, but only the boundary between past and future, a boundary which is never stationary, but always shifts further ahead. It is the moment we can never prevail upon to stay, for always it has already gone or not yet come. In practice, the present can be experienced only in the form of recollections and expectations. Whether it is a matter of our personal present, or present history ecclesiastical or secular, we can pin it down and describe it only in historical retrospect, in descriptions of a situation already created, or in the form of prognostications, hopes and fears, and the corresponding postulates and programmes. We are and live out only what we were in a partly forgotten, partly remembered past and will be (perhaps) in an unknown future, i.e., in all the questionableness of our being in past and future time. In the present in which we think we have it most securely we have no time.

This is our being in time. "Thus we live all our days." Of course it is possible to shut our eyes to all this. But we cannot escape it. We cannot be as men—our reference is to man in himself and in general—except in this way, in this riddle of time. If the being of man in time is interpreted in any other way; if either as an individual or as a representative of the race man is said to have time now and not just to have had it or to be about to have it, to be in time and not just to have been and (perhaps) to be about to be; if an attempt is made to interpret positively the temporality of man in its three dimensions, the venture is nurtured either by illusions or by secret borrowings from theology. A human self-understanding genuinely orientated by a general picture of man will be halted by the riddle of human temporality, and will have to be content to assert that we must live our life in the absolute uncertainty given with this riddle because we are not asked whether we would prefer a different possibility.

Whether we realise it or not, we are up against an ultimate truth about the [515] being of man in time, which we can neither evade nor contest. It is a truth which doubtless finds suitable expression in the metaphysical conception of the infinity of time. Infinite is the abyss into which the past and all that it comprises, all that we have been, sinks and disappears before our eyes; an abyss which is deeper than all the virgin forests of pre-historic times, with the fabulous monsters that inhabited them. Infinite, too, is the future (perhaps even that of nothing) to which everything is bound to hasten, whether it likes it or not. Infinite, above all, is the flight which is also a chase, the chase which is also a flight; what we call the present; the succession of moments, or rather of constant shiftings of the boundary, between the darkness there and the darkness here. Infinite is the impossibility of escaping time, of not accepting time, of not being in time. Infinite, also, is the impossibility of escaping its enigma as the enigma of man himself, man who is, and who would like to be in time and have time, who is in point of fact temporal, and whose being in time is of this nature.

The metaphysician is usually silent at this point, and silently enjoins resignation. Hence the last word rests with the seer or poet who can dream of beings very different from ourselves, of beings which are eternal, and thus tell us that our being in time is in its infinity an infinitely tragic destiny, which it is the final task of those to whom the gods give the means to describe in a pious song, yet which eschews all cheap and easy consolation. Perhaps Friedrich Hölderlin has given us one of the best examples in his "Hyperion's Song of Fate":

> Ye soar above in light,
> Softly borne, blessed spirits!
> Radiant winds divine
> Caress you lightly,
> As artists' fingers
> Playing on holy strings.

> Unbound by fate, heavenly beings
> Breathe like the sleeping infant.
> Their spirits bloom eternally,
> Chastely inviolate
> In a modest bud,
> And their happy eyes
> Look out serenely
> In calm, eternal clarity.
>
> But to us poor men
> Is given no place to rest.
> Harried by pain,
> We grope and fall
> Blindly from hour to hour.
> Like water dashed
> From cliff to cliff,
> In lifelong insecurity.

[516] This is what *we* are. This is how we are in time. And now let us recall the beginning and conclusion of our christological investigation. "I am ... which is, and which was, and which is to come, the Almighty." This is what the man Jesus is. This is how He is in time.

Yet we cannot be content with this simple contrast, for Jesus is not only God and therefore different from us, but also man and therefore like us. He is not only the Creator, but also a creature among creatures. He is not only eternal, but—in His own particular way—with us in time. To compare our lot with that of "blessed spirits," with very different and purely eternal beings, may produce a gloomy Hymn of Fate, but it gives us the easy evasion that we men in time are so totally different. Our comparison, however, is with the man Jesus. And although as the Son of God He is so utterly different from us, yet as the Son of Man He is wholly like us. Hence we cannot escape the contrast by pleading His absolute dissimilarity.

Nor can the painful contrast between Him and us be the last word on the subject. For it is intolerable to be able to develop the statement that we have time only in the form of the antithesis that we do not have it at any time; that we no longer have the past, do not yet have the future and certainly do not have the present, because it is only the step from the one darkness to the other. The monstrous nature of this situation may perhaps be overlooked or forgotten, but once seen and remembered, it cannot be denied. Nor can it be explained by invoking the contrast between man and God, creature and Creator, time and eternity. Along these lines, the only possible way of accounting for it is to shift it back into the Godhead which has made man in this way, into the will of the Creator which has created this type of creature, into the eternity of which this temporality is the foil. In this case we should have to resign ourselves to our fate, not hymning it like Hyperion but defying it like Prometheus. But its monstrous character remains. That this is the case, that neither questioning, complaint nor protest can be suppressed, is shown by the innumerable theoretical attempts to reinterpret this disconcerting picture of man's being in time. Perhaps a fulness of time, and a prolongation of human being in time, is sought in a deepening of the recollection of the past by relating man to his origin in a world of immutable being. Perhaps expectation of the future can be understood along similar lines with the help of the idea of endless progress. Perhaps the present as the step from the past into the future may be regarded as a creative, saving, redeeming and liberating act, as a divine or at least a God-like work accomplished in the act of our existence, a work which makes man eternal in every "moment." But it is painfully obvious that these interpretations gloss over the reality. And the reality is so monstrous that it asserts itself against these interpretations, like the original of a picture which has been badly painted over. It is worth noting, however, that it has always been felt necessary to cover up the original. For this shows us with what cares and questions and protests man faces this reality, how hard he finds it to accept his [517] being in time as normal. We all run away from this picture. We would all prefer it otherwise. This comes out even more plainly in the fact that in practice we usually close our eyes to the problems of our being in time, that we try not to see or consider the matter but live as if our past and future were really ours, as if we really had time. For when we prefer not to look or think, trusting that we can find help in a resolute "as if," what is hidden beneath the surface is definitely something abnormal and unnatural: not an inevitability which we can calmly recognise and accept; but a contradiction in face of which we are powerless, yet which we try to escape by hook or by crook, even by putting it right out of our minds. In other words, the difference which emerges between our general being in time and that of the man Jesus does not seem to be one which is original or natural.

On the contrary, when we make this comparison between Jesus and ourselves—and the presupposition of our whole enquiry is that we have to see and understand man in this comparison—the antithesis between Jesus and ourselves points not merely to the contrast between man and God, creature and Creator, eternity and time, but to God's judgment upon man; not merely to the nature and order of God and man, but to God's indictment against man, to His sentence and punishment, and to man's existence under His wrath. What we have been describing is *sinful* man in time. The man who lives in that monstrous situation, in that loss of time which cannot be denied, reinterpreted or even forgotten, is the man who is alienated from his Creator and therefore from himself, from his creaturely nature, and who has to pay for his rebellion against God by living in contradiction with himself, in contradiction with his God-given nature. The enigmatic reality of our being in time is a perverted and disturbed reality determined by this twofold contradiction. And the real reason why we cannot accept it calmly, or gloss it over, or forget it, or effectively deny it, is that man is not left to his own devices in this contradiction, but that in the existence of the man Jesus with His very different being in time a divine protest is made against his perverted and disturbed reality.

81

Whether man hears and accepts this protest is quite another matter. The protest has been registered, and registered for all time. It is an effective protest, upsetting all our attempts to call black white. For within humanity and men generally, whose being in time consists in that continual loss of time, the man Jesus exists as the Lord of time. God did not undertake to recognise and accept our monstrous being in time. In the existence of the man Jesus it is decided and revealed that God did not at all create man in that state of falling "from cliff to cliff"; that it is not at all His will which is manifested in the fact that our being in time is very different from the creaturely nature given by Him; and that He is determined to vindicate and protect His right as Creator [518] and ours as His creatures in face of the monstrous perversion and corruption in which we exist. Because this protest is made, we may look our situation in the face and either handle it with metaphysical profundity or hymn it as our fate, or we may refuse to look it in the face, either glossing it over or simply living on in spite of it, but we cannot escape its monstrous abnormality or accommodate ourselves to it. We may think we have succeeded in doing so, but this is sheer illusion. For it stands under the divine protest. It cannot be our situation as willed, created and recognised by God. It is one of the exponents of divine judgment, of the indictment, condemnation and punishment under which we now stand, having placed ourselves in this position, in this sphere of His wrath, as sinners against Him. But God has vindicated His right and ours. He has come to our rescue, and therefore to the defence of our true creaturely nature against the unnatural condition into which it had fallen. He has come to save us. This divine protest, effective and revealed in the existence of Jesus Christ, makes it objectively impossible for man to be content with his being in time, to accept the abnormal as normal or the monstrous as the rule. Man is uneasy at this point because God is uneasy before him. And God is uneasy because man, even sinful man, is His creature and even His covenant-partner whom none can pluck from His hands, to whom neither the devil nor man himself can give another nature, another being in time, than that which God has given. God is uneasy because His grace, His grace towards man as His creature, is not broken or limited by the fact that man has sinned and thus incurred His wrath. God is uneasy because He has not ceased to seek and find lost man, even the man who exists in the loss of his time. This reality of God the gracious Creator is the power which combats our direct and indirect attempts to escape, and which does so victoriously, however we may writhe and turn. And if it is asked whether and how and how far it really does this, the answer is that this takes place and is revealed in the existence of the man Jesus as the Lord of time.

But the being of Jesus in time has this power to unmask and sober man, to recall him to the truth from every height and depth and reinterpretation and forgetfulness, because the monstrosity of general human being in time is overcome in Him. Thus the primary significance of His being is not critical. It is critical only as it actualises and reveals positively the real being of man in the time really created by God and given to man. It depicts our general being in time as the plunge into falsehood against which God protests. It allows us no rest in this falsehood, because it is itself the truth which confronts it; the truth of human nature as God created it; the truth of our being in our time. We have already maintained that the existence of the man Jesus does not mean only that God confronts man, the Creator the creature, eternity time. If this were all, there would be many easy or more costly ways of resolving the antithesis. It would then be possible and necessary to accommodate ourselves somehow or other to the situation. But the existence of the man Jesus means that God became man, the Creator a creature, eternity time. It means, therefore, that God takes and has time for us; that He Himself is temporal among us as we are. Yet He does this in a manner appropriate to Himself. He is temporal in unity and correspondence with His eternity. But what can this mean but that He is temporal in a way which also corresponds to man as His creature, in the original and natural form of the being of man in time before it was perverted and corrupted? That Jesus is the Lord of time, He who was and is and is to come, is of course unique to Himself. In this respect He is incomparable. It is the divine determination of His human being alone. But this unique determination includes a being in time which is true and genuine in contrast to the plunge into falsehood. For Jesus, to live in the present does not mean the flight and chase from darkness to darkness, but being which is independently filled and therefore self-resting and lasting. For Him the past has not become being which has gone, which is lost, which is no more, a mere shadow, but being which is also present in the present, filling it and filled by it. Similarly, the future is not just being which comes, which is therefore dark and empty, which has to be filled artificially, which is not yet, but being which is self-filled and therefore fills both present and past. As Jesus is in time in this way, He is the object of the Father's good-pleasure, not only as His unique, eternal Son, but also as man like us, in His likeness to us. And it is because of Him, of His life and death, of His existence, that God does not turn away from us whose being in time is so utterly different from His, but rather turns to us. [519]

God is righteous. He sees that our being in time is condemned to disintegration and extinction. He makes this plain to us as He is merciful to us in this One. But first and foremost He sees this One Himself. He judges us according to His judgment on Him. He finds in Him the fulness which He cannot find in us. He sees this One, and us in Him—not alongside or beyond Him, but in Him. Thus He finds in us all that He finds in Him. In our disintegrating being in a lost time He finds His true and genuine being in the time created by Him and given to man. Because we are the men loved by God from all eternity, He places our being in time in the light and under the promise of the true and genuine being in time actualised in this One. This is the righteousness of God in the mercy in which He encounters us in the man Jesus. For what is revealed by His mercy in this One is His will in the creation of man, and therefore the true nature of man as he was created, the right of the Creator over His creature

[520] and also the right of His creature. What is actual and true and revealed in Him is no more and no less than our own natural condition as willed and planned by God and pleasing to Him. If we see this man as He stands before God in our place, we see ourselves in Him in the nature from which we have fallen by falling away from God, and in which God has not ceased to know us in spite of our apostasy. The existence of the man Jesus means that God is not deceived by the two-fold contradiction in which we have entangled ourselves when He confesses us as His creatures and covenant-partners. It means that before Him—and therefore in truth—our true nature has not been destroyed or invalidated by our corruption; that our human nature as God willed and created it has not ceased to be true and actual even in respect of our being in time. It is still our true and actual nature in the truth and actuality of the righteousness in which God willed to turn, and has actually turned, to us in this One from all eternity. We cannot and will not find it in ourselves. We do not have it in ourselves. What we find and have in ourselves is our perverted, corrupt nature, a being in time which is one long loss of time. Yet we find and have our true and actual nature in the One in whom God has loved and loves and will love us, and therefore in Him our true being in time. As He is the pledge of the faithfulness of the Creator, He is also of the continuity of His creature, of its preservation and maintenance. Surprising as it is, it is to the free grace of God in Jesus Christ that we owe the fact that the nature in which we were created, and from which we have fallen by falling away from God, is not taken away from us, but is maintained and preserved; that in spite of the falsehood in which we have become involved we may be genuinely in time and have true and genuine time.

To see the truth of this, we have only to cease trying to ignore the free grace of God in Jesus Christ. We have only to cease trying to make use of "natural" theology and therefore anthropology. Illusion always results when we seek light on human nature from any other source than the man Jesus Christ. To do so is to trifle with the fact of sin. It is to dig leaking wells. It is to entangle ourselves in conjectures and reinterpretations. It is again to seek final refuge in oblivion. The profound unrest concerning our corrupted nature and our forfeiture of time remains unassuaged. The only real way to meet it is the way which the righteous God, who is merciful in His righteousness, has taken, takes and will take to all eternity in Jesus Christ. The only genuinely victorious protest against it is His protest against our contradiction, which is also His protest against its consequences and therefore against our perishing, against the possibility that His creature will cease to be His creature. This divine protest is the rock on which we take our stand when we count on it that there is a human nature preserved for man in spite of his fall, and therefore a true and genuine being of man in time. There is no other ground on which we can seriously make this claim. But on this ground the claim can and must be made seriously.

The anthropological truth with which we are here concerned may be combined with its Christological basis in a first proposition which must occupy us in this sub-section. It is that the existence of the man Jesus in time is our guarantee that time as the form of human existence is in any case willed and created by God, is given by God to man, and is therefore real.

84

2. *Given Time*

It is real. We are, therefore, in time. Time is not, therefore, the abyss of our [521] non-being, however perverted and corrupt we may be in it. We have time. Threatened though we may be, we are not in time in such a way that it continually slips away into infinity and is therefore lost forever. Time is. It is the form of man's existence, the form of our existence. To be man is to live in time. Humanity is in time. This is involved in the fact that the being of man is his life, and that his life is reception and action, rule and service. If this life of his is real, so too is his time as the stage on which he lives out his being.

We can say this in the strict sense only of man. We do not know what time means for animals or plants, or for the rest of the universe. We live in constant relationship to the rest of the universe. Therefore, since we ourselves are in time, we may conclude or suspect that time is the form of existence of everything created. At any rate, the mode of existence of the earthly cosmos as observed and conceived by us shows countless analogies to our own to support this view. Even the apparently timeless truths of mathematics may be observed and conceived by us only in the form of temporal acts of consciousness, analyses and syntheses, demonstrations and definitions. Moreover the biblical accounts of creation, especially the first, seem clearly to imply that time was created simultaneously with the universe as its form of existence. Like man, the whole universe is in time as created by God and therefore real. But to the universe there also belongs heaven as the upper cosmos—the inconceivable and inaccessible side of created reality. And we would be making a bold step to say that this has time as its form of existence. Indeed, we do not know what it means for beings in the earthly cosmos to be in time. We have no means of observing or conceiving their temporality. But we can observe and conceive our own. We can and must see and apprehend that we ourselves are in time and only in time; that—whatever its significance—we are only in the movement from the past to the present and no mere "presupposition" of human reality, as though the positing of it, or the reality as such, were really timeless. Man is, only as he is in his time. Even in eternal life he will still be in his time. For he will then be the one who, when there is no time but only God's eternity, and he is finally hidden in God, will have been in his time. Just as he is the soul of his body, so he exists in his time. We might almost say that he is himself his time in the sequence of his life-acts. He is himself his time fulfilling itself in the sequence of his life-acts. So close is the relation between the real being of man and the real time in which he is.

So close is the relation between them that we may ask (although we cannot give a conclusive answer) what is the exact nature of this movement from the past through the present and into the future. Is it time that moves? This is how we generally think and speak of it, because the hands of the clock move, and because our external environment is always chan- [522] ging and never stationary. But does time really move before our eyes like a film, or the carriages of a railway train, so that we stand still and look on? Or is it we who move? Is time the constant dimension in which we move about like ramblers, riders, drivers or airmen? Is it a landscape through which humanity as a whole marches on a broad front, the nations and other historical social entities in narrower formations, and the individual on a linear track, his so-called path of life? Are the times only stages on this journey? Are they stopping points which have been awaiting our arrival, but which, once reached, will be left behind? Or are both views equally true? Are we ourselves on the move, but time also on the move in and with us, only in the opposite direction? Are we speaking of something external to ourselves when we speak of yesterday, to-day and to-morrow? Can we speak of ourselves apart from our yesterday, to-day and to-morrow? This much at least is certain—that it is as difficult to separate time as the form of our existence from ourselves as it is to separate ourselves from time. All such abstractions are as absurd as the separation of body and soul.

Humanity is temporality. Temporality, as far as our observation and understanding go, is humanity. The first of these two statements is clear. However we may interpret it, human life is that movement from the past through the present into the future. Human life means to have been, to be, and to be about to be. Human life means to be temporal. The second statement is not so clear. But at any rate we do not know what we are really saying when we ascribe to "temporality " a different content from "humanity." We cannot espouse with confidence even the more modest statement that the concept of temporality might have other contents.

How intimate is the relation between man and time may be seen from the fact that such decisive relations for human being as that between God and man on the one hand and man and man on the other are purely temporal, i.e., historical relationships; actions the reality of which consists absolutely in their performance and therefore in the sequence of their initiation, execution and completion. What God and my fellow-man are to me, they are to me in the history of their being and action, and therefore in the time they have for me. And what I am to God and to my fellow-man, I am in the history of my being and acting, and therefore in my time, to the extent that in some way I am in my time for them.

God would not be my God if He were only eternal in Himself, if He had no time for me. That He loves and elects me, that He wills and intends me, that He calls, judges, punishes, accepts, delivers, preserves and rules me, that He is my Light, my Commander, my Succour, my Comfort, and my Hope—all this is history, and has its time, and refers to me in this time of mine, even in God's eternity before I was and when I shall have ceased to be. And that I recognise it or not, that I refuse or accept it, that I am grateful or ungrateful, that I hear His word and in some way respond to it, that I sin against Him but also believe in Him and love Him and hope in Him—all this must take place, and does take place, as I live before Him in my time.

[523] And the same applies to my fellow-man. He does not confront me as an abstract idea, but for good or evil in his historical reality, in the totality of what he was and is and will be, and in this totality as the Thou without whom I could not be a human I. That I see and understand him or not, that I help him or ignore him, this, and anything else my relation with him might involve, has reference to his being in time. Similarly I for my part cannot be for him just an

abstract idea. I encounter him in my historical reality. I may be a source of joy or a burden to him, an encouragement or a temptation. But whatever I am, I am in my temporal reality, in the totality of what I was and am and will be.

We have no knowledge of an analogy to our relationship to God and our fellows in the being of plants and animals and the rest of the universe, but in this respect are left in the sphere of inference and conjecture. Hence we do not know whether being in time is as essential and inalienably peculiar to them as it is to us. In the last analysis we do not know what we are saying when we call time the form of their existence too. It may be that this is the point of difference between man and the rest of the universe. It is equally possible that there is no difference in this respect. We do not need to know the answer to this problem. What we must know is that it is essential to us, that it belongs to our nature, to live in time, as is conclusively proved when we recall our relationship to God and to our fellow-man.

It is of a piece with this that the message of the Old and New Testaments, unlike any other religious tradition, and even more so any philosophy, is the concrete message of a history wrought out in time. God's relation to His creatures, as attested in Holy Scripture, is quite unlike anything we find in mythology. It is not a permanent, universal relation (as that between finite and infinite, matter and spirit, good and evil, perfection and imperfection, the sovereign and the dependent, etc.), which develops and differs only in local manifestations, and which only fortuitously and not necessarily is more or less evident at a particular point, in a particular way and in particular individuals. God's attitude to His creatures as attested in the Bible is a necessary action in its concrete particularity. It occurs at this particular place, in this particular way, as a relation to those particular men with definite names in a definite environment, each with his own particular origin, determination, burdens, capabilities, perils and promises, each with his own character, prejudices, experiences and functions. It is in these concrete relations, in His acts, that the God of the Bible is Himself, and always the living God. He is this in the history initiated and continued by His acts and conducted to its particular goals and ultimately its final goal. The history of these acts both individually and in their interconnexion forms the content and time of Holy Scripture. And not merely subjectively and from below, as the manifestation of a totally different being somewhere above it, but from above and objectively it is the individual and interconnected history of these particular men. It is their history before Him and with Him and with their fellow-men. It is the history in which no man in his time is just an instance, a representative figure. None may be confused with any other. Each has his own special part to play, each his own special, divinely given endowment and responsibility. The God of Holy Scripture does not hover motionless above the flux of human history, above the times with their kaleidoscopic variety, above the passage of each individual from yesterday through to-day and into to-morrow. God accompanies them in person. "God is not ashamed to be called their God," says Heb. 11^{16} of those who left their native land in faith and wandered about the earth seeking a new country. He calls Himself the "God of Abraham, Isaac and Jacob" (Ex. 3^6). The New Testament calls Him "the Father of our Lord Jesus Christ." His eternal will is embodied concretely in the lives of these men, each with his own existence in time. His acts are identical with the history, so trivial compared with His eternity, of the people of Israel and of the Christian community which has its centre in the history of Jesus, to this which His people first look forward and then look back. "To everything there is a season, and a time to every purpose under the heaven" (Eccles. 3^1). This does not have only the restrictive meaning that everything is confined to its own time. This is, of course, true. It is true that no man—no individual in his time, and *a fortiori*^{EN150} in any of the times which go to make up

[524]

---

^{EN150} all the more

his life as a whole—"can find out the work that God maketh from the beginning to the end" (Eccles. 3¹¹). He has his place and function in the history of the acts of God; but these acts are not exhausted in his history, still less in any one part of his history, however important. Before him, contemporary with him and after him there are other times than his, while even his own life contains other than these particular times, however full of consequence they may be. Man is not called to know the beginning and end and therefore the totality of the divine work. Yet Eccles. 3¹¹ also, and primarily, tells us that God "made everything beautiful in its time." In the context of His work, God has given every hour a perfection of its own. Again in the context of His work, He has set eternity in the heart of every individual human being, each in his own time and in his different times. He has allowed him to share something of the meaning and content of all created time, and therefore of all times, even those which are not his own. He has made the history of each individual, *in nuce*^EN151 and *pars pro toto*^EN152, the history of His own mighty acts. "I know that, whatsoever God doeth, it shall be for ever: nothing can be put to it, nor anything taken from it: and God doeth it, that men should fear before him" (Eccles. 3¹⁴). In each man's time God is unreservedly with man, for him and against him. Similarly, God's covenant with man is not just an idea, but a connected history in a continuum of time in which individuals share in its initiation and execution, its grace and judgment, having their own particular part in it with their own history in their own time. Hence this covenant can be proclaimed and believed only as the meaning and secret of all human history and time, and all individual histories and times. But this means that it necessarily directs anthropology, the understanding of human nature, to regard temporality, the being of man in time, as something necessary and essential, and not just incidental and fortuitous.

But it is not enough to assert the inextricable unity of man and time. It is equally important to remember that man is in the time given to him. Unless we remember this, we shall fail to realise that time is our real form of existence. We have no control over time and our being in it. We can only have it *de facto*^EN153, and the question arises what this fact is. On the basis of what fact do we really have time? We do not have it in virtue of our being. We cannot create it. We cannot either take it or keep it. Do we really have it at all? Would it not be better to say that time has us? However that may be, there can be no doubt that we must have it; that we cannot escape from it. In relation to its movement past us or over us we have no option but to go with it. And even if it really consists in our own movement, we can only make this movement. We cannot contract out of it. We cannot arrest it. We cannot jump the queue. We cannot accelerate or retard it. Above all, we cannot reverse it, making it move back from the future through the present and into the past.

[525]   We can run a film backwards, but not human reality. Allusion may be made to the remarkable phenomenon that in their conscious utterances dying men often seem to survey the whole course of their lives in reverse. Perhaps this is an extreme instance of something which is characteristic of old age generally. A dying man often imagines himself to be getting younger and younger until he reaches his childhood. It would be interesting to know whether the moment he reaches his birth coincides with the moment of his death. If the

---

EN151 in a nutshell
EN152 the part for the whole
EN153 as a matter of fact

phenomenon is patient of explanation, we might perhaps say that it is the rebounding of the whole course of life and movement of time against its *terminus ad quem*[EN154] in death which is proclaimed prophetically in this process with its retrogressions in the direction of the *terminus a quo*[EN155]. The strange contradiction between this phenomenon and reality would thus seem to confirm our thesis that the life of man and the movement of time proceed steadily in one and the same direction so long as they are not broken off as such.

All this supports the view that time as our form of existence is no less ordained by a higher power than existence itself. Time can and must be seen in the most intimate connexion with ourselves and our being and action. We are and work only in this connexion. We cannot possibly persuade ourselves that it is we who can create or assume this form, or even set and maintain ourselves in this connexion. We can only see that we are actually in this connexion. What we have here is obviously an exact parallel to the other anthropological fact that man is as he has spirit, i.e., as he is established, constituted and maintained by God as the soul of his body. Indeed, it may even be said that the fact that we are in time and have it is simply another aspect of the same fact. What emerges in both is that man is not God, but a needy creature of God. He does not have his existence and nature autonomously, but as they are given by God. He does not have his time as his own possession, achievement, acquisition, or choice. He has it as he acquires it. And he acquires it—we must again add—as and because he is not without God, though not himself God. He would not be in time if he were without God. But he is in time. Hence he is not without God. To say "man" or "time" is first and basically, even if unwillingly and unwittingly, to say "God." For God is for man as He has time for him. It is God who gives him his time.

The presence and gift of God cannot, therefore, be ignored in this matter if we are to think of human nature. For it is in virtue of the presence and gift of God that temporality too belongs to human nature. All man's unbelief, error and superstition cannot alter this original relationship of God to him or its far-reaching implications. Unbelief, error and superstition certainly involve a misuse of the time given by the presence and gift of God. By means of them man may very well compromise himself. His being in time may acquire the character of dissipation and corruption. But it cannot be destroyed. For God Himself, His presence and gift, cannot be abrogated or destroyed. Time as the form of human existence is always in itself and as such a silent but persistent song of praise to God. This is not merely because it is laid upon us, because we [526] cannot escape from it, because we cannot alter its implied conditions, or because we cannot take and keep it of ourselves. All this simply serves to call our attention to the fact that time in itself and as such proclaims the praise of God. It does not do so, however, because it is so powerful and transcendent, but because it is the dimension for the history of the covenant between God

---

[EN154] ending point
[EN155] starting point

and man, thus making possible a history between man and his fellow-men, a history of humanity. If man were not in time there would be no dimension for this history, for the history of the divine covenant and his own salvation, and therefore for the history of humanity. But the time which he has, the hours and days and years which he is given, are as such the declaration of the acts of God's righteousness and mercy, of His wisdom and patience, whose witness and object he is privileged to be in virtue of his existence in time. The time given to man tells him that he is not only the creature of God, but His covenant-partner. It speaks of God's faithfulness to Himself and His creature. That is why it is so inseparable from ourselves. That is why it is so irresistible and immutable in its own way. That is why it is so powerful an ordinance, which we cannot produce of ourselves but can only accept. In all its hiddenness it is the rustling of the Holy Spirit by which, however deaf to it we may be, we are surrounded in virtue of the fact that we are in the movement of time and are obliged to make this movement in and with our own life, so long as we have it. And in the modest garment of time, this mere form of our existence, given in such sovereign freedom, we are actually confronted by the presence and gift of God's grace. If we are to speak of prevenient grace it is difficult to see in what better form it may be better perceived and grasped than in the simple fact that time is given to us men.

Time, then, is willed and created by God as the form at any rate of human existence. A few words of explanation are needed here. Time is not eternity. Eternity itself is not timeless. It is the simultaneity and coinherence of past, present and future. Thus eternity is the dimension of God's own life, the life in which He is self-positing, self-existent and self-sufficient as Father, Son and Holy Ghost. It is this in contrast to time as the dimension of our life—the dimension in which past, present and future follow in succession. Eternity is not created. Eternity is God Himself. For as God is self-existent, He is also His own dimension. But time is willed and created by God as a reality distinct from Himself. It is willed and created as the universe is willed and created, and in the universe man. It is willed and created to be our dimension, corresponding to His. This must obviously mean that God willed and created time as the dimension of the life He ordained for us when we were willed and created, and therefore as the dimension of a life in communion with Himself as the eternal [527] and living God, and also in relationship with our fellow-men, to whom He has given that same dimension for the same life in communion with Himself. Time was in fact willed and created in order that there might take place His dealings in the covenant with man, which finds its counterpart in the relationship between man and his fellows. It is for this reason and in this sense that time is the form of our existence. As our existence is not an end in itself, neither is time as its form. It is our time and we have it only to the extent that we belong to God, i.e., to the God who turned to us even in His eternity. It is ours and we have it only to the extent that as our time it rests in His hands, which from beginning to end are of course at work for us. It is in this sense and to this extent that time is given to us, and this mighty ordinance of time, which we can only accept as such, is as we receive and possess it a hymn of praise to God, a proclamation of His mighty acts, the hidden rustling of the Holy Spirit, the garment and form of the grace in which God wills to meet us. Everything depends upon the fact that God willed and created time for this purpose.

But it is to this extent that time is real, and we are in time and have it. Its secret is the will and act of God—the Creator who will not be thwarted or confused by human sin, but remains faithful to Himself and therefore to us in defiance of sin and its consequences. The dangers to which the reality of our time is exposed may bewilder and terrify us, as indeed they must. But they do not invalidate the truth of His presence and gift. They cannot frustrate His creative will or reverse His creative act. Bearing in mind the ground on which alone all this is possible, we shall now attempt a second and very different analysis of the being of man in time.

1. Let us consider it first in the tense in which its reality is most impressive and palpable, but also most vulnerable—as our being in the present. That man is in time means at its simplest that he always is now, i.e., that he is always crossing the frontier between past and future which one moment is just ahead and the next just behind, only to be ahead again, to have to be recrossed, and again to be behind. If man really is in his time, if he really has time, it is always now, in the crossing of this frontier. Every conception of human being, life and activity (even when ostensibly concerned with the past or future) has to do concretely with this step from the past to the future. It is always now that I am or am not, that I have or have not, that I know or do not know, that I do or leave undone, that I enjoy or eschew, love or hate, am sad or happy. It is always now that my reaction to my environment both human and non-human is positive or negative, critical or neutral. It is always now that decisions are made concerning me, and my own decisions are taken. The reality of all this—for it might, of course, be only a dream or empty show—and my own reality in it, depends upon the fact that I really have time for it, that I am really in time with all my being and life and action. It depends upon the fact that this present moment, which I need for it all, is real. Is it real? I am. But is it really true that I [528] am? The question has a comprehensive reference. Always when I take this step from the past into the future I distinguish between the two. Always when I take this step I engage in recollection and expectation, living my whole life. And I do this in such a way that from this point I recollect the past as a Now like that in which I now cross this frontier, and also expect the future as a Now like the present. If I say "I was," this implies in principle and in certain recollected outlines a present which is now past. And if I say "I shall be," this implies in principle and in certain expected outlines a present which is to come. In other words, from the standpoint of the present I always see and understand my being in time as the totality of the previous and subsequent times now distinguished by me and meeting in my Now; and I always see and understand my past and my future, and therefore the totality of my being in time, as a present

like my actual present. But is this present real? And if not, what about the reality of my whole being in time?

It is true, of course, that nothing is more impressive and palpable than our being in the present. How many sceptics have thought they could take refuge in the boast, "I am"! And what structures of assurance have been erected on the foundation of this boast! But what does this boast mean on the lips of man and as an expression of his conviction that he really exists in the present and therefore in time? The insecurity of our being in the present is no less impressive and palpable. For the present is merely the frontier between past and future, and our being in it is merely the crossing of this frontier. The present is without duration or extension. What then do we mean by being in the present? Where am I, and how, as I am now? How far am I now in time? We are sometimes assured that our being in the present is pre-eminently our proper, immediate, absolute being in time. But this is only to make a virtue of necessity. Is it not obvious that in the actual present we have no time? Schleiermacher's contention that we are eternally in every moment would seem to be nearer the mark. All this boasting about being in the present really amounts to Schleiermacher's contention. But this suffers from two disadvantages. First, by speaking of eternal being it abandons the problem of man's being in time; and secondly, by claiming for man what can only be postulated of God, it rules out the problem of human being altogether. We cannot evade the question how far man is really in time merely by boasting "I am." So if by "I" we really mean man, and by "am" his being in time, the phrase "I am" simply begs the question. But if we surreptitiously take the "I" for God, and the "am" for His eternal being, we are left with an answer which has nothing whatever to do with the original question.

If we ourselves had to secure and safeguard our being in time, at this crucial point where we are faced by the problem of the present our only alternatives would be either to abandon the attempt to find a solution at all, or to adopt one of the illusory solutions which are possible and have been attempted on the basis of the boasting "I am." But we are not left to our own resources in this matter if we have reason to believe that the will and act of God are the secret of our time, of our being in it, and therefore of our being in the present moment, in each present Now.

[529] It is clear that of all the prophets of "I am," the Christian theologian, Schleiermacher, came nearest the truth. If only, instead of all his exaggerated and confusing talk about our own eternity, he had spoken of the eternity of God, of the eternity of His righteousness and mercy, of His wisdom and patience at every moment of our lives, in each successive Now in which we cross that frontier! And if only we could interpret in this sense all those who boast about the present! But since this is out of the question, we must pass them by and proceed as follows.

It is true that we are now, as we cross the frontier and thus distinguish between past and future, so that we are always sure that our past was a similar now and that our future will be. It is thus true that the present seems to be the basic form of our time as a whole. It is true again that the very reality of this basic form, and therefore the reality of our time as a whole, seems to be hopelessly called in question by the fact that our present is without duration or extension, disappearing as soon as it comes. Primarily, however, it is not we who are now but God who is now: God who created us and is in process of rescuing and preserving us; God who is not dismayed at our sin, and does not cease to be for us, nor reverse our determination to be for Him and in mutual fellowship; God in all the defiance of our unfaithfulness by His own faithfulness. He is now primarily; and we secondarily. He is in the height of His majesty; we in the depths of our creatureliness and sinfulness, which even in conjunction are shallow compared with the depth of His mercy. He is in His wisdom and patience; we in our folly and anxiety, in the flight and chase to which we referred earlier. He is in His self-existence and self-repose; we "pass hence, and wander from one year to another." He is now properly; we improperly in relation to Him. But more important for our present purpose than these differences is the relationship. He, too, is now in His way as we are in ours. He is now as Creator. But this means that there is first a divine stepping from the past to the future. This is His present. We speak of His eternity, in which the past is not "no longer" nor the future "not yet," in which therefore the Now has duration and extension. It is in His eternity that God is now. But we do not speak of God's abstract eternity, but of the eternity of His free love, in which He took and takes and will take time for our sakes, in which He wills to be for us and also wills that we should be for Him and therefore in mutual fellowship. That God is now means that all this is now the meaning of a divine stepping from the past to the future, of a divine Word spoken now, a divine action performed now. And we now continue that there is also—in relationship from the very first to what God is and does—our human stepping from the past to the future. This is our present in our time, in which the past is no more and the future not yet and therefore the Now is that middle point between the two with neither duration nor extension. Yet as we may not speak of God's abstract eternity, we may not speak of our abstract time. For us, to be in time, to be now, is to be under and with God, to be under and with the eternal God, who wills to be, and actually is, not merely for Himself but for us, not merely in the heights but in the depths. That we are in the present means that we are in the present of the gracious, judging, commanding will and action in which He has turned wholly to us, but claims us wholly for Himself, for fellowship with Him, and therefore for human fellowship. It is in doing this that He gives us time, and first of all the present, and what the present is in our time, that moment between the times which is without duration or extension. It is our past on the basis of His, in His and for His. That is why it takes the form it does. That is why it is a stepping from the past to the future. That is why it means a leaving of the past which is "no longer" and a grasping of the future which is "not yet." And finally that is why it is in itself only that frontier and our crossing of that frontier and therefore apparently nothing intrinsically its own. That God is present to us is what fills our present: from the past, for He is not "no longer," into the future, for He is not "not yet"; and therefore also in the centre, because His movement from the past into the future has the duration and extension which escape our own Now. That I am now—with all the inescapable problems which this involves—means that as I am continually

[530]

93

there in movement from my past to my future, I am referred wholly to Him and cast back upon Him, upon His being in time addressed to me. Without Him, without the fact that He is for me, I should have no time and therefore, since I can be only in time, I should not be at all. The very fact that I am now far from giving that boastful certainty of my real being, would then show me only that I am in process of sinking into nothingness. But I really am now because God is, and is first, and is not only for Himself but for me. Because God loves me without cause or merit, I am now. And I can add with confidence, and with a precision of which the prophets of "I am" have not the slightest inkling, that because God loves me I really am now, and really have time as I have it. I do not sink into a void, although I still have that great "no longer" behind me and the great "not yet" in front of me, and although I have only the unstable moment, the ice-floe of the present, beneath my feet. If I have God (or rather, if God has me), I need no more. I have space and therefore time. Time is given me, and with all the certainty and solidity that I could desire because it is given me directly by Him, because, as I am in time in this way, I have to do with Him, and therefore with eternity as the fount and sum and source of all time. His presence as such is the gift of my time. He Himself pledges both its reality and its goodness. I am His creature. All I need to be this is time. Only if I want to be as God can I desire more, and suffer and sigh and complain because I only have time, and my now has the remarkable form of this transition. Only if I had to be a creature without God should I have to regard this transition as my destruction. But I am a creature under God and [531] with Him. I have time. I have my now in the form in which I need it. I am where I may live neither threatened by illusion nor enmeshed in falsehood, i.e., in real time, in the present of God. Tersteegen is right after all: "Content is he, who hath Thee, Whose spirit to Thee cleaveth, Every yearning leaveth."

We next ask concerning the significance of the fact that man is always now. We have seen that all human being, action and experience is either now or else unreal. Even as past and future it can be understood as a totality only in relation to the present, as a past or present now. We are always in this transition. Our own reality depends upon the reality of this transition. And this transition, and therefore the Now in which we are, is real as and because the present of the eternal God as the Creator of time is the secret of our present. What is this transition, then, but the offer, the summons, the invitation, to be with God now, to be present with Him, to make this transition with Him, recognising that He always precedes us, not without us, but for us and on our behalf? He always does this now. This is what gives our present its distinctive weight, but also its distinctive lightness; its distinctive seriousness, but also its distinctive radiance. God is primarily and continually present. He is always the same, yet always new, always with a particular offer and summons, always with a particular invitation. In this way, in this particularity, God's present is the secret of our own. It is not merely like the dominant undertone of a painting, or the sustained basic note at the beginning of the St. Matthew Passion. It always has its own particular sound, character and lustre. It is the present of the living God, not of an exalted but static picture of God. And this means that our present is not like the millions of identical oscillations of the clock with which we measure it. It would be like this if we had to live it without God, if our present were lost time, if it were not real but non-existent. The fact that the living God is present makes our present not only real but weighty and therefore important. It encloses the mystery of what God has for us now, of what He has to say to us, to allow, to command us, to give us. It encloses the opportunity which He wills to be realised in and through us now. It encloses, therefore, the mystery of the grateful response we now owe to Him and in consequence to our fellow-men.

Only now can we see how significant it is that every Now, in its particular relation to the past and future, is an opportunity which comes only once and then, perceived and grasped or not, passes never to return. Only now can we see that each Now is indeed a "now or never." Schiller was quite right when he said: "What thou abstractest from the minute can no eternity restore." How do we know that what we now consciously or unconsciously omit is only a paltry thing and not the turning-point which determines our whole being in time both past and future. There are moments like this. Indeed, in the strict sense all moments are like this. At any rate, we have to reckon with each moment because God Himself has particular moments, καιροί, in His being, speech and action in relation to us; moments which continually come and go. Now is no time for dreaming about past or future. Now is the time to awake, to receive or act, to speak or be silent, to say Yes or No. Now is no time to send as our proxy a recollected or expected picture of ourselves, a ghost or an ideal, to act under our mask. Now we must step out and act as the men we really are. The urgency of the moment demands absolute sincerity and readiness. A general and therefore ungodly view of time and of the present certainly cannot give this weight and promise and claim to our being in the Now. But it is given with supreme clarity and necessity by the concept of the time and present given by God and therefore real. Because we are under God and for Him, as we now are, there is no evading the importance of the Now, and no excuse for missing or misusing it. But there is also no absence of His grace and mercy even in our Now. Our present is indeed joyful, for in it, since God is He who is primarily and properly present, even in our weakness and stupidity, even in our missing or misusing of what is offered, we are not abandoned by Him or left to ourselves, to the power and wisdom of our own decisions, but may always count on the fact that the first and final responsibility for us is in His hands, that He forgives sins, protects erring children and causes tired wayfarers to take their halting steps, that His wisdom exceeds our folly and His goodness our evil, that He is wakeful even though we fall asleep and dream about the past and future when we ought to be buying up the Now which will never come our way again. Even in the particularity of His presence which we have failed to see or use, or perhaps misused, He will not have been present to us in vain. Without us,

[532]

against us, but finally for us, He will have filled our Now according to His will even though we have not responded to His offer, summons and invitation. When have we ever been a match for Him or done justice to His claim? Of what past can we think without being driven to seek refuge in His grace and mercy? What future can we imagine when it will not be our consolation that He will always be much greater with His presence and gifts than our greatest skill and exertion to do justice to the opportunity offered? This, then, is how the present is filled. It is real. And from this we are entitled to conclude that all our time is real, that we are really in time, that we really have time. God's presence and gift creates, delivers and sustains this reality. This means judgment and grace. This is the mystery of the whole Gospel and the whole Law. But this means that though we are sinners who have forfeited our time, and indeed ourselves, we are not lost, but as we were created, so we are sustained and delivered.

[533]   2. Now let us turn to our being in time in the past tense: "I have been." The juxtaposition of present and perfect—"have" and "been"—raises at once the whole problem we have to solve. In the first place, and positively, it means that I am now the one who has been. As I reach the frontier and cross into the future, I am not a mere cipher, a blank sheet of paper. I am gifted and burdened, freed and enslaved, enriched and impoverished, credited and committed, strengthened and weakened, inclined, directed and determined, by the many earlier transitions I have made in the past and right up to this point. I am what all my past life has made me. It does not matter how insensible I may be to it, how few my clearer recollections. When the hour strikes and registers my present Now, when I embark upon the new transition, I am what my past has made me, formed and moulded by all my previous transitions. Whatever I may be and do and experience now, and whatever I shall be and do and experience after this Now, the prejudices and assumptions which I have brought from the past are in varying degrees significant for this Now and will continue to be so for my future.

Certainly a new page is now turned, a new opportunity is offered, and the whole problem of life is posed afresh. Perhaps it will not merely bring a few or many changes but alter the whole picture of life, revealing it in an entirely new light, and placing it under an entirely new sign. For all I know the present moment may be the most critical turning point in the whole of my life. What I am on the verge of receiving, saying or doing may leave an indelible mark on the whole of my future course. Yet this new page still belongs to the same book as the earlier pages. In some way or other the entries on the earlier pages are connected with the entries which will be made on the pages yet to come. The good and the evil, the achievements and failures of my past are not simply written off; they belong inalienably to me, whatever changes the future may have in store. I am what my past has made me, even though I may be quite different now from what I was then. I am what I have been.

But is this really so? What guarantee is there that I am really the same to-day as I was in the past? What guarantee is there that my past is real? "I have been"—this juxtaposition of present and perfect may have quite a different meaning which casts a wholly new light (or shadow) on the first. It may mean that I once was—in a present now past—but then something irrevocable happened. That present was followed by another, and my then being became a new and different being which covered over the former and therefore the former present. My being in time was transformed and became a thing of the past. This is what is really meant when we say that we have "been." What we were in the past is past, *passé, vorbei*. A line has been drawn across the page, separating what I was from what I am now. I am what I was, but only underneath this line; only in the present; only in so far as this contains my past in a diluted form, as a product or extract; only to the extent that to-day and in the new form in which I am to-day, I am still the same person that I was yesterday. But what I was yesterday, above that line, has now perished. It is only in the [534] sense that it has been, that the being has been taken out of it. It lives on only as I who lived then still live now, and live as the one who lived then. But I have no more life as the one who lived then because that time has passed. What is marked off from the present by that conclusive event has been put behind me. It has become a "pluperfect." The change it underwent was indeed an absorption to the extent that its then being was deprived of extension and duration, i.e., that its time was irrevocably taken away from it. What was then still exists only as it is to-day. It no longer exists in so far as it was then.

This aspect of the matter is profoundly disquieting. For we know how things stand where the past ought still to exist in that diluted form, in our being to-day, now, in the present. We know that it cannot enjoy duration or extension, and therefore genuinely live on, even here. And this raises the disturbing suspicion that even our present and future are hastening towards the past; that that fatal line will be drawn again and again; that our present and all our future being are incontrovertibly condemned to undergo that transformation and therefore to become past being in the sense described, and as such to be no more. From this standpoint again it would seem as if we have no real time. And there are two ways of meeting this disturbing situation: the one by memory; the other by oblivion. Though diametrically opposed, they both lead to the same result. For they are both equally incapable of remedying the situation. Neither can guarantee that our past being also is as such. Neither can convince us that we really have time. And so both are equally unsatisfactory.

In memory we start with an awareness of the problematical character of our being in the present and therefore in the future as well. But at least it seems certain that we were once: "I once possessed this priceless boon." So we seek refuge from the present and the future in this "once upon a time." Memory is an attempt to restore to the past the duration and extension which it obviously does not have any longer. It is an attempt to recall our then being in time as such. If it were possible to do this, we should have a solid, though limited guarantee of our being in time, a partial assurance of the reality of time and therefore of our own reality. When a man regrets to-day and has no hope for to-morrow, he has recourse to memory. And when the same thing happens to a whole generation, it resorts to historicism, romantically or scientifically investigating what was. The attempt may be partially successful. It is possible to conjure up more or less clear-cut, colourful and animated pictures of the past. This is what happened, and this is how it happened. And in so doing a good deal of light and shade is thrown on the present, for the past lives on in the present, and therefore *historia vitae magistra*[EN156]—a reconstruction of the past can help to a knowledge of the present. But the real purpose of the study eludes us. Our reconstruction of the past and the past itself are poles apart. The actual past never returns, however vivid and accurate the reconstruction. Indeed, the clearer and more accurate our memory, the more vividly it throws into relief the line which is drawn beneath the past, and its absorption into the present. In its own being it was, and does not return. Its time is up. If ever it was real, it is real no longer. And it is clear that in its initial intention as flight from the present and the future our enterprise is doomed to frustration. Time marches on, with all its problems, even while we are daydreaming in our memories. We can make this attempt only in our own problematical time, and therefore we fall victim to the very thing which we seek to elude.

[535]

In oblivion we start from the opposite end. We know how problematical is our being in the past. It is gone, and memory is powerless to retain or recall it. What is certain is that we are now, and shall be—or at any rate want to be—in the future. So we run away in precisely the opposite direction. We flee from the cathedrals, prisons, inns and catacombs where we were yesterday, into the light of to-day with its promise of even greater light to-morrow. When we try, consciously or unconsciously, to forget the past, we simply let it lie to the extent that it is not absorbed into the present. We do this so as to be free to give all our attention to the solid, though limited, assurance of the being which seems possible now and therefore in all our future Nows. When a man cannot be happy about the past, he seeks happiness in the present and future. And when a whole generation finds it impossible to make sense of the past, it glories all the more readily in the "spirit of the age," that is, of its own age, and succumbs to the belief in progress. This too, as we know, can be partially successful. When we are tired of our old letters and diaries we can tear them up and burn them. We can suppress all that we were and experienced and said and did. We can replace it by a picture of what we think we can and should be and experience and say and do now and in the future, finding freedom and beginning life all over again, and this time real life in the admiration and service which it evokes. But again our real intention eludes us. Our being in the present and future is not a secure refuge from the problems of the past. We can paint rosy pictures of our being in the present, but these pictures bear no relation to the reality which is just as problematical as our being in the past. It is as foolish to flee from Scylla to Charybdis as *vice versa*. So far from solving the problem, we are confronted with it in oblivion even more acutely than before. In fact, there is no escaping it. The Scylla of the past haunts us, even though we forget it, in our flight to the Charybdis of the present. It is not merely that a man cannot live down his past or be other than his past has made him. It is not merely that, however cheerfully he may pursue his way, he cannot enter the present and future except *omnia sua secum portans*[EN157]. The real trouble is that he has behind him the great lacuna of his past being, gone never to return; that his being in time, even if it had (which it has not) a safe haven in the present and future, has sprung this leak, and would therefore sink even if it were in port. After all, he comes from the past. He is the same person as he was then whether he contrives to forget it or not. And what is he now, what is all his being in time, if his past being in time has gone (as he foolishly seems to confirm by his forgetting), if in the fact that it is now past it is without reality?

Yet we could only choose memory or oblivion, or possibly a combination of the two, if we were dependent on ourselves for assurance of the reality of our

---

[EN156] history is life's teacher
[EN157] carrying all his past with him

being in time, and therefore of our real being even in the past. But we are not dependent on ourselves if we accept the fact that the will and act of God are the meaning and ground of our being in time, and therefore in the time which is behind us. If we really accept this truth, the position is as follows. To be sure, we were. That line has been drawn and will be drawn continually. One day, indeed, it will be drawn for the last time, thus denoting that our whole being in time belongs to the past, and apparently denying it any reality at all. Primarily, however, it is not we who were, but God. Even then God was our Creator, Deliverer and Preserver. He then continued to be for us in spite of our enmity against Him. He then opposed His faithfulness to our unfaithfulness. He was first in the heights; then we in the depths. And even then there was not only opposition but relationship between us and Him. Above us, for us and with us, God has also been. For there is a Then, a genuine past, in God's eternity, as surely as it is the eternity of the living God. Of course, no lines are drawn there. The past is not left behind, nor does it fade. The God who was, is now, and ever shall be. It is in the coinherence of past, present and future that His eternity is original, authentic and creative time. And the eternal God was then, in the past, the surety and pledge of the reality of our created time and of our real being in it. Again, of course, we are not concerned here with eternity in the abstract, but with the eternity in which God willed, wills and shall will that we should be His creatures, and therefore that we should not perish and cease to be. We emphasise that God's eternity is the eternity in which He willed this. No line is drawn under this "He willed." It is not subject to any "no longer." It includes the fact that He wills and shall will. And in this "He willed" He was over us, for us and with us when we were in that past reality which now seems to have perished, so that it can only be either remembered or forgotten. More than that, God's eternity is the eternity in which He did what was necessary for our being, for our deliverance and preservation, for securing us against destruction. He was from of old our Creator, Father and Redeemer. He was moved in Himself for us long before He executed this movement, and especially as He did so, and does not cease to do so. In this "He did," which does not come to an end, finally becoming a "no longer," He was over us and with us when we were in our highly problematical being as a past being. [536]

But again we continue that, in relation to what God was and willed and did, there was also at that time our being, experience, volition, action and inaction, the totality of what we were and the way in which we were it. We are invited not to see or understand ourselves abstractly in this our being in the mode of past being. Our time in this dimension is no more to be thought of abstractly than God's eternity. What were we? We were what we could and should and had to be under and with God, on the basis of His past being. And in what form were we? We were as those already loved by Him, to whom He willed to give time, and actually gave it. But He gave this time for life, and therefore for continuing life, in the present in which we now live, and the future towards which we move. That we were then and may still be to-day is a proof of the patience of

God already shown us then. It is for this reason that our then time could not be permanent or stationary, but could only come and go. It was time which as we had it was marked for dissolution in new time. As our then life-time it had to become what it is now from the standpoint of the present, past time. But this does not alter the fact that, because God was then, it was real and full time. And because God was then, its reality and fulness cannot be taken away by the fact that it has gone. God does nothing in vain. What He willed and created cannot disintegrate into nothingness. It has merely lost its character as our present, which it once had. But it has not perished as one of the terms of our time. "Thine eyes did see my substance, yet being unperfect; and in thy book all my members were written, which in continuance were fashioned, when as yet there was none of them" (Ps. 139[16]). All our members were in God's book and plan and purpose even before they were. How then, when they have once been, can they be no more? There is a being in the past tense, a past being which is real as such. Our being in time is real in this tense too. But we can say this only in relation to God. We cannot cling to its then reality nor can we recall it. Apart from Him, it would be idle and quite inconceivable to maintain that our being in this tense, our then being, is as real to-day and to-morrow as it was then. Without God the fact that the past is irrevocably behind us, and that even the present hour and our future days and years rush irresistibly into the past, would be the leak in virtue of which we could understand our whole being in time as one which is condemned to perish. But we are not without God. We can understand this fact in relation to Him. And God, the eternal God, whose yesterday is also to-day and to-morrow, He loved us even then. And this means that our then being as the object of His love, which He will not allow to be taken from Him, has not ceased to be real in His eyes and therefore in truth. What He has once given He does not take back again. What was by Him and before Him still is. Nor does this mean only that our past is included in our present and is present with it. It has a further, less obvious, but decisive meaning. Our being in time with its regressive duration and extension not only was real but is real. It is not lost. It has not escaped us or ceased to be. It is as genuinely ours as our being in the present and future. We are in our whole time, in the whole sequence of its parts, and not just in the one part we call the present. For our time is the dimension of our whole life. If our whole time is the gift of God, then God also pledges to maintain its reality as a whole. It is only time. It can and must be past, and continually pass, and even in the future hasten towards the past. But again it would be quite wrong for man to try to be God and therefore eternal instead of being cheerfully and modestly man and therefore temporal. The passing of our time would only mean destruction if we had to be men without God, outside the covenant He has established with us. But this does not correspond to the reality of man as God has created it. His covenant with man has stood from the creation of the first man, from the beginning of the world, from God's eternity. The truth is that we may really have our time as given by God; our whole time, even in its character as past and passing time. [538]

But the further question arises what is meant by the fact that we were. That we were is real because primarily, beyond us and for us, God was, in His omnipotent grace and mercy, holiness and righteousness. He loved us in our time then, and because He has not ceased to do so, we are real even in that time. But this means that our past being, which accumulates with each succeeding day and hour, and which we bring behind us, stands wholly under His judgment. In this whole sphere, there is no more divine offer, summons, invitation or opportunity for us. The die has been cast. What we were, we were; with all that we did and omitted to do, all that we discovered and overlooked, all the good and evil that we did and suffered, all the beauty that we enjoyed or in our stupidity failed to notice, all the joys that we experienced or missed because we were not equal to them. Everything was exactly as it was. Nothing can be taken away from it or added to it, nothing improved upon or made worse. It was all before God, and it is still before Him in all its reality. No recollection is needed, nor can oblivion alter the fact that it is still before God and therefore as real now as it was then. Even our present, the remarkable result of our past, is not needed to establish this. We are really the persons we were in the whole duration and extent of our past, because in it we were before God, to whom we owed everything but were also responsible for everything. He it was who even then gave, withheld and took away. He it was who even then helped and encountered us. He it was who even then rewarded and punished us according to His wisdom and justice. He it was who even then knew us through and through, however much we tried to disguise or conceal ourselves. He it was who even then was greater than our heart, who could use us or find us unserviceable and yet use us otherwise than we perceived. All this past of ours stands under His judgment and sentence. As those we were, in all the unalterability in which we really were it, we are delivered up wholly into His hands, for grace or condemnation. That this is so, that we are simply in His hands and at His disposal, unable to do anything about it ourselves, is what is meant by the fact that we were. It might seem doubtful in the present and especially the future tense. For in the present and especially the future tense our personal plans, decisions and actions might seem to be a secondary and co-operative determination of our existence. But our being in time also has this tense—the past. One day, indeed, it will have only this tense. This does not mean that it is destined to perish. Because God exists, it is real even in this tense. But even the blind is surely compelled to see that in this tense it is in God's hands. If he willed to accept it, it is accepted. If He willed to reject it, it is rejected. And He owed us nothing—we owed Him everything. What was it then? Exactly what his decision, His judgment, His verdict made it; exactly [539] what we shall see it to have been when the book in which it stood, the book of God, is opened. No more, no less, no different. "It is God who rules."

In conclusion, this throws a new light on our retrospective view of the past. If this stands before God and under His judgment in all its unalterable reality, the possibility both of recollection and oblivion acquire a new character.

As regards the former, we may say that it would reveal either a strange ingratitude or a strange timidity to refuse to live in our past, in the history which is behind us. Why should we? After all does it not belong just as really to our being in time as our present and future? Is not God alone its Judge? What reason can we possibly have for shutting our eyes to the past? Have we not every reason to look in this direction as far as we can? And when we do look carefully, what else do we discover but traces of God's judgment? If they are encouraging, why should we not rejoice? And if depressing, why should we not be summoned to humility and modesty? God does not need to remember, but we cannot live without memory, even to-day and to-morrow. A man without an awareness of history, without definite pictures of what was and the patience to learn from them, would be an escapist, running away from reality and God, and quite unreliable in his dealings with his fellow-men. There is no occasion for this escapism, not merely because it is doomed to disappointment, but above all because as we look back over the past there is so much cause for gratitude and shame that no place is left for evasion.

At the same time, however, we must insist just as seriously that we can never live in the past as if it were our true home and the present and future an exile. We cannot seek in it a picture of the life we do not hope to find in the present and future. This flight in reverse is equally unhealthy. It may take the form of a *laudatio*EN158 or a *contemptus temporis acti*EN159, but either way it is impossible. For what matters is not our then being in itself and as such, but the fact that it was our being under and with God. If it was under and with God, then it is so to-day and to-morrow. Memory can enable us to live also but not exclusively in the past. We can live in the past but not by it. We can be conservative in relation to it, but we cannot be genuinely reactionary, either by restoring it or even by reacting continuously against a past artificially restored by our own aversion to the present. In clear and living memory we think to-day and with a view to to-morrow. There is thus no temptation to falsify it, either whitewashing or blackening it in our own favour, i.e., for our own justification. Above all, we realise the limitations of memory. It can give us pleasant or terrifying glimpses of the past, but it cannot recall the past itself. As it really was and is, it is before the eyes of God and not of man—our own but a hidden reality. Because it is [540] safe in the hands of God, we are freed from any positive or negative paralysis in relation to it. We do not feel the compulsion of positive or negative historical ideologies. We are delivered, not from living, but from dead and deadening memory. We are delivered for forward-looking life now in quiet contemplation of the past.

EN158 commendation
EN159 scorn of past time

2. *Given Time*

We shall also have a different view of oblivion when we remember that what has been is in God's hands, and therefore real. And the first point to notice is that we may forget. God never forgets, any more than He needs to remember. But we need to forget. And we are enabled to do so. If it were otherwise, we should be in a terrible plight. We should never be able to bear the sight of our whole being in time, even in our own pictures of its reality. This is because our past stands under the judgment of God. None of these pictures can justify or save us. And the sight of them all might well overwhelm us. It is a good thing that we are able to forget, that we can pray, *quod vixi tege*[EN160]. And it is a good thing that God draws this veil over the past even without our asking. In so doing, He allows us to live to-day for to-morrow with just the few memories we need of what was. The deep and salutary meaning and purpose of forgetfulness is that for large stretches we are not compelled to consider our past being in time even in the form of pictures, and therefore that we are not condemned to the constant agitation these pictures cause us. It is enough to have those which actually are before us. Above all, it is enough that our being in time is before the eyes of God in its reality, and stand under His judgment.

It must also be said, however, that we do not have to forget in order to be able to live. If so, we should again be paralysed, for we should have no history. If God is the Judge of our whole life in time, then none of our memories of the past can be a source of regret. Of course, there are things in our past we should prefer to forget but cannot. Since this is the case, God must have ordained that it should be so. There is every reason to think that it is God's good purpose that these fragments of the past should belong to our life in the present and the future, and that it would not be salutary for us if we were able to forget them. Hence nothing could be worse than to try to forget them. No, there is nothing which ought to be torn up and burnt! How much harm comes from the forcible suppression of memories contrary to the will of God: memories which we ought to have, but for some reason or other seek to avoid; memories which we try to conceal under images of the present and the future, but which God Himself has not concealed; memories which we cannot really succeed in obliterating, but which merely become the cause of psychological disorders. Enforced oblivion is as bad as enforced recollection. To try to live in oblivion is as bad as to try to live on memory. If we know that God was when we were, we are free in this respect too. In this knowledge we must not and shall not try to forget even what we might otherwise prefer to forget.

3. Finally, let us consider our being in time in the future tense. "I shall be." [541] Here, too, our first reference is to the present and to a distinctive filling of our being in the present. That I shall be has its beginning in the present, and then reaches out beyond the present into the future. We know that the step from the past and the step into the future are not really two steps but one. In popular terms, however, we may think of it as a further step. I am now leaving the

---

[EN160] cover over what I have done

103

Now previously entered, crossing its forward frontier. Like a wayfarer who finds no room in the inn, I am coming out again and continuing my journey in the hope of finding lodging further on. The future is the further side of the present, just as the past is its nearer side. In the present they touch one another. As the past moved towards it, the future moves away from it. I am now awaiting a new present. I am eagerly stepping towards it. I am grasping it. But this eager waiting and stepping and grasping begin now. They immediately cease to be now, but it is worth insisting that they begin now. Hence our Now is always full of the future as well as the past. As we are, we anticipate the future. We project ourselves into the future. We see and will ourselves as we shall be. We act as though our future being had already arrived. To this extent we are determined by it. Our thoughts, feelings, actions and reactions are coloured by specific hopes and fears. All our human activity, but also all our human experience and suffering, hastens towards a *telos*. The farmer's work in springtime is to sow seed for the summer. His work in summer is his harvest for the winter. His work in autumn and winter prepares for next spring's sowing and next summer's harvest. All our present joy is at the decisive point a foretaste of the new and true joy which is still to come. Similarly, every present pain is only a sinister herald of what we fear will be worse pains. And conversely, as we all know from experience, there is always in present joy a foreboding of coming pain, and in present pain a promise of coming joy. Till Eugenspiel was right perhaps to be more anxious in times of ease and more lighthearted in toilsome ascent. At any rate, whether we are conscious of it or not, the present is always openly or secretly pregnant with the future. Coming events cast their shadows before. In the experiences and decisions of to-day, the developments are prepared and proclaimed which we shall have to live through and for which we shall have to answer to-morrow. I am not only what I was, I am already, even if only *in nuce*, what I shall be.

But am I really what I shall be? On that further side of my present, will I be the same person just a stage further on? Is there a forward continuity of my being? Is there still room for my life? "I shall be," I say. But I may not be at all. And in any case, I have not yet reached the place I am aiming at when I say, "I shall be." I am not yet the person I shall be. And it might well be that this [542] undeniable "not yet" threatens my future being no less inexorably than the "no longer" my past being. The "not yet" is no sure guarantee of a coming "then" or "one day." It may even contain a threat, the threat of a "never." For the step in which I transcend my Now presupposes a place in front of me in which to plant my feet. But from a distance there is no certainty that I can do this. That step forward may be a step into the void, into the abyss. There may be time for others, but not for me. My own time may be up. The future of which I am full may be a preparation leading to nothing. It may be an indicator pointing into the void, a presentiment resting on an illusion, a prophecy which will never be fulfilled. The future of which I am full is not my real future. It is not even a pledge of it. It proves only that I now live as if I had a real future, a real being in time in this third tense. As I was and am, I take it for granted that I shall be. But this is not self-evident. A Now will come when I can no longer maintain this "as if" or deceive myself with this assumption. And I never know whether my next Now will not be the Now of this great illusion which will be followed by the great disillusionment of the fact that I have no more time. The further side of my present may turn out to be the further side of my being generally. This is the possibility of an acute threat ahead of us—a threat from the very point at which my life aims. Life means time, but we may find that our time has no more duration and extension, but is a thing of the past, so that life itself is over, and has only a past and no future. Can we console ourselves by reflecting that this threat can be serious, and that the catastrophe can break over us, only once, and that on every other occasion we shall escape? Or, to put it another way, is there any comfort in taking a chance that the next moment will not be that of the great illusion and therefore of the great disillusionment, but that we at least still have time, perhaps quite a bit of time? There would be some comfort in this if we had a clear view ahead, and could see the real catastrophe from a distance or even when it is close at hand, and if that final crisis, which is bound to come sooner or later, were not the term of all the being in time still ahead of us, thus impressing its character upon the whole. In fact, however, the whole space of life before us, beyond the present, is chronically and therefore continually threatened by this catastrophe. To be sure, the terrible end can come only once, and it may still be a long way off. But come it will, and therefore the future which precedes it cannot be other than unending terror. There is little true consolation in a prospect like this. But this is in fact the prospect which faces our being in time in this third tense.

Again there are two ways of facing this prospect. We can shut our eyes to it, or we can look it straight in the face, and act accordingly. We can be unreflective and frivolous with regard to the threat which lies ahead, or reflective and preoccupied. We can be optimists or pessimists, activists or quietists. These are obviously very different attitudes, and they are both clear and simple possibil- [543] ities. They embody the two classical views of life which have always divided men, and will always do so. But they have one point in common—that they both end in a *cul de sac*[EN161].

The unreflective way is to stand firmly on the pretence and to assume that it affords solid support, never giving a thought to the fact that our future being in time is enclosed by a great bracket; that one day—we do not know when—we shall step and fall into the abyss, having a present without a future, encountering the further side not only of our present moment, but of our whole being in time; and that with every step we take our being is a being of unending terror under the threat of this catastrophe. It is possible to ignore these unpleasant facts, to speak and act as though that bracket would be removed. It is possible to persuade ourselves and others that the fear is not so terrible and that we are not really afraid of it at all. This is to posit absolutely the future of which our present is full. It is to treat it as though it were already past and lay behind us. We then speculate as in Jas. 4[13]: "Today or

---

EN161 dead end

tomorrow we will go into such a city, and continue there a year, and buy and sell, and get gain." We then live by planning, arranging and managing everything. We then live for our programme in the preparation of its execution. We live for the principles and ideas and pictures, both theoretical and practical, which we have projected and made for our own personal future, and perhaps for the future of a greater or smaller or perhaps all human society. We fondly imagine that such dreams represent the future as it really will be—in germ, at any rate. As we contemplate them and enjoy a foretaste of the reality, we imagine we are already there. The barrier posed by the question whether everything might not turn out very differently from what we had expected, since there might be no future at all or only a threatened future is triumphantly surmounted by the assertion that the worst has not yet happened; that we still have a future; that where there's a will there's a way; that the future has never failed yet and will not do so on this occasion. This view is superficial, no doubt, but there is something healthy and brave about it. It is certainly a happy thing to gather rosebuds while we may. And we can certainly do so if we are prepared to live without reflection. But this is hardly possible in practice. This is the *cul de sac*[EN162] to which this kind of outlook leads. When all is said and done, it is not really possible to be careless and unreflective. No one can. We cannot persuade ourselves and others that we are. We can only act as though we are. The facts are stronger than all the healthy assertions and certainties exploited by this outlook. They are stronger than all the cheerful grasping at the future in which we try to put it into practice. It is an illusion to think that we can posit the future absolutely even in the present. We have not the means to do so, and we know very well that we have not. No intention or purpose, plan or programme unless it is that of a madman can fail either consciously or unconsciously to take into account factors unknown as yet, or to be limited by the conditions, needs and demands even of the present itself. No one ever lives exclusively in the future. And in so far as we do, the triumph in which we think we can do so is more like the effect of a self-administered dose of morphia than of genuine, healthy achievement. We are no match for the future which really comes and is so terribly menacing. Our own projected images of the future, now present in us, are not the future itself, or even the germ of it. We do not seize the future; it seizes us and overpowers us. And at bottom everything always turns out to be very different from what we expected, and in the end totally different. A broad shadow of uncertainty lies over all the time we still have. And we know this, and reflect concerning it. We may stifle or suppress this reflection, but we cannot extinguish it. We are terrified even when we maintain that the unending terror to which we move is not so dread-

[544]

ful after all. We should not be men, living in time, if we did not reflect on the hazards to which our being in time is exposed, from the very point to which we must now and continually push forward.

We are thus left with the way of reflection, i.e., reflection avowed and acknowledged and allowed to dominate the scene. Since we cannot stifle our fear of the future, why not bring it out into the open and allow it to be normative and determinative for our whole attitude to life? Sooner or later we shall step and fall into the void; we shall have a present without a future; we shall meet the further side of our being in time. This terrible threat may overwhelm us at any moment, surprising us like an armed man and depriving us of all the consolation we had forged for ourselves against it. Once we are aware of it, it becomes depressingly clear that we have nothing else to look for but unending terror, even before the dreaded prospect actually comes, and we must order our lives accordingly. The way in which we look and step from the present into the future is determined by the fact that we see the whole of the path before us in this shadow. It is always with diffidence and uncertainty, hemmed in and unconcerned, that we now look and move into the future. It is only with

---

[EN162] dead end

broken pinions that we can make the venturesome flight from the present to the future. The present itself now comes to me, to the extent that it is inevitably full of the future as foreseen in this way, as a source of anxiety, a burden to be borne and only to be endured. Here, too, we have a triumph, another victorious way of facing the future. But this time it is to the negative aspect that for some reason we give the preference and dominion. And once finally triumphant, it will quench all hope of a better future, all confidence in ideas and plans, all resolution to put them into effect. We will simply plan and perform the bare essentials, and then just wait in fear and resignation. Here is another view of life, a definite view, if not exactly healthy, brave or cheerful. It is a view which because of its ostensible honesty and realism is often compared favourably with its opposite. Is it not the view of a mature man, of one who has plumbed life to the depths? Is it not better in the long run to be reflective than unreflective? Yes, so long as we are really able to be exclusively and totally and definitively reflective. But again we are in a *cul de sac*EN163. No one is a pure pessimist. Even Schopenhauer was so only on paper. Even the suicide is not a pure pessimist, for his very attempt to "make an end" shows that in spite of everything he is looking for a better future. We can only behave as if we were completely reflective. As long as life lasts, we hear the call of a fresh possibility of something to be attained and won. For we cannot help considering that our terrible end may still not be just round the corner; that the immediate future at any rate is not unending terror, but in spite of all our fear and anxiety it may also offer positive opportunities. No one can manage to live without some plan for the future, however modest. No one is so reflective in his attitude to life as to have no room for a modicum of the unreflective spirit of childhood. Even the reflectiveness of the most reflective is nourished in the last resort on dreams, on dreams of the future fed by his contemplation of the final limit of his being in time, and not on the future itself as it actually comes upon him and overwhelms him. The reflective man, too, forgets that on this side of that final limit everything may turn out very differently from his gloomy prognostications. But he only forgets it. In spite of his forgetting, his future is still open and all he can do is to proceed towards it with a certain openness, which means with a certain unreflective intrepidity. Once again, the conditions under which we have to live in time are stronger than our own view of them. They do not allow even the most unreflective to posit their future absolutely in the form in which they think they know it in the present. So we cannot say without qualification that the reflective are altogether superior to the unreflective.

But we are not left in this dilemma. We do not have to choose between these two equally futile attempts to escape our being in time. On the contrary, we [545] can count on the fact that the will and act of God are the meaning and ground not only of our being in time generally, but also of our being in the future. True, the future stands at every moment under the question whether it will be our future, our time at all. But in the first instance it is not we who will be in the next moment, to-morrow, or a year hence. It is God, our Creator, Deliverer and Sustainer, who will still be for us and faithful to us. In the first instance it is He in the heights, and then we in our depths. But between Him and us there will be a connexion, for in His eternity—it is the eternity of the living God— there is also a genuine Then. Not, of course, a Then under threat of extinction! For God there is no "not yet" which might possibly be a threatening

---

EN163 dead end

107

"never." But as He was and is He also will be. As He was, is and will be simultaneously without limit or separation, His eternity is original, authentic and creative time. But this eternal God will guarantee the reality of our future too (however long or short it may be), just as He guarantees it even now and has always done so. He will give it to us as the dimension of the life which He has appointed for us. He will do this because His eternity is the eternity of His will which has as its goal that we should live as His creatures and not have to perish, and therefore have our time. This is what God will also will for us in our long or short future. We can know this for a fact because He wills it now, always willed it, and never did not will it. Never did not do it—we must say even more strongly. For He was never not our Creator, Father and Redeemer. He never did not do what had to be done for us to have time for life. He did it as He initiated our particular time, and before He initiated it, as He initiated all time and before He initiated it in His eternal counsel. And with the same definiteness He will do it in our particular future in all the future, and beyond the end of all time in His eternity. Thus He will be over us, for us and with us, as we shall also be in all the uncertainty of our future being.

Furthermore, it is in relation to what God will be and will and do that we too shall be in the short or long time which is our future. And as we are invited to see the eternity of God, not abstractly, but as His eternity for our future, so too we must consider our own future, our being in this tense, not abstractly, but in relation to the eternity in which God is also future to us. What shall we be? Come what may, we shall be what we shall be under and with God; what we can and may and must be on the basis of His eternal future, i.e., those who are loved by Him, to whom He will give time to live. It is because it is given for this purpose as the dimension of our life that in the future tense it is the time which we do not yet have, and of which we do not know how long we shall have it. We do not have it yet because we do not need it yet. And we do not know how long we shall have it because we do not know how long we shall need it. But it will be given, and will really be our time, as the time which we need for the life given us by God. We can be sure of this because there is no "not yet" with Him. He always is, even though we are not yet. He is always the Creator and Lord of time, of the time we need for the life which He will also give us. That is why it does not matter that it will end in a catastrophe, and that in view of its approaching end it stands always and inevitably under a threat. If God is taken into account, we have to say that even in the future tense time is a reality which is assured and which assures our life. It is the framework of our being, and its end will not be terror and cannot terrify. This could not be said, of course, without God. The end of our time could then be understood only as a catastrophe, and our whole being in its movement towards this end as a threatened being. But we are not without God. The same God who has loved us and loves us will still love us as surely as He is eternal. And this means that even our future being, as the object of His love which He will not let slip, is real before Him and therefore in truth in all its allotted and salutary compass and to its

[546]

108

appointed limit. Come what may, it is genuine space for life. *Amabar, amor,* and therefore *amabor*EN164. We not only have lived and do live, but we shall live. We ourselves cannot guarantee this, but God does. The fact that our time hastens towards its end would be intolerable only if we wanted to be God and therefore eternal instead of real men under and with God, and therefore temporal. And the future tense of our time could terrify us only if we had to be men without God, strangers to His covenant. But there is no natural urge compelling us to be without God and strangers to His covenant. As created by God, human reality has been embraced by God and His covenant from all eternity. It is the case, then, that we may have our time—our whole time, and therefore our time in the future tense as given by God. Its end is not a terrifying end, but the goal which He has set us. And therefore its course is not an unending terror, but the way on which He is always before and over us as well as behind.

From this standpoint we may again ask, as in respect of our present and past, what is really meant when we say that we shall be. Since God will be over us and for us then, in every "then" allotted, including the present in which we shall have no further future, this obviously means that in all our long or short future this side the goal we shall always be under His judgment. We do not yet know— this is the particular nature of our future being—to what this judgment will refer. Even less can we control that which will come under His judgment. As we try to gaze and reach into to-morrow from the vantage point of to-day, this to-morrow comes upon us dark and triumphant: dark because we cannot really see it for all our inklings and hopes and fears; and triumphant because, although we prepare ourselves to meet it, it cuts right across our preparations, according to its own will and not ours. In spite of our good resolutions we shall make innumerable mistakes both old and new. Our plans and projects will be [547] thwarted by all kinds of obstacles, expected or unexpected. But shall we not also realise positive possibilities which now seem to be dormant in us and of which we are not aware? Light will come from expected and unexpected quarters. Help will be proffered which is both anticipated and astonishing. And it will all develop and interweave so concretely that when it comes we shall be as much surprised by it as a child turning over the pages of a new picture-book. It will all be as it will be. But again, it will all be before God. No reflectiveness or unreflectiveness on our part will alter the fact that it is before God and therefore genuinely real. We shall still have to thank Him for everything, and answer to Him for everything. And if our future gives advance notice of itself in our present in the pictures we make of it, if even now we begin to be what we shall be, we must still remember and insist that even our present is placed anew before God and under Him. No alien fate is laid upon us as a burden to be reduced, borne or rejected. It is not we who have to decide what our future will be as we advance into it. It is not we who have to decide what form it will take. For God has already arranged it, and the point of our stepping into the

---

EN164 I have been love, I am loved, I will be loved

future, and therefore our present in which we initiate this step, is to look for this arrangement of God.

With this in mind, it is possible and necessary to return to our dilemma, to the question whether it is better and more advisable to take the unreflective or the reflective way in relation to the future.

Surely the unreflective way is right, and it is better and more advisable to step unreflectively from to-day into to-morrow, if we must fix our eyes on God alone. After all, we move towards the more imminent or distant end appointed, and therefore we always move into a future rushing on to this end. If this provokes concern, it is not our concern but God's. In other words, we can cast our care on Him, freeing ourselves from the reflectiveness to which it gives rise by realising that it is really His concern, that He cares for us, giving us time and its end, and therefore time which rushes on to this end. Why should this frighten us? Surely this gives us firm ground on which to set our feet confidently and therefore unreflectively as long as we can. Whatever happens, we shall have God with us and over us. That being so, there is firm ground ahead which will certainly carry us. There is room for us to live and move and have our being. Why should we not proceed with confidence? And if the judgment of God is already over us, why should we not be allowed and commanded calmly and confidently to show a little interest to-day in the things of to-morrow? Why should we not plan ahead a little so as to be ready for the forward movement which we are about to make? There is no need to suppose that we are masters of our future, or that we posit it absolutely in the form in which we conceive it. But we are surely free to live to-day responsibly for [548] to-morrow. Is not this the freedom to pray the fourth petition of the Lord's Prayer: "Give us *to-day* our bread for *to-morrow*"? For to-morrow, even if it be our last, we shall still be under God and with Him. It cannot, therefore, be wrong, or illusory, if to-day—since we unavoidably live to-day for to-morrow—we make the unthinking presupposition that we may and should do this, that it is not arbitrary or presumptuous to do so.

It is certainly not arbitrary or presumptuous to do so. It is not a flight from God into the idea of a beneficent fate or chance as the clue to life's perpetuation. Nor is it a flight from God into the idea of our own mastery as the key to our preservation. An unreflecting consideration and apprehension of the future—limited by all kinds of reflection—is justifiable if it is confidence that the future is that which God gives, and this confidence alone. It is justifiable so long as we remember that in our future we shall be judged and limited by God: not overshadowed by our end, but irradiated by the goal He has set for us. This unreflectiveness which is legitimate and commanded, wholesome and cheerful, has nothing whatever to do with optimism or pessimism. The only thing that we can do with our anxiety for the future is to cast it resolutely upon God. Otherwise all the counter-arguments to this cheerful view are back in full force. It is mere frivolity or even paralysis, day-dreaming or intolerable affliction, and either way an idle and futile pretence, if we expect to maintain ourselves in life even in the near future, even to-morrow. We can only approach this kind of success as a gift. But we can approach it with confidence as a gift actually given, knowing that God will be over and with our future being. So much is undoubtedly to be said in favour of unreflectiveness, and by way of a summons to it.

But there is also something to be said for the reflective way, even from the same standpoint, and we have to realise that from this standpoint we are summoned to reflectiveness. The being which we approach as future being is not any kind of being, but again our being under God and with Him. It is His judgment which will be pronounced over us at the end, and under which we continually stand as we move towards this end. That He constantly gives us life, and the time needed for it, means that we are again and again, and in the end conclusively, challenged to gratitude towards Him and responsibility before Him. To be a man is to live before God and therefore in this gratitude and responsibility. There are indeed good reasons for fearing this future. Indeed, if our knowledge of the God who is over and with us banishes all false fears of the future, enabling us to live unreflectively, the very same knowledge evokes and inspires the necessary and serious fear of God Himself. If we are to continue to live within our appointed limits, how can we stand if it is wholly a matter of standing before God? What are all other anxieties compared with the anxiety which must overwhelm us from this quarter? Are they not all removed in order that we may bear this particular anxiety? It is an indisputable fact that we shall [549] have further time only to live under God and with Him. And at the end we shall be asked whether and how far we have really done this. Indeed, this is the question which is with us all the way. And to-day, coming from the past, we stand in our present before advance into the future, and therefore before this question, as those we now are. All to-day's preparation for to-morrow should correspond to the fact that we shall always have to answer this question of our gratitude and responsibility towards God to-morrow, and that finally the totality of our being in time will have to form a suitable answer to this question. But how can we expect to stand when in relation to our past we can only fall back upon the prayer: *quod vixi tege*EN165? This is not just ordinary pessimism. How insecure our whole position is, and how comical and empty all optimism and activism, emerges in all its frightfulness at the very point where we are summoned so urgently to be unreflective. This is one aspect of the matter which is quite incontrovertible.

But again we must turn the page if we are to see the decisive aspect of the reflectiveness which is also clearly and inexorably required of us. The infinite terror without which we cannot go into the future must be fear of God Himself, and not of an idea of God invented or constructed by ourselves, not even of the idea of a Supreme Judge of absolute holiness and sovereignty. Otherwise it would not be genuine or lasting. Otherwise—for man is astonishingly

---

EN165 cover over what I have done

111

fickle and powerful in relation to his own ideas—it could be only too easily cast off. But it is fear of God Himself only when we clearly realise that as our Judge, to whose judgment we move every day and conclusively on our last day, He is also the One who from the very outset has intervened and made Himself responsible for us in His almighty mercy. We shall be in the hands of the Lord who from all eternity has been our Covenant-partner and Friend. This will make it impossible for us to escape terror before Him. It will not leave us even the line of retreat which is still left open by any idea of a supreme Judge that we might easily construct for ourselves. It will enable us to stand even under the whole weight of the question addressed to us. Indeed, it does so now. It is this which makes the question serious. The God who is gracious from eternity is the One who calls us even now to gratitude and responsibility, and who will continue to do so to-morrow and every day of our lives. God is not mocked. He is the God who is really to be feared. And it is to Him—the God to whom, looking back over our past, we can only pray for the forgiveness which He does not owe but will not refuse—that we must render an account. It is with Him that we have to do in our genuinely established and unending concern about this future reckoning. That we for our part will be completely unequal to this grace of His is the basis of the only concern about the future which really matters. And in the light of this concern—far surpassing even the religiously most profound pessimism, e.g., of a Schopenhauer—it is right to be reflective concerning our future being. And true reflectiveness on this basis will be distinguished from a false and finally relative one by the fact that it is fruitful and practical. If the gracious God is the Judge to whom we move we cannot be mesmerised before him like a rabbit before a giant snake or a condemned criminal before his executioners. This might be the case if we were dealing with the idea of a supreme Judge, and then at the last moment we might discover that the danger is not so great after all. But this is not so when we have to do with the real God who will judge us in His grace. We cannot escape Him, because all our attempts at evasion cannot alter the fact that He loves us, that we belong to Him, that we are engaged and committed to Him, and must render account to Him. And our terror before Him is not one in which we are transfixed, but the terror of a movement in which we unconditionally acknowledge that He will always be in the right and we in the wrong, yet in which we shall demand that His divine right prevail over our human wrong, His grace over our ingratitude, His word over our poor response; and that even though we are sinners who have not merited the honour, and are quite incapable of doing so, we may be continually taken into His service. We shall really be terrified before this real God. We shall never fondly imagine that we can stand before Him, or that in the end we are not utterly dependent upon the fact that He is always this gracious God and Judge, even as and though we cannot stand before Him. We cannot escape the fear of Him by trying to forget that with each step into the future we are face to face with Him. The reflectiveness in which we venture this step will always consist practically in the fact that we

[550]

112

place ourselves in His hands just as we are, with all the inadequacy and failure which we have no prospect of overcoming, holding ourselves in readiness for Him even as the sinners we are. As we prayed *quod vixi tege*EN166 in respect of the past, so we must pray *quod vivam rege*EN167 in respect of the future. It is only in this movement that we are really afraid of this real God. However serious our reflectiveness in face of the expected judgment, if it did not take place in this movement it would merely be a new form of the bad old unreflectiveness which is out of the question if we really expect to be under God and with Him in our future. For in this movement, too, we really let Him be our faithful God, who loves us from all eternity and therefore reliably intervenes for us, who genuinely cares and therefore provides for our gratitude and responsibility; and we therefore enter into the validity and power of that genuine and well-founded unreflectiveness. "Teach me to live according to thy good-pleasure"—with this song of praise in our hearts and on our lips, we are not only genuinely afraid of our future under God and with Him, but we confess a genuine fearlessness in which, in spite of even our future inadequacy and failure, we can find comfort and even joy in relation to the future.

This, then, is how man is in the time given him by God; this is how he is [551] before God in his present and moving from his past and into his future. The time which we have been considering in these three tenses is the time created by God. We have not been speaking of God's eternity, but of our time as God created it and gave it to us; yet not of what it must become and be on the presupposition of our alienation from God, but of time as God gave it to man in creation, and as He constantly renews it in allowing him to live; of the time which as the form of his existence belongs no less to his natural reality than the fact that man is the soul of his body. Always against the background of God's eternity, we have tried step by step to isolate human time—the time created and given by God—from its distorted and obscured manifestation, and to study and present it in and for itself. We began with an analysis of time in the distorted and sinister form we know only too well; and we found that Hölderlin has the last word on that subject. We then proceeded to analyse time in the reality in which it may be seen as the time given us by God.

In conclusion, however, we do well to remember the presupposition on which alone the second analysis can be meaningful and its result—a view of real time—tenable and secure. We reached this view by taking into account at every stage—starting from the present and looking back from it to the past and forward to the future—the factor which was left out of account in the line of thought which reached its zenith in Hölderlin. We understood time and our being in time as real by considering it as the form of human existence willed and created by God. We thus purged the concept of time from all the abstractions by which it is inevitably confused and darkened when the divine will and

---

EN166 cover over what I have done
EN167 direct what I shall do

action are left out of account and time is not understood as His creation. All the way through we have expressly taken account of God's presence and gift as the open secret of time. We understood man, and therefore his time, as God's creation. Only in this way could we regard it as real. But we must remember how we came to introduce the new factor which enabled us to banish those abstractions and therefore to think and speak of past, present and future as we did. We did not do it merely by introducing the word "God" into the discussion and treating it as an Open Sesame to every problem. If God were merely a word or systematic principle, if we had merely "introduced" Him, or taken Him into account, or made use of Him in our thinking, our second, revised analysis of the concept of time would have been a web of speculation, revealed as such, and scattered, by the first puff of wind. The first and obvious view would then have returned with its absurd infinity (the infinity of its contradictions, impracticability and sterility), and all its emptiness and cheerlessness would have seemed to be more illuminating than the alternative worked out with the help of the idea of God. The mere thought of God as such—even the

[552] thought of the living God, to which we have tried to keep as faithfully as possible—is of no avail. No bare concept is adequate to accomplish or even clearly to indicate the inversion depicted.

To recall the clear indication and actual accomplishment of this inversion, we must return to our starting point. We first established that the existence of the man Jesus in time is our assurance that time as the form of human existence is willed and created by God and given to man, and is therefore real. Our whole presentation rests ultimately, not on itself, but on this assurance. We start with the name of Jesus when we introduce the new factor. It is in His light that we can and must see time so very differently, as real time. It is necessary to introduce this new factor because in Jesus it is already present, even in our reflections on the subject. If we leave Him out of the picture only for a moment, our thinking on the subject may have all kinds of other results but it will not enable us to see time as it really is. In Jesus God is not just a word or a systematic principle, but the reality and *prima veritas*EN168 which of itself sets itself at the head of all other thoughts and gives them a specific direction and content. In Jesus God is eternal, i.e., eternal in the only way that really matters here—eternal for us. He is this in a twofold sense. First He is not far from us in His eternity, but near us; not turned away from us, but turned to us; not indifferent or hostile, but gracious, the One who loves us. And second, He is not just hidden from us in His eternity, but also manifest. The "Lord of Time," as the man Jesus came to be known by us in the first sub-section; He who is and was and comes, is also the eternal God, who is for us and manifest to us.

This Lord of time stands at the beginning of all our attempted thinking about time, ruling and establishing, illuminating and proving. In Him it is the case, and by Him we may know, that time is real and that we have it. In Him

---

EN168 first truth

God utters His gracious and saving contradiction of man without God and therefore of a concept of time without God, checking self-perverting and ignorant man and arresting the development of all false and cheerless conceptions of time. In Him who, as the eternal Son of God, is the Lord of time, there is shown to us who are not the eternal children of God, and therefore not lords of time, that time is real, that we are in this real time, and how this is the case. As His time, it is the time created and controlled by God and given to men. And we live on the basis of this reality and think on the basis of the promise which it gives. In Him we see ourselves as God willed and created us; in the nature in which God has not ceased to see us, and which has not therefore ceased to be our true nature in spite of all the disruption and error caused by sin. Christology gives rise to a definite anthropology in respect of the concept of time too; the anthropology of the man who is under and with God in his time, not of a second Jesus, but of the man who exists with the one Jesus (as the recipient of the divine promise addressed to him in the man Jesus) in the time [553] created and given him by God. This is the man who is seen and understood in the light of the fact that the contradiction uttered in the man Jesus was not for nothing, that Jesus did not fight and suffer and triumph for all men in vain. The man seen and understood in this light is natural man. But he is more. The man delivered and kept by Jesus, translated into eternal fellowship with God, and one day to be manifested beyond all time, is certainly more than natural man, who as such is exposed to the perils of sin, disintegration and error. If Jesus had not fought and suffered and triumphed for him, man would be a very different creature. But He has in fact fought and suffered and triumphed for him, and therefore even as a natural man he is to be seen and understood in the light of His resurrection. Neither ontological godlessness nor ontological inhumanity is to be ascribed to him—even in respect of the temporality of his existence. It cannot, therefore, be said of him that in himself he is nothing, or that he exists in an empty time and therefore has no real time. It can only be said that he is at least threatened by this peril—for it doth not yet appear what he shall be—and that he would undoubtedly have succumbed to it if it had not been divinely contradicted. But it has been contradicted. Jesus is risen and is the Lord of time. And therefore we can say positively of man that in the true nature in which God sees him he is not destroyed, but has real time and may live in it.

This conclusion, developed in our second analysis, rests on the promise given us in Jesus, on His resurrection and lordship over time. For on this depends the fact that we can relate man's time to God's eternity, and that God's eternity can and must be seen and understood as His eternity for us, God Himself as the Creator and Giver of our time, and therefore our being in time as a reality. All this depends on the reality of the divine being, intervention and work for us as it has taken place in Jesus. All speculation—even that which is based on a perfect idea of God, let alone any other—will inevitably end in a vicious circle. But in theology we are not free to ignore the reality of this divine being, intervention and work, or to start our thinking at any other point. And if we make this our starting point, we shall find it possible and necessary, compelling and illuminating, to break through and invert the concept of time along the lines attempted. Yet we shall not forget that this starting point is not a formula to be adopted and appropriated at will, but an actual encounter with the reality to which theological presentation can only point.

3. ALLOTTED TIME

[554] In the preceding sub-section we have been looking at time as it were from the inside. We have examined the structure, way and movement in which man was and is and will be. We have been occupied with the problem, the riddle, posed by these three forms of time, the question of the reality of time raised at all three points and in their mutual relationship. We have answered this question by understanding time in all its three forms as the time created by God, as the divinely given space for human life.

But this is only one side of the matter. We shall now take it for granted. We shall assume that man has time, that he is really engaged in this movement. To live as a man is to be in time, to be temporal—in relation to God's eternity—because God is eternal, not merely in and for Himself, but as the Creator for His creature, man; because as the Eternal He is the Giver and Guarantor of his time.

But the fact that it is "his" time, the time of the creature, the time of man, opens up a new aspect of the subject. We shall now consider time as it were from the outside, as the totality of that movement, as the succession of those moments of transition in which we continually come and go, continually leaving ourselves behind us and having ourselves before us. We shall now consider it as the series of moments, and the acts which fill them, in which we are continually present "between the times." In this totality, succession and sequence it is our creaturely, human time. For in this totality, succession and sequence, in its inter-connexion, it is the sphere of human life, of the life of man and men. God gives us time, and we have it, as we need it for life and may actually have it for this purpose—no more and no less. And so this space is not unlimited, but limited. The totality, succession and series have both a beginning and an end. It is the self-enclosed form of human reality which can actually be observed from outside, if only in intellectual perception, just as *mutatis mutandis*EN169 man himself, to the extent that he is the soul of his body, can be observed from outside in physical space, and therefore in physical perception. As in the latter sphere he does not have unlimited space, but supremely limited, so it is in respect of the fulfilment of his life. His time is the allotted span, i.e., the limited space, which he needs for this fulfilment and which is given him for this purpose. This span begins at a certain point, lasts for a cer-

---

EN169 allowing for differences

tain period and finally comes to an end. Man is, therefore, in this span, and not before or after it. It is only in this way, as allotted time, that time is his time. At a certain point this movement began, and it continues and constantly repeats itself until it finally reaches its goal and climax and comes to an end. At this point we have ourselves wholly before us and not at all behind us. Now we have ourselves both behind and before us. One day we shall have ourselves only behind us and no more before us. For at a certain point life began. Now we are somewhere in the middle or before or after the middle. One day it will be over. This is how we are in time. It is our allotted time, and no other.

This raises the new problem to which we must now turn. It is by no means [555] self-evident that human life requires for its development, and therefore acquires and has, only this limited space. Human life demands permanency, or rather duration. Human life would always like to regard itself as an unfathomable, inexhaustible reality. Human life as such will always abhor the suggestion that once it was not and one day it will be no longer, and that it is really to consist in this fulfilment which has a beginning and end, and has duration only between these points. Human life protests against this "only." It protests against the fact that the space for this development is to be that allotted span. And, pending further clarification, we may allow that its demand for duration and protest against the barrier set by the allotting of time are neither mistaken nor presumptuous. Indeed, we must say that it would have no knowledge of itself if it did not know anything of this demand and therefore this protest, if it did not have any question at this point, if it could be readily content with the allotment of the time given it, if it could approve and even welcome it with joy.

As we shall very soon see, it is not simply a matter of accepting this allotment of our time, but of welcoming it with gratitude and joy. But we cannot start at this point. It can only be a deduction from an answer which we give to that question. It ought not to suppress the question itself, otherwise we should fail to appreciate the significance of the answer which we are actually given. If it is not a deduction from the answer which we are actually given, if the protest is silenced and transformed into its opposite, the position is far from satisfactory. It is part of the disorder occasioned by the fall if nothing is known of the longing for duration, or the allotment of a set span is not felt to be a threat, or there is a resigned acceptance of the fact that we can only have allotted time. Resignation of this kind is incompatible with the fact that life is created by God. It is an acceptance of sin and its consequent punishment as though they were our original and authentic destiny. It is acquiescence in a condition in which we cannot and should not acquiesce. It casts doubt on the unfathomable and inexhaustible character of our own reality, treating it as if it were a matter of indifference, or even making it appear to be terrifying and unwelcome. The allotment of a set time ceases to be a problem crying out for an answer, and becoming something to be accepted with more or less complacency. But human life is ignorant of its own true nature when it accepts the fall as its original and authentic destiny, and therefore when it is not troubled by the demand for duration and finds no problem in the allotment of its time.

The reason why human life must be conceived as an unfathomable and inexhaustible reality is that from the vertical standpoint it is created by God and for Him, while from the horizontal it is created in relationship to other men. From both standpoints it is human life and remains so even when it falls and denies its true nature in both directions. For man belongs to God. And he belongs to his fellows. Divinity and humanity are his original and authentic determination. In both these directions human life demands no less than perfection. In both it demands duration, for its determination rests upon its creation by God and is therefore enduring. "Enduring" means without limitation or lack. It means inviolably self-subsistent. But surely there is a serious violation, an obvious limitation and a clear lack in the duration of human life, if its only dimension is an allotted span of time. As though in both directions it could be satisfied in practice with something less than perfection! As though it could develop according to its determination, and do itself justice, in either or both directions under this limitation! As though, in view of its determination, it could endure the idea that once it was not and one day it will no longer be! Why not always? What but an unlimited, permanent duration can be adequate for the fulfilment of this determination?

[556]

If all this were only an abstract desire for life, life hungering for life and never satisfied, but always beating angrily against the barrier set up by the fact that its time is allotted, that it once began and some day must end—if this were all, it would be easy to dismiss the question as foolish and the protest as unjustified. It would simply be necessary to point out that man has no right to an extension of life, no claim to more than an allotted span, merely for the sake of continuing in life.

It would then be easy to show him that in this world there is no life which lasts for ever. Everything has its time, man included. Instead of demanding an unlimited life, it would be better for him to accept the fact that his life, with all its opportunities, is neither unfathomable nor inexhaustible. It is in no way destined to last for ever. So he had better be modest and cease craving for more than a set span of time, which is to cry for the moon. The craving of sinful man, i.e., of man who considers his life and his desire and hunger for life apart from his determination, his divinity and humanity, is indeed futile. Hence there is no great difficulty in silencing it. But again this does not mean that the problem is removed. It may still come up again in a new form even when silenced in the old.

But human life is more than the satisfying of an abstract craving for life. Man can, of course, pretend and protest that he lives in this abstraction. Indeed, he does this, and in the most dreadful way. But even when it seems to be lived in this abstraction, human life is still primarily and ultimately a fulfilment of the determination given with its divine creation. Even in its wildest perversions and distortions, it is human life, and has the determination to be lived for God and one's fellow-men. To be unfathomable and inexhaustible is proper to it, as its craving for duration is legitimate. It rightly protests against the fact that it has an allotted span of time, for if it is to fulfil its determination it would seem to need unending time. And often the demand for unlimited space may well be most insistent at the very point where man is most estranged from his determination in both directions, where he denies it most emphatically in his life, for in this case he constantly robs himself of the time he actually has, thus showing himself all the more plainly that he has too little time, far too little time, to live his real life. However that may be, when the question is raised on this ground it cannot be so easily suppressed or dismissed. There can, of [557] course, be no question of man's original and authentic determination conferring upon him a right or claim to duration. Where man insists that duration is his by right in virtue of this determination, and where his protest against the allotment of time is directed against his Creator, he is guilty of folly and presumption. The creature can make no demands on the Creator. But supposing that in this demand and question and protest man does not make any demand, but appeals to the promise given with his creation in relationship with God, to the gift and task given him with his creation in relationship to his fellow-men? Supposing he does not present his own right and claims before God, but simply pleads God's own Word? Is not God's Word—both as a summons to God Himself and a direction to fellow-men—the real reason why human life must regard itself as an unfathomable and inexhaustible reality? Does not God's Word provide the real reason why duration must be demanded, why there never seems to be enough time, why the allotment of a particular span is a problem? Does not the difficulty which confronts us have its source in the fact that our twofold determination by the Word of God is revealed to us, and that we are deaf and disobedient to this Word if it is no problem to us that we have so little time, that we have only this limited span of life? Of life? Life under the Word of God demands duration and therefore more than an allotted span. For it never seems as though it can have enough time to fulfil the determination which it is given under the Word of God, and every "only," every limit, can only mean a lack or non-fulfilment. Raised from this standpoint—as it always is at root—it is not a question which we can dismiss by saying that it ought not to be asked. On the contrary, we must try to answer it from the same angle.

The question is undoubtedly right to assume that human life demands duration in the light of the determination given in and with its creation. The demand is not unwarrantable. In fact, it would be an unwarrantable denial of itself not to demand duration. In the light of its determination it has the appearance of, and is indeed, an unfathomable and inexhaustible life. No depth from which it comes is deep enough for it; no height to which it strives high enough; no space in which it develops is wide enough. How can it ever be adequately either life for God according to its promise, or life with its fellows according to its gift and task? In both these directions it may and will and must endure. It has an urge for perfection; it is impatient with all limitations; it storms all barriers; it is by nature the denial of all denials. Man as he really is, man under God and with his fellow-men, cannot accept the fact that once he was not under and therefore for God, and with and therefore for his fellows, and that one day he will be so no longer. Man as he really is, as God created him, stands questioning before those frowning walls of rock which enclose him

[558] in the narrow gorge of being, and seem to fling at him the twofold taunt: Once you were not! and: One day you will be no more! But what about his determination then? And since his life stands wholly under his determination, what about his life? What will happen when duration is denied it, when the path to perfection is cut off, when it is neither an unfathomable nor inexhaustible life? How is it to be lived then? How is it to suffice when in spite of its determination it is only this short—and for other reasons very disturbed and broken— approach to God and one's fellows. The question is justified if at this point it takes account of a demand necessarily inherent and proper to human life, theologically understood.

But it is also right to make the further assumption, viz., that it needs time as its dimension, and that this time is allotted. It has margins. It has a definite measurement, which we may depreciate, which can really be measured very differently from our depreciatory estimate, but which is in any case a definite, limited and fundamentally calculable measure.

1. God also lives in His time. But His time is eternity, which has no fixed span, no margins, no other measure but Himself. Eternity is not time without beginning or end. Time is the mode of existence of the creature. To identify eternity with time without beginning and end would be to attribute to it an idealised form of creaturely existence. This would be wrong; for to say eternity is to say God. And God does not live in an idealised form of creaturely exist- ence. God Himself is not only the ground and content but also the form of His existence. To the extent that He is His own form of existence He is eternal, and He is in eternity as in His time. When we say this, we say only that He is in Himself. Hence in His eternity He is indeed the Creator of time, but as its Creator He is the One who was, and as such is and will be; who is, and as such was and will be; who will be, and as such was and is. In His eternity He is beginning and middle and end. He is not, therefore, apart from all these. If He were, we should have another false definition of eternity. Eternity is not timelessness. It is beginning, middle and end in fulness, for it is all three simul- taneously. It is always the first and second as it is also the third. Thus God is His own dimension. And this dimension underlies, conditions and includes that of His creature, so that that of His creature is always His own, and where His creature is, He is also. But His dimension has no fixed span, no margins, no measure but Himself.

Man on the other hand lives in the time created and given him by God. If he were God and not man, the allotment of his time would not be a problem, for his time would not be allotted. For he would be eternal. But that is a dream, and a bad one at that. Since man is man and not God, and he is not therefore eternal, the dimension which he is left, and over which he has no control (as God has over His, because He is His own dimension), is created time, which in

[559] distinction from the eternity of the Creator has a beginning, middle and end which are not simultaneous but separate, distinct and successive, so that it has

margins and a measure in its beginning and end, and is thus allotted time, the time between its beginning and end.

But these boundaries are necessarily the boundaries of human life. This brings us to that narrow gorge with precipitous walls on either side. Where does our life come from? From its beginning, i.e., the beginning of its time, before which it did not exist. Where is it going? Towards its end, i.e., the end of its time, after which it will be no longer. Why not? Because it is creaturely life in this its creaturely dimension. Because by acquiring creaturely time it acquires as its time the dimension appropriate to it as a creaturely life. The life of God requires and has a different dimension. For the life of God is not only unfathomable and inexhaustible, but self-grounded and self-creative, welling up from within itself. That is why it is eternal life, and why eternity is its dimension. In clear distinction from His, our life too acquires the dimension it needs, a dimension which fits and suits it like a tailor-made garment. *Suum cuique!*[EN170] The proper dimension for the life of the creature which is not self-grounded or self-creative, welling up from within itself, but has its basis in the life of God, is the time in which beginning and end are distinct, and therefore constitute its boundaries.

Human life as created by the eternal God has its proper boundaries in respect of which we must speak as the Bible does in relation to man: "They are like grass which groweth up. In the morning it flourisheth, and groweth up; in the evening it is cut down, and withereth" (Ps. 90^5; cf. Isa. 40^6; Ps. 102^{12}; Job 14^2). "Behold, thou hast made my days as an handbreadth; and mine age is as nothing before thee: verily every man at his best state is altogether vanity. Surely every man walketh in a vain shew" (Ps. 39^5). "We bring our years to an end as a tale that is told" (Ps. 90^9: R.V. Marg: "as a sound or sigh"). "For ye are a vapour, that appeareth for a little time, and then vanisheth away" (Jas. 4^{14}).

Is not our question already answered when we say that God has His dimension, unallotted eternity, and we ours, allotted time? Yet the fact is that man stands in relation to God. He has a life with God in virtue of the determination given in and with his creation. Hence he cannot abandon the demand that He should endure and burst the limits of temporality. He cannot possibly acquiesce in a *suum cuique*[EN171]. That he has with his life in time that promise, gift and task from the eternal God is the cause of the discontent of which we have been speaking, and the reason why it cannot be stilled by a reminder that God is God and man is man. This reminder can only prepare the ground for the answer we require.

2. But we advance a step further if we grasp the following point. Is it really the case that the legitimate demand of human life for limitless duration, its character as a striving after perfection which can brook no denial, would be genuinely served if unlimited dimension and therefore infinite rather than allotted time were placed at its disposal? We are now assuming that human life [560]

EN170 To each his own
EN171 To each his own!

is content to be creaturely and not to be the eternal life of God. We are assuming that it has no desire to leap over this boundary. For if it were divine and eternal life it could not entertain such a desire at all. By the very acknowledgement of this desire it resigns itself to being a life different from the life of God. On this presupposition—and assuming that it is not content with a set span as its dimension—its only option is to want the idealised creaturely dimension which we mentioned above, i.e., an enduring time without beginning or end. We have met the idea of infinite time before. It is the expression of the infinite embarrassment into which man without God is plunged by the question of the reality of his being in the present, past and future. Considering the source, we have no great confidence in the notion. But let us assume for the moment that it has some substance in it. Time is then an unlimited dimension in which human life can develop as an infinite quantity, in the form of a process without beginning or end. It thus has the opportunity to do justice to its determination to live for God and for others.

But would it really do justice to it in this form? Would it really correspond to man's legitimate craving for duration and fulfilment? This would obviously be the case only if an infinite quantity of human life could guarantee a duration adequate to its determination and the perfection to which it aspires; only if it could guarantee that in its relation to God and to others, from the standpoint of its divinity and humanity, it would be the life which it ought to be in correspondence with its determination. It is understandable that it should require and demand time for this purpose, and it receives it. It is understandable that it should require much time rather than little; that it should rather be a long life than a short; that in any case it wants a sufficient measure of days and years for its development as the fulfilment of its destiny.

This is the meaning of the "long" life promised to the children of Israel (Deut. 4^{40}, 25^{15}) in the promised land on condition that they remain loyal to the covenant with the God who will bring them into this land. This is what is meant when the bloodthirsty and deceitful men are told that they shall not live out half their days (Ps. 55^{23}), and even the righteous complains: "He weakened my strength in the way; he shortened my days" (Ps. 102^{23}), and prays: "O my God, take me not away in the midst of my days" (Ps. 102^{24}). It also explains the jubilation in Eccles. $11^{7f.}$: "Truly the light is sweet, and a pleasant thing it is for the eyes to behold the sun. Yea, if a man live many years, let him rejoice in them all." In particular, it is in this sense that long life is attributed to the king (e.g., Ps. 21^4), and, in the familiar exaggeration of courtly language (which must not be taken literally), the salutation even goes the length of wishing the king should live for ever (e.g., 1 Kings 1^{31}). It is also in the same sense that the Old Testament (Gen. $5^{4f.}$) recalls the exemplary longevity of the patriarchs from Adam to Noah, Methuselah (v. 27) having reached the astounding age of 969!

[561] But if even the idea of a "long" life is a doubtful one in relation to its determination—"Because thy lovingkindness is better than life" (Ps. 63^3)—"long" life is certainly not life without beginning or end, nor are many years the same as everlasting time. And in any case it is hard to see how everlasting life can guarantee duration and fulfilment in relation to its determination. Short or

long time is no guarantee of this duration and fulfilment. Time is only the *conditio sine qua non*[EN172], only the indispensable opportunity, both for life itself, and for the realisation of its legitimate craving for duration and fulfilment. And for the latter and decisive factor, for the realization of this craving, even an infinite quantity of human life in a correspondingly infinite time is no guarantee. If life as such, in the light of its determination, is God's good gift to man, the normal man will not only desire but seriously pray that the gift should not be niggardly, that his life should be long and not short. But even length of life, and therefore a great or infinite number of days, cannot guarantee real duration and fulfilment. Long life and an ample measure of time can only mean more opportunities. And an infinite measure of human life can only mean an infinite number of opportunities. But this is not what human life really asks if it has a true understanding of itself. It does not ask merely for the constantly repeated and ultimately infinite possibility of duration and fulfilment, of perfection in accordance with its determination. It does not ask merely for more and ultimately infinite space, although it undoubtedly needs this space and the opportunity to reach out for duration and fulfilment. What it does ask for is the reality of duration and fulfilment, the removal of the restrictions which stand in the way of this realisation, the negation of everything which negates it. No infinity of space or everlasting time can achieve or even guarantee this negation, this removal of restrictions, this realisation, which consists in the perfection of the relationship to God and fellow-man to which it aspires. Even if it were in unlimited time, this could only mean the possibility of a constant reaching out to this perfection. In relation to what he really asks for, because he really lacks it, man would still be no better off on the presupposition of the reality of this notion of infinite time than in the allotted span in which he has actually to live. We may thus conclude that no serious renunciation is demanded of him, no resignation in face of a blessing which he may rightly ask and seek, if he accepts the fact that he does not have to live in an everlasting time, which is in any case illusory and invented only in the illusion of a dilemma, but in the real, allotted time created by God and proper to him as the creature of God. He does not lose anything in so doing. In his temporally restricted time he has only opportunities to live up to his determination. But even in a temporally unrestricted life he would still have no more than opportunities.

3. But we must go further. He would actually be worse off rather than better in an unrestricted life. For in a life without beginning or end he would not only be able but compelled to aspire continually to duration and fulfilment. He would come from an infinite series of opportunities and move towards an infinite series. The actuality of his life before and behind would be a continual reaching for the perfection of the relationship to God and fellow-man. He [562]

[EN172] necessary condition

could only be perpetually *in via*[EN173]. He could never have reached the goal, and never do so. He would have infinite space before and behind, but only for his creaturely human life, which always seeks satisfaction because full satisfaction, duration, fulfilment and perfection are promised and assigned to him by creation, but which can never attain it because it is not divine. If it were without beginning or end it would always lack and seek this satisfaction, unable to escape its determination or to shake off either its divinity or humanity. Indeed, it would neither come from a beginning of this imperfection and dissatisfaction, nor move towards its end. It would be condemned to perpetual wanting and asking and therefore dissatisfaction. Could there be any better picture of life in hell than enduring life in enduring time? Do we not have to say that life on this condition—on the assumption of the reality of that notion—would be a life of misery which it would be folly to describe as a good creation and gift of God? But if this is so, the scales which previously seemed to be equally balanced are tipped against the notion of infinite time and in favour of the allotted time which we actually have. We do not desire a good thing but a bad if we are dissatisfied with the set span God has given us and want unrestricted space. For in it we condemn ourselves to a continuation of the unrest which gives rise to our problem. If it is a restless craving for perfection in our relationship to God and fellow-man, it cannot remain unrest, positing itself absolutely as such and finding pleasure in its perpetuation. If it is genuine unrest, it aspires beyond itself to realisation and therefore to the peace of a permanent life under God and with other men. Life as an endless process, and therefore space for it, is the last thing any one conscious of the humanity of his life can desire. Rather, he will appreciate the fact that the exact opposite, life confined to a set span, is what he has been granted, and that in comparison with that other possibility it is not only equally good but far better.

4. But the real answer to our question has still to be given. Our conclusions thus far are (1) that life in an allotted span is appropriate to man as such in his difference from God; (2) that it is certainly not to man's disadvantage to live in a definite and not an indefinite span; (3) that it would be fatal for him if he had to live in an indefinite instead of a definite span. The real answer to our question can be given only as we now try to show that positively as well as in relation to that other possibility it is good and salutary for man to live in allotted time.

[563]   Let us first examine what it must mean to be positively good and salutary. It must obviously mean first that the allotment of time, the fact that it begins and ends, has to lose wholly and utterly the character of a restriction and threat to human life in the development corresponding to its determination. The picture of the narrow gorge and its enclosing walls has to cease to be valid. There must be no more occasion for care and anxiety lest the natural craving for duration and perfection should not be satisfied. All our chafing against the

---

[EN173] on the way

limitations of our life must be irrelevant and superfluous. The apparent threat and restriction must be overshadowed by a mighty, beneficent promise. The rock walls must have become the protecting walls of a living-room or work-shop. Fear and anxiety must have yielded to confidence and trust, dissatis-faction and complaint to praise and thanksgiving. All this, not in spite of the fact that the time given to man is allotted, but just because of it. The answer must exactly fit the question, and yet the whole prospect alter, so that the ques-tion is made meaningful and fruitful by its positive answer. But there is more to it than that. Life in our allotted span must cease to be a series of opportunities with the persistent unsatisfied demand for duration and perfection, and only the possibility of their satisfaction. With the fact that life is a set span an offer must be made which is greater and more powerful than its deepest need or the most urgent question to which it is an answer. In virtue of its beginning and end, and therefore its limits, it must be guaranteed and presented with what is necessarily demanded. The allotment of its time must actually assure it of what its time, whether long or short, or even unending, cannot of itself either achieve or assure. In virtue of its limits, it must be a life which is upheld and sustained, sheltered and provided for, and finally satisfied for all its dissatisfac-tion. In these limitations it must be engaged in the realisation of its determin-ation, and find full satisfaction in this movement.

All this is true if, as in the previous sub-section, we again have reason and cause to see and set the time in which man is in relationship with God; with the God from and to whom he may be and live as His creature. Here too, then, we shall have to divest the problem of the being of man in time of the abstraction in which we have had to regard it to see it as a question. It makes all the differ-ence in the world whether we conceive our life as one which is abstractly limited or limited by God; and whether we have to accept it as a general truth that our time is allotted or realise that God has given it to us in this form. If we regard the matter abstractly and generally, the question of duration and per-fection leads us nowhere. It remains a question, and inevitably takes on the character of a complaint and accusation. It is no help to remember that the distinction between Creator and creature rules out any other possibility. Nor is it any good suggesting that things would be just as bad if we lived in unlimited time instead of limited. Nor is it any use convincing ourselves that it might well fare much worse with us if we lived in unlimited time. In itself, this is no reason [564] why our limited time should be the right time for us, or why we should cheer-fully and happily and gratefully accept it. It is far more likely that we shall finally and basically shake our heads and bite our lips and simply make the best of the fact that we have no option but to take what we are given—a limited life in an allotted span of time. And this simply brings us back to the starting-point. Does life really have to be like this? And when we raise this question again we again shake what we think are our prison bars and angrily or anxiously contrast our determination with the conditions under which we are forced to live. And the question itself is still unresolved. We still do not see why things have to be as they are, and not otherwise. The whole picture changes, however, if we are not concerned abstractly and generally with the limitation of our life, but with the God who limits it; if we are not concerned abstractly and generally with our allotted time, but with the reality of the God who allots it. In both cases, of course, we are concerned with the same thing. But the same thing now becomes quite different. It becomes so different that—if we really count on the reality of God—we are not merely confronted by the convincing and definitive answer to our question, but the question itself is resolved.

Let us assume that we do have good reasons for seeing that the time in which we are stands in direct relationship to God. The relationship consists simply in the fact that He is all round us; that He is our Neighbour with whom we have to do on the margin of life, at the frontiers of our time. Whether it is our "not yet" or "no longer," our being or not being, He is there behind and before. Therefore the question of our Whence? and Whither?, of the duration and perfection of our life, cannot lead into the void, like a broken bridge in a sea of mist, but always to Him. It is not in relation to an indistinct something that we are limited, that we are called in question, with our legitimate demand for life, by the allotment of our time, that we are a vapour, a shade, a sigh, a breath, or grass which flourishes and fades, as the Bible puts it. It is in relation to Him that we are all these things. If we ask concerning the beyond, which undoubtedly compromises and threatens us even in our deepest and most legitimate concern, there is only One either behind or before us, either before our beginning or after our end. He, God, is this beyond. And God is not an "it," a "something," even the negation of a "something." He is absolutely Himself: the One who reveals Himself to us in His Word; who, according to His own Word, is the Creator and Lord of all the reality distinct from Himself; whose sovereignty extends even over chaos, the sphere which he purposely excluded from reality; who, again according to His Word, intervenes and makes Himself responsible for His creature because He loves it; whose aim, again according to His Word,

[565] is to manifest the fellowship which He willed to grant it, and continually does so, as His glory embracing even the creature. God Himself is at the point to which we look in our question how the duration and perfection of our life can be attained in the brief and transitory span which we are allotted in this time of ours. We ask concerning Him when we ask concerning this possibility. We are moved by a concern which always is His concern, and always will be. At this point, if we are not blind, or dazzled by our illusions, we shall see Him, and Him alone.

And we shall see Him indeed as the One in relation to whom our life has its limit and our time is allotted. We shall see Him as the One who has created and wills to have us within this limit and allotted span. The final longing for an unlimited life in unallotted time necessarily falls away once we realise that the limit and set span of our existence is the condition which must be fulfilled in order that He, the eternal God, may be our Counterpart and our Neighbour as described, and that we may be His counterparts and His neighbours. Limit in the creaturely dimension means a clear-cut outline and contour. Man would not be this man, here and now, the concrete subject of this history, if his life did not have this outline and contour, if it did not have these limits and boundaries. A being in unending time would be centrifugal. It would not be that of a concrete subject to whom God can be an equally concrete Counterpart and Neighbour, with whom He can enjoy communication and intercourse.

This shows us again that we are not to think even of the being of God as being in an indefinitely enduring time. If it were, it too would be centrifugal. And it would be quite nonsensical to say that God was, is and will be, that He is beginning, middle and end, because in Him there could then be no beginning or end. God, however, is eternal. That is to say, He is simultaneously and in fulness beginning, middle and end. In this respect He is utterly different from us. But in this respect too, for all the difference, He is a concrete Subject, which can encounter us and be our Neighbour on all sides.

If this is to be the case, however, we as His creatures must not be without limits or boundaries, but must be defined in our life and in our time: not abstractly and generally (in contrast to indefiniteness); but by Him and for Him (in contrast to an indefiniteness in which we could be concrete subjects neither by Him nor for Him); and therefore genuinely defined. The fact that we are in a set span is thus a benefit, an expression of the divine affirmation under which we stand, for it—and it alone—makes it possible for us to be those whom God encounters in speech and action and who, impelled by the legitimate demand based upon their determination, may look to Him, stand before Him, hear Him and have a part in His action, all their care and anxiety being removed by Him. He really cares for us by giving us an allotted span instead of unending time. For in so doing He sees to it that between Him and us there can be a relationship and fellowship. For this reason, formal if we will, [566] it is wrong to rebel against this limitation or merely to resign ourselves angrily or anxiously to its inevitability. Even for this formal reason gratitude is the only proper response.

5. For a deeper understanding, however, we must first take up again the earlier point that it is the determination given to our life by the same God which makes the craving for duration and perfection a serious, legitimate and weighty craving as distinct from a mere desire for life. This raises the very real question whether our life is not too brief and our time too short to satisfy this demand. In the light of our determination, we are compelled to regard them as unfathomable and inexhaustible. But our determination is given by the God with whom we stand in relationship in our allotted span. And this can mean only that the matter which gives rise to our questions and complaints and protests is not left to us; that although we have a part in it and responsibility for it, it is not our task to see to its successful accomplishment. The very fact that our life is temporally limited under its God-given determination tells us unmistakeably that with the task which He has laid upon us we are wholly in the hands of God. We are right to ask for duration and perfection in our life; and to exist in

127

this request. To do this is the task undoubtedly given us with our determination. Our life would not be human, it would not be the life which God has created and given us, if it were not spent in carrying out this task. But we should be wrong if we were to conclude that we ourselves can and must achieve duration and perfection by a power immanent in our life as such, that the fulfilment of our determination consists in this forceful effort and attainment. The fact that our time is allotted is an obvious negative refutation of this view. Its positive refutation is that at the very point where the appointed limit can be clearly discerned at the beginning and end of our lives, there is no prospect of infinite processes of activity and achievement, but we stand quite alone, although genuinely confronted by the eternal God who has given our life its determination, whom we are summoned to obey in our allotted span, who confronts us a the eternal God in a superiority in face of which we can only give up ourselves for lost or surrender in implicit trust. It is in Him, who has determined and limited us in this way, that we have the duration and perfection for which we rightly crave. It is in Him, in His eternal counsel and work, that God and man, and man and man, are brought into the intimate fellowship which we necessarily but disturbingly see to be the goal of our life. We misunderstand ourselves if we think that we can seek and find the object of our legitimate demand elsewhere than in Him. Indeed, we cannot demand it rightly if we do not long for Himself above even the highest good. Apart from anything else, we miss the basic thing—that with our limited life in our allotted

[567] span we can stand in confrontation and proximity to the eternal God. If in our being in time we have to do so concretely with Him, how can we have to do concretely with anyone or anything else when it is a matter of the fulfillment of our determination? If our determination by Him will not let us go, so that we must anxiously ask concerning its fulfilment, and can never meet its requirements in relation to Him or our fellows, our limitation by Him will not let us go either, so that even if we do all that we are commanded we can never satisfy Him, but must always recognise and confess that we are lost before Him, or rather saved and kept by Him. He is the same God who, as He gives our life its determination, summons us to throw in our lot with Him, and who again, as He sets our life its limits, shows beyond all doubt that the cause we serve is not ours but His. From this standpoint, the fact that our time is allotted is quite in order. And it would not only be rebellious but eminently inadvisable to question this order. What would happen to our legitimate craving for duration and perfection if our discontent did not continually issue in the profound contentment of the knowledge that God Himself undertakes to gratify this craving? Once this is recognised, so much of its realisation is seen that until its final realisation we can dare to go on living from hour to hour and day to day under the determination which is given our life and which we cannot suppress, but also in the time, our allotted time, which we can receive and have as such as the good gift of God.

6. But a final step has still to be taken if full clarity is to be attained, for again

it is not enough merely to bring in the word "God." Here, too, this may well be an empty formula. The contention that it is good and salutary to be restricted and limited by God must be decisively proved. Why should we welcome the fact that at the point where our being and non-being seem to collide so inexorably and so menacingly we have to do with God, with the same God under whose determination our life is human and therefore impelled by that craving for duration and perfection? We must now bring out into the open something which so far has received only incidental mention. And we must give it such emphasis that all the other associations which the word God has for us will seem trivial when they are measured and illuminated by it, namely, that God is the gracious God. Everything which we have said about the God who restricts and limits us has been leading up to this point. We have been speaking of a God who is not without man or against him, but for him. He is the God who far from thinking it beneath Him made it His glory eternally to elect Himself for man and man for Himself. He is the eternal self-grounded and self-satisfying majesty, but in the full freedom and sovereignty of His work as Creator, Reconciler and Redeemer addressed wholly to another, to man who cannot do anything for it, who cannot merit the divine address, or correspond to it, but can only receive it as a gift, the gift to which he owes everything. This is the free grace of God, which is not just a benevolent attitude towards man, but the turning to him of God in person; of the God who, in inverse ratio to his deserts, enters into solidarity with him, thus interposing Himself, making the life of man His concern, the salvation of man His need, the peace of man the cause for which He fights and wins, so that all human affairs, be they great or trivial, individual or collective, are first and last His concern, ordered and solved by Him. That He Himself receives us to Himself is God's free grace. And this God who is gracious to us in freedom is the very One who limits our life and bounds our time. He does not only do this. He bears and sustains our life even with the span allotted to it. In willing to have it so, He disposes and fashions that it may always be life, so long as He permits. He protects and preserves it from the disintegration from which it cannot protect itself and which would be its inevitable fate if it were to run its course without Him. He governs it in accordance with the determination which He has given it—and against the intentions with which we would like to govern it. He leads it towards His revelation; the revelation of His glory which consists in the fact that we may live under Him and with Him. Yet in doing all this He also limits it. And thus He is certainly present to us, so long as we have our time and are privileged to be grateful recipients of His gifts and responsible executors of His commission in this time of ours as knowing and acting subjects. There is no part of our time which is not as such also in His. It is, so to speak, embedded in His eternity. But as we are thus in God's time, He limits ours. He appoints its beginning before which we were not, and its end after which we shall be no longer. And in this He is to us in a particular way the gracious God. This is shown in the fact that at the very points where we emerge from non-existence and return to non-

[568]

existence, we are confronted in a particular way by the gracious God. For at these points we are referred wholly and absolutely to the fact that He is our gracious God. For what are we, or were we, or shall we be, if He were not already and still there as our gracious God even when our own life and being is not yet or no longer?

If He is not there for us, who is? If He is not there for us before we were and when we shall be no longer, then our only prospect is annihilation. And if that is not our plight, if we do not sink back into the void, if our life and being are sustained, it is because—but only because—He is there for us. To be sure, even during our life and in our span of tune we are utterly dependent on the grace of God. But during our journey from our beginning to our end this truth may be veiled from us. During our life and in our span of time it appears and the appearance is very strong though it is only an appearance—that we have to do not only with God, but also with all kinds of elements and factors which bear us, maintain us, protect, preserve, vivify and control us, and especially with our [569] own selves, so that we may at least ask whether man is not his own gracious Lord and God. But in relation to our beginning and our end in time there can be no place either for the appearance or the question. We are faced by the simple alternative. Either the gracious God (and He alone) is for us, or nothingness is the abyss from which we have emerged and to which we shall return. But if we are confronted, not by nothingness, but exclusively, unequivocally, fundamentally and definitively by the gracious God, we are obviously near this God at these two points in a way which cannot be said of our being in the time between, though He is certainly near us there as well. What characterises the nature of man at these frontiers of his being is that, as the God who is wholly and utterly for us, God is wholly and utterly outside us, namely, beyond all our other possibilities. This is generally true as He is near us. But it is clear and essential only at the point where we can cling to no one and nothing but Him who as outside us is for us; neither to the world nor to chaos, to angel nor devil, nor even our own selves.

Thus the fact that our time is allotted, and allotted by God, simply means the proximity of His free grace in this clarity. In this way, in this clarity of His free grace, He alone being our help, comfort, assurance and hope, His free choice our sole ground and promise, God confronts man from the very first as He gives him a limited life in an allotted span of time. He would obviously not confront him in this way if He gave him an unlimited life in unallotted time. Even then of course—if for the moment we may make the monstrous assumption of man as an infinite subject—it would still be true that man lives solely by the grace of God. But it would not be natural or obvious. He would be blinded by the illusion that he can rely on many other things as well as God, and especially on himself. In the supposed inviolability of an unlimited life in unallotted time in which he is endlessly alone, he might even be tempted by the foolish question whether he himself is not God. The free grace of God would then be relegated to an infinite distance, not in its truth, but in its compelling, exclusive and unequivocal clarity. Even if known, it would be a mere notion without concretion or practical significance. He would then be almost irresistibly invited and enticed to sin, to make idols, to try to justify and save himself. If this is not so, if he is urgently warned against this, it is because the limitation of his life, whether it be long or short, refers him concretely and practically, with supremely unwelcome but supremely valuable proximity and clarity, to the fact that apart from God he has no support, basis or goal, that without Him his existence would merely be a journey from nothingness to nothingness. Thus from this standpoint too his nature does not permit him to sin. If he does so, he cannot blame his nature for it. His nature, as that of a temporally limited being, is a powerful invitation and direction to throw himself upon God's free grace, to give Him alone his trust and full obedience, and in so doing to fulfil his determination and satisfy his craving for duration and perfection. If he fails to do this but falls into sin, he does not conform to his nature but denies it. By his nature, in virtue of its peculiar character as an allotted span, he is referred and bound to the gracious God as the One who is wholly and utterly outside him but wholly and utterly for him. It is now clear how much depends on the fact that our being in time is ordered as it is. From the standpoint of the most basic understanding of man, i.e., in confrontation with the gracious God, we have no reason to reject this order. In fact, we have every reason to recognise it in all its severity as good and wholesome, to accept it as a unique benefit, and to love and praise its Author for it. What greater ground could we have for loving and praising Him than the fact that by nature He has ordered our being as men in time for His free grace, and for this grace in all its clarity? [570]

Here, then, is the basic answer to the problem raised by the fact that we are given only an allotted span. We had to take the successive steps in our analysis to show how it is to be given with increasing definiteness and clarity. Our next task will be to develop it in detail: first, and more briefly, in relation to the fact that our existence and time have a beginning; and then, more fully, in relation to the more pressing problem presented by the fact that they come to an end. But before we take up these questions, we must remind ourselves of the way in which we have reached this answer. The limitation of our life and restriction of our time is too serious a fact for us to produce a positive answer as it were out of the hat, with no realisation of how we have attained it or on what grounds we may and must hold it. We will therefore recapitulate the various assumptions which we made to come step by step to the point of gratefully and joyfully affirming what at the outset it seemed possible only hopelessly and grimly to deny. We found in the determination of human life for God and our fellowmen the basis of the craving which makes the set span of our life seem so painful at a first glance. We accepted the necessary difference between the eternal existence of God and our temporal existence. We counted generally on the fact that between God and man there is nevertheless encounter and fellowship. And finally and decisively we presupposed that the God with whom

131

we have to do is the God who has turned to us in His grace, who is not only for Himself, but in very truth for us. The conclusive form of our positive answer rested wholly upon this last assumption. But we must now recall that this last assumption (and therefore all the others as well) cannot be taken for granted, but can be adopted only as it is given to us. In our whole assumption that the gracious God is the limit of our time, and our conclusion that it is therefore good and salutary for us to be limited in time in this way, our starting-point has been the man Jesus in His time, but He also as the Lord of time, and it is only

[571] in view of this man that we have been able to consider man in the abstract and in general, and therefore his temporality. Was not the life of the man Jesus a limited life in a restricted time? Yet we saw that that life, with all its limitations, was the life of the eternal Son and Word of God. We saw that His restricted time as such was fulfilled time, filled by the coming of the kingdom of God. We saw that in His resurrection the perfect realisation, based in God Himself, of the true relationship between God and man, and man and his fellows, is revealed as the perfection of this limited temporally restricted life; and He Himself, this man, is manifested as the One who is in God even before He was and when He was no more, and as the man who will come and reveal the aim and purpose of God in respect of all men. We look at this man, who like us has lived a limited life in its restricted time, when we adopt our understanding of the nature of man in respect of his temporality. We keep to the determination of man revealed in Him when we accept man's craving for life as such. But we also keep to the fundamental difference between God and man also revealed in Him (in His distinction from us) when we acquiesce in the fact that we are temporal and not eternal like God. Again, we keep to the presence of the kingdom in His life in His time when we see the eternal God and temporal man in relation to one another. And again and supremely we accept the scope of His being in God both in His time and before and after it; we accept the revelation of His lordship over time, inaugurated in His resurrection and to be consummated at His coming again, when we understand the limitation of our time as the clear proximity of God's grace for us. The gracious God of whom we spoke is not an abstraction but the concrete reality of "God in the flesh," the man Jesus, who was in time and the Lord of time. The formulation is bold but not inaccurate that He is the One by whom we are surrounded on all sides. For what time before or after our time is not His as well?—the time in which and over which, as He is in God and God in Him, He is Lord. "God in the flesh," the man Jesus Himself, is God for us in the whole majesty and condescension of the divine being and action. He Himself is God's free grace. And He is it in the clarity which can enlighten us only from the two frontiers of our life. It is impossible to regard human nature in the light of the existence of this man without realising that it is good and salutary for us to have a limited life in a restricted time because here the grace of God is near and clear to us. But we cannot realise this except as we regard human nature in the light of the existence of this one man. At this point, too, a definite anthropology results from

Christology. But this anthropology can be based only on Christology. Here we have the assumption behind all our other assumptions in this matter, and it ought to be clear by now that we can recognise and accept it and count on it and start from it, only as one which has already been made for us. Where for any reason we cannot do this, the answer which we have now given will never have the specific weight which carries conviction, and the question which it is supposed to answer will still be unsolved.

[572]

4. BEGINNING TIME

The problem raised by the fact that the time given us is an allotted span has two aspects which we must now consider in detail. Our time begins, and it ends. Attention is usually concentrated on the second aspect—that it ends. There, somewhere ahead of us, lies the term of our life, the frontier of our time, which is firmly drawn at an unknown point, and which we approach with every day and hour. At that point we shall be no longer. But the first aspect is just as real. There is a term and frontier from which we come, a point where we were not yet. The only difference is that we move further and further away from this point with every day and hour, so that the question posed by our beginning seems to decrease in urgency in proportion as the question posed by our end increases. That our being in time will one day come to an end, when our present will never again be followed by a future, appears far more disquieting than the fact that it once began as a present without a past. And it is indeed far more disquieting. For our life, and with it our time, is set irreversibly in this direction, so that what looms before us is the approaching end and not the receding beginning, which we have no urgent or pressing cause to consider, since it is plainly and self-evidently given and lies unquestionably behind us. The two aspects are seen together in an old German proverb: "I come and know not whence … I go and know not whither. I marvel that I am still so happy." But it is easy to see why the two aspects are not usually brought together. They do not have equal weight. All the same, the statement: "I come and know not whence," has a weight of its own. The fact that we feel no need to concern ourselves about it does not prove that there is no intrinsic reason to do so. And if we are really troubled by the second aspect: "I go and know not whither," and are surprised that we can still be so happy, this may be connected with the fact that there is a riddle at the point which we do not usually consider because our being in time faces the other direction, but which reveals an ignorance no less complete than in respect of our Whither? Our beginning is indeed behind us and constantly recedes. It does not attract our attention or arouse our concern. Yet it points to the same fact and confronts us with the same problem as our end: that our being is bordered by our non-being; that our non-being behind and before is a most terrible threat to our being; that we

133

[573] are menaced by approaching annihilation; and that our being thus seems to be a mere illusion and our life irretrievably forfeit. Why are we afraid of our end? Obviously because, consciously or unconsciously, we carry and bring with us from our beginning a lurking terror which in virtue of the irreversible direction of our life and our time takes the opposite form of fear of our end, but which in both its latent and patent form is essentially one and the same fear of the term set to our life, of the allotment of a fixed span for our time. Since this is so, it is worth spending a few moments in consideration of the first aspect of our problem, and thus realising the scope of our basic answer in this respect too.

Our life once had a beginning. Nor does it make any difference at what point we locate this beginning.

The older theology created difficulties in respect of the soul and its origin which we can spare ourselves because they do not really touch the heart of the problem. Its only theological justification was that unlike ancient and modern Gnosticism, it rejected *a limine*[EN174] the so-called doctrine of "emanationism." According to this doctrine the human soul is an efflux or emanation of the divine substance. It is not a creature, but of divine essence. This view clearly rules out our problem in advance. It is as pointless to worry about where we were before we were born as to worry about the previous existence of the Deity. Yet it is equally clear that this advantage is purchased at the price of blurring the distinction between divine and human being which is one of the fundamental assumptions of all Christian knowledge and of thus taking up a standpoint from which no theological teaching or discussion is possible. The early Church and its theology, while rightly insisting on the gulf between Creator and creature, thought that the problem of the origin of the soul, and therefore of human life, could be solved in various ways between which we do not need to choose. Some, following Plato, and within the Church Origen, talked of the pre-existence of created souls. These were either represented as a kingdom of spirits which had to relate themselves to the material bodies allotted to them—the theory of a pre-temporal or at least pre-historical fall, championed in modern times by Julius Müller, might conceivably be adapted to this view— or it was assumed that when God created the first man they were all breathed into him and therefore created with and included in Adam, to be later distributed among his posterity. On both views it was possible to hold the particular doctrine of the migration of souls (metempsychosis or reincarnation), i.e., that the same souls could enter into many associations with different bodies. Partly in opposition to the doctrine of pre-existence, yet inevitably connected with it, and represented particularly by Tertullian in earlier days, and later (surprisingly enough) by Luther and Lutheran theology, was the traducianist doctrine that the soul originates in the act of conception. A soul-seed, distinct from the body-seed, is supposed to be detached from the soul of the parents, thus becoming the independent soul of the child. The doctrine prevailing in the Roman Church, which (again surprisingly) was followed in traditional Reformed theology, is creationism. On this view each individual soul originates in a divine creative act, an immediate *creatio ex nihilo*[EN175]. This creative act is supposed (cf. F. Diekamp, *Kath. Dogmatik*, Vol. II, 1930, p. 119f.) to take place at the moment of conception when the parents create the requisite physiological conditions for the existence of a human being in this act. The parents are, of course, only *causae secundae*[EN176], God

---

[EN174] from the outset
[EN175] creation from nothing
[EN176] secondary causes

Himself being the *causa prima*[EN177]. And simultaneously God in heaven, this time as the *causa unica*[EN178], creates the soul and associates it with this new human body. There is, of course, room for discussion as to the differentiation and unity between the vegetative and sensitive and the properly human or rational soul, and whether the former is progressively shaped to the latter in the period of pregnancy. According to Thomas Aquinas (*S. theol.* I, qu. 118, *art.* 2, *ad* 2) the actual creation of the characteristically human *anima intellectualis*[EN179] would seem to be relegated to a later stage of pregnancy, whereas the dominant view to-day tends to assert that the intellectual life-principle is created and begins to function immediately upon conception, since the human body is apparently antecedently disposed for the reception of this life-principle. [574]

We may have various reasons for refusing to enter into this strange discussion about the date of the inception of human life. In any case, however, none of the various attempted solutions, each of which outdoes the other in abstruseness, leads us even the slightest step forward from where we stand, i.e., face to face with the fact that, if we exclude the pantheistic solution, we are bound to reckon with a beginning of human life, and therefore with a time when we were not, which was not yet ours. Before the being of the individual as of the race there was somewhere a non-being. And this non-being from which the individual and the race come is the non-being to which we also move. In the language of traditional theology (which we now find obscure and unacceptable), there was a time when my soul did not exist. In the terms of a more biblical view of man, there was a time when I myself as the soul of my body, I myself as the unity and totality of my psycho-somatic existence, did not yet exist, but I began to be. That this is the case is the occasion of a serious theological concern to which it is possible to give a serious theological answer. For it means—and none of the theories attempted can help us to escape this conclusion—that even from my origin I am threatened by annihilation, being marked as a being which can only advance towards nonexistence. Before a certain point I had no past; the time before this point was not my time; I had there no dimension to live in. And even if I associate myself with the whole human race, and regard my soul as an individual member of that kingdom of spirits or as included in the soul of Adam, before the time of Adam there was for him, and before the creation of that world of spirits there was for its individual members and therefore for me, no time, no dimension to live in. This is the shadow which has lain over my being in time ever since it began; the deficiency which now lies heavily upon me as I pursue life's journey; the shadow and the deficiency with which I now move towards my future. One day, it will no longer be my future. When I have had my last present, I shall have no more future, but shall only be past and have been. The latter point is not so easily forgotten as the former. But even if I can forget the former, I still live under the shadow and deficiency. I can be only as one who once was not, with all the

---

[EN177] primary cause
[EN178] sole cause
[EN179] intellective soul

135

threat which this entails. I can be only as one who is definitely confronted from behind by his own non-being. Whatever this shadow and deficiency may lack in urgency because it is not before us, it gains in actuality over that which still belongs to the future. For the decision that we were once not yet has already been taken, whereas the decision that one day we shall be no more, for all the certainty with which it awaits us, has still to fall. We still have a present with a little future. We still live. The door to our future non-being is still unopened. But the door through which we came to being from non-being is wide open. It has already been decided that at that time, beyond that door, we had no time. And we must live as those who come from this decision; as those who are always suspended with all that they were and are and will be. It is as well, therefore, to address ourselves to the further question of our Whence? so easily forgotten and apparently irrelevant, yet all the more urgent in fact. What are we as those who inexorably come from this point?

[575]

That this question is a relevant one, whether we are aware of it or not, is shown by the phenomenon already touched upon at an earlier point, viz., the general interest and concern to know as much as possible about the past, the phenomenon which we usually call the human interest in history in the narrower sense of the term, namely, the history which lies behind us. That a man can be concerned with his own personal past is understandable, for there, as we have seen, he is concerned with himself, as well as with his present and future. But it is far more difficult, and in fact quite impossible if we ignore this latent question, to understand why man in every age and clime, with varying degrees of zeal and ingenuity, yet with a remarkable unanimity, has always been exercised about what lies beyond his personal recollection and its possibilities, his own life and times; why he has always wanted to recover and bring within the range of his vision and picture as vividly as possible what happened before his time, and how it happened, in spheres which were not his. Why cannot he let the past remain past? After all, it was not his past and it has no bearing on his life to-day or to-morrow, as his own personal memories have. How are we to explain the remarkable demand for sagas and legends, for epic poetry or for assured traditions handed on from generation to generation, and finally for the most accurate historical research and presentation? What do we expect from it all, from these distant figures of the past, from life and times long dead, from the thoughts, words and deeds of men long since departed, from the circumstances under which they lived, the emotions and experiences by which they were actuated, from their achievements, successes and failures? Why must all these things be called back into this strange second life in the pictures which he forms? It would be superficial to put it all down to the playful or serious urge of mind or imagination exercised in this as one of many fields. Nor is it sufficient simply to say that man goes to his predecessors to learn about himself and his own present and future, hoping to find in these realms, which were not his, the inspiration, motives, criteria, stimulation, encouragement and warning he needs in order to live a meaningful life in his own sphere. Nor is it the whole story if we point to man's legitimate and serious need of human society—a need which might lead him, and will necessarily do so if he does not find true contemporaries in his own age, to generations long since departed, to the encounter with their needs and hopes, resources and responsibilities, with their particular way of meeting the demands life lays on us all. All this, of course, is perfectly true. Yet at the same time there is a deeper and more powerful force at work. Man is impelled to penetrate beyond his own life and time. He has an urge to carve out for himself living space and therefore time at the point where he was not. He is anxious to dispel the shadow which haunts him from the past, and make good the deficiency under which he suffers from this quarter. He seeks light and fulness there too. He would like to have been and lived at that point. He would like to be "transported" to it—the real aim of every imaginative or scientific attempt at historical reconstruction. He wants to be then as well as now; to hear and see Bismarck and his opponents; to be a contemporary of Napoleon I; to feel and think and hear and smell as people did in the 18th century; to look over the shoulders of Leibniz and Kant, Luther and Calvin, and countless others as well; to think with their minds and have direct access to their thought. He finds it intolerable that all this should have happened then, i.e., long before his own day, as though it were no business of his. He cannot bear to think that this dimension of life never belonged to him. Therefore he cannot leave history alone. He cannot accept the fact that he comes from non-being. Therefore he fills the gap by plunging into it with his historical investigations and discoveries. Therefore he must dream and write poetry, preserve monuments and documents, and when he has the tools for it, endeavour scientifically to bring the past within the range of his own experience just as it was. The process is usually stigmatised by its critics as a "flight into history." And there are, of course, certain aspects which justify this criticism. But there are others which give it the appearance of an all-out offensive, a vigorous crusade, a passionate attack on our allotted span of time in which we try to reach out into that field of the past which is so visible and broad that by comparison the expanse ahead which we can exploit for future enterprises and achievements may seem wretchedly obscure and confined. It need hardly be said that this endeavour, which rightly understood is truly titanic, is nevertheless afflicted by a final impotence in all its forms and can never lead to the desired goal. Just as our personal memory is in the last resort confined to recapturing and preserving a few more or less clearly defined and detailed images, so it is, and even more so, when we try to reach out beyond our own time into that of other men of the past. However clear our reproduction, however scientific our research, we can never actually be there ourselves. However hard we try, we can never be in an area where we were not. Of course, pictures of this area can enrich our life, and in this way belong to our life. But our life as such remains within its confines. There can be no backward extension of our being in time. The genuine historian is no stranger to the pathos of the fact—and the more strongly the more clearly he sees it—that even the most vivid pictures can only testify that a recurrence of its reality, or our own return to it, the desired backward extension of our life's dimension, is necessarily an illusion. But the force of the historical impulse in its many different forms does at least show that man is aware of the abyss of non-being which lies behind him, and that he is basically more concerned with the question of his existence in this direction than might at first sight appear, or seem to be demanded by it.

[576]

That this problem of the origin of our life, of the beginning of our being in time, is so great, is due supremely to the fact that the theological answer to the problem of allotted time which we have just given has reference to and embraces not only the more obvious problem of our exit, but also the less obvious of our entry. The result of our radical examination—that it is good and salutary for us to be limited because it is the eternal, gracious God who limits us—tells us that we derive from this God. We certainly come from non-being, but we do not come from nothing. We do not come from an abyss which has spewed us out only to swallow us up again. God is not nothing nor chaos. As the Creator of heaven and earth and of man, He is the Victor over chaos, who in His omnipotence has negated and still negates nothing, who intervenes against it for the creature which of itself is no match for it, who protect it

137

[577]   against its onslaught, who rescues it from its most dreadful triumphs, who has made Himself its Pledge and Helper in all the inviolability of His self-grounded being, who has always and will always prove Himself to be such. There was a time when we were not. Nothing can alter this. We should not be creatures but God if we had been eternally. And we should not have been concrete creatures, existing as well-defined subjects, if we had come from an infinite previous time. But the eternal God was before we were. He was in that past before our present which our being in time so utterly and painfully lacks. He was in the "then" which was not yet ours. He was in the unattainable life-space before ours. We can never regard Him as belonging to the past like everything before us, as something lost which cannot be recaptured because only our non-being was before us. He has preceded us in time, in all the times of our non-being. Indeed, He has preceded the non-being of all creation, the beginning of all time as its dimension of life. Where do we come from? From the being, speaking and action of the eternal God who has preceded us. This is the particular answer to this particular question. Before we were, this gracious God was our gracious God: the God who even when we were not was not without us but in all that He was Himself was for us; therefore God for us; wisdom and omnipotence for us; holy and righteous, merciful and patient for us; eternal and ineffably glorious for us; for us the origin and fulness of all perfection. His inner life as Father, Son and Holy Spirit, His will and purpose in relation to heaven, earth and ourselves, His already accomplished and uninterrupted work in execution of it—this was the content of the time before our time, the meaning of the pre-history before our history. Hence there is nothing mysterious or terrifying about the time before we were. It does not really entail any deficiency or shadow. Our yearning to expand our being backwards into the past is pointless. Whatever our end may be, our beginning does not lay us under any threat or curse. Regarded in the light of its beginning, our life in our allotted time is tolerable because at this point it does not hang lost and helpless over an abyss but is reliably held and supported, secured and guaranteed. Indeed, it stands under a promise. Its progress and even its end are set in the light of its beginning. From the point where we derive we can go further, treading to the end the road which begins there. Because of this beginning, we have no reason to fear that it will be impassable or lead us finally to catastrophe. On the contrary, we may be confident that the road on which we find ourselves and the goal to which we are moving will prove good and salutary. For the eternal and gracious God, who is the boundary of our beginning, will surely guarantee the whole of our life, the span which we are given, and its final end. Obviously the theological answer which we have given to the problem of allotted time is not properly understood if it does not really have this

[578]   dimension, if it does not lead us to take seriously the question of our Whence?, and give us light and comfort in respect of it. For this reason we cannot just ignore the question.

4. Beginning Time

Nor is Holy Scripture silent in this respect. That Israel was perfectly alive to the problem of our Whence? is shown by Job 8[9]: "For we are but of yesterday, and know nothing." And we have a classic expression of the answer given to this question in the prayer attributed to Moses, the man of God, in Ps. 90[1f.]: "Lord, thou hast been our refuge, from one generation to another. Before the mountains were brought forth, or ever the earth and the world were made, thou are God from everlasting, and world without end" (P.B.V.). No violence is done to the text if we then emphasise v. 3: "*Thou* (who wert our refuge from one generation to another, and God before the world was made) turnest man to destruction; again thou sayest, Come again ye children of men." But if we are to arrive at a concrete understanding it is essential to give full weight to the first sentence: "Thou hast been our refuge, from one generation to another." According to the Old Testament revelation, when the Israelite contemplates the beginning of his individual existence he is confronted with God Himself and with the history of the people of which he is a member. His thinking is indeed "historical," but under a particular token. For the Israelite God is not a first principle or an idea. It is significant that passages like Ps. 90[1f.], which at a pinch can be regarded as the expression of a physico-metaphysical world-view, are extremely rare in the Old Testament. And it is clear that even Ps. 90 is not meant to be taken in this way. Yahweh has been the refuge of Israel and of all Israelites from generation to generation. This massive historical reality is the form of the God who was before man was, before ever the earth and the world were made. And the fact that He was Israel's refuge before man was, is not, e.g., subordinated to the earlier point (viz., that He was before the earth and the world were created), as the particular to the general. On the contrary, the general point is included in the particular, and can be stated only in the light of it. The true way to put it is that in the first place Yahweh is Israel's refuge, and only then and as such the God who was before all the world. For Yahweh, the God of Israel, is in an absolute sense the Founder and Inaugurator, the Lord, Legislator and Guarantor of the covenant in which Israel alone can have its historical existence as a people. He is the Lord of this covenant from all eternity. He has proved Himself as such and acted as such from generation to generation. This is His form to which the individual Israelite looks back when he thinks of the time before his time. This past confronts him with the challenge (again attributed to Moses): "Remember the days of old, consider the years of many generations: ask thy father, and he will shew thee; thine elders, and they will tell thee. When the Most High gave to the nations their inheritance, when he separated the children of men, he set the bounds of the peoples according to the number of the children of Israel. For the Lord's portion is his people: Jacob is the lot of his inheritance. He found him in a desert land, and in the waste howling wilderness; he compassed him about, he cared for him, he kept him as the apple of his eye: as an eagle that stirreth up her nest, that fluttereth over her young, he spread abroad his wings, he took them, he bare them on his pinions: the Lord alone did lead him, and there was no strange god with him" (Deut. 32[7f.]). The same challenge to remember the former days or years is to be found in Deut. 4[32], and also in Job 8[8], Is. 45[21f.], 46[9], as well as in Jer. 6[16]: "Thus saith the Lord, Stand ye in the ways and see, and ask for the old paths, where is the good way, and walk therein, and ye shall find rest for your souls." And how man lived up to this challenge and responded to it is shown in Ps. 77[5ff.]: "I have considered the days of old, the years of ancient times. I call to remembrance my song in the night: I commune with mine own heart; and my spirit made diligent search. Will the Lord cast off for ever? And will he be favourable no more? Is his mercy clean gone for ever? Doth his promise fail for evermore? Hath God forgotten to be gracious? Hath he in anger shut up his tender mercies? And I said, This is my infirmity; but I will remember the years of the right hand of the Most High. I will make mention of the deeds of the Lord; for I will remember thy wonders of old" (cf. also Ps. 44[1f.], 78[1f.], 143[5]). That is the particular token under which Old Testament man thinks "historically." The historical element is Yahweh's election of Israel,

[579]

139

Yahweh's acts and miracles in fulfilment of His covenant, Yahweh's commands and instructions, Yahweh's faithfulness which abides even though it is so often obscured by Israel's guilt. This is the pre-history, the time before his own history and time, to which the Israelite looks back. He sees and understands his life as integrated into the great context of the past. He is a member of the people which Yahweh brought out of Egypt and led through the Red Sea. This happened, it was, before he himself was. Here it is that he sees and finds his refuge with all who from generation to generation were before him. However Great his perplexities and complaints in relation to the present or future, he is here sustained, directed and inspired. By this event God lifts him up and sets him on a rock (Ps. 27⁵). Deut. 32¹⁸ can even say that this rock "begat" his people, and therefore himself. It is of this rock that he thinks when he thinks of his God, whether in gratitude and joy or in remorse and contrition, dereliction and despair. And it is of this living rock that he thinks when he contemplates his own life and origin. This is the real source of his life.

It is in this context that we must understand the exalted role played in Israelite thought by the "fathers" and "forefathers" right back to the patriarchs, and from these down to their own particular racial and tribal ancestors. On a superficial level all this may be due to family piety and a love of genealogy. But on the vital theological level of the Old Testament it is something very different. The fathers, their names, succession and history (however fragmentary), are important to the Israelite and worthy of the utmost attention and reverence because they are either the direct witnesses or the accredited narrators of the event of which he thinks when he calls to mind the holy name of God. His father and his father's father, and behind them all the ancestors from whom he is directly descended, serve as his sureties. For they in their day were children of Israel, standing under the promise and command of Jacob, the incomparable "before" of Yahweh, the Lord of the covenant, who was as such before the earth and the world were created. Yahweh is the God of his fathers, and finally and supremely the "God of Abraham, of Isaac and of Jacob." This is what binds and joins the Israelite to his forefathers. Hence the prominence of the fifth commandment, which comes immediately after the commandment of the Sabbath and before all the ethical commandments, and obviously belongs in sense, if a distinction is to be drawn, to the first table rather than to the second. That is why it is also combined with the promise "that thy days may be long in the land which the Lord thy God giveth thee" (Exod. 20¹²). Life in the land depends upon God, or, to put it concretely, on the *prius*[EN180] of His election and covenant, His accomplished miracles in the past, His given commandments and directions. Father and mother are the concrete, visible embodiments of this divine *prius*[EN181]. They are to be honoured because they represent the living God of Israel and therefore the eternal consolation of the Israelite at the beginning of his existence. For this reason "ye and your fathers" often appear in the Old Testament as a collective unit both in good and evil. That is why the children had to suffer under the curse laid upon them for the "sins of the fathers," but could all refer to the older covenant which God swore to their earliest forefathers and which they could invoke in respect of their own sins as well as the sins of the later fathers, as in the concluding words of the Book of Micah (7¹⁸ᶠ·): "Who is a God like unto thee, that pardoneth iniquity, and passeth by the transgression of the remnant of his heritage? he retaineth not his anger for ever, because he delighteth in mercy. He will turn again, he will have compassion upon us; he will subdue iniquities; and thou wilt cast all their sins into the depths of the sea. Thou wilt perform the truth of Jacob, and the mercy to Abraham, which thou hast sworn unto our fathers from the days of old." That is why the Israelites call themselves after the man Israel-Jacob, the youngest of the patriarchs, in whose kaleidoscopic career they found a prefiguration of the

[580]

[EN180] presupposition
[EN181] presupposition

whole history of their people, and from whose sons they derived their twelve tribes. But it is also why they call themselves the seed, race or children of Abraham, after the first of the patriarchs, whom Yahweh took and led out from the nations, and to whom He also showed the land and gave it.

We can now see why blessing is regarded in the Old Testament as the epitome of all the good things which the father can pass on to the son and the son receive from the father. A blessing is the word which has divine power to pass on good things. It is thus clear that originally and properly the Word of God alone can be a blessing. All human blessing, as Num. 6^{24} shows, is contingent upon the blessing of God: "The Lord bless thee, and keep thee"—"(he) shall bless thee with blessings of heaven above" (Gen. 49^{25}). "Blessing," according to Rudolf Kittel's definition (cf. *TWzNT*, II, 753), is a "supernatural challenge to human action and behaviour emanating from the deity." But in this connexion with divine blessing there is also a human blessing. The name of the man Abraham becomes a word of blessing (Gen. 12^2, 22^{18}, 26^4). His name, so it is promised, will become a blessing to "all nations of the earth." The existence of this word of blessing means first that at the beginning to which every Israelite as such may look back as his own beginning, there stands the word, spoken in power as God's own Word, of election, covenant, salvation and hope—and all embodied in the person and name of Abraham, and therefore valid for all his descendants. It is this word which is testified to the people when the high priest blesses them; and it is this word which is testified to the son when his father blesses him. The testimony to each and all is that each and all—and this is the blessing which they receive—come from here and may live as those who do so. It is to be noted that this is never a self-evident reality or natural condition like membership of Israel by physical descent. It is the living word which must be repeated by Jacob (Gen. $49^{28f.}$), by Moses (Deut. $33^{1f.}$), by Joshua (Jos. 14^{13}), by David (2 Sam. 6^{18}) and by Solomon (1 Kings 8^{14}). It must be specified according to time and occasion. It must be declared afresh with every generation, just as circumcision has to be performed constantly on fresh male descendants. Nor should it be forgotten that while the good thing, the benefit, the gift which the person giving the blessing passes on to the person he blesses, includes a whole wealth of external salvation, its kernel and substance lies in the fact that the people blessed derive from Yahweh and may live in the light of His countenance and under His grace (Num. 6^{25}). "The Lord shall preserve thee from all evil; he shall preserve thy soul. The Lord shall preserve thy going out and thy coming in from this time forth, and even for evermore" (Ps. $121^{7f.}$). That He does this; that He has done so from the beginning of Israel's existence, and continues to do so from generation to generation; that in His mighty acts in history He is the refuge of each living Israelite in turn; that this is repeatedly attested from old to young; that the word of blessing, the name of Abraham, who is at once the source and recipient of the blessing, can be handed on in supreme reality from fathers to children and children's children—this freedom to bless and to receive blessing is the Old Testament's answer to the question of the Whence? of man's natural life. According to the Old Testament, only Israel has this freedom. But the promise that one day the blessing will extend to "all nations of the earth" shows that concealed in the soteriological we have to do with an anthropological determination; that the position in relation to the Whence? of man's natural life is really that we come from God, and from the God who as our Creator is also the Lord of the covenant of grace, the Lord of the history of His grace and of our salvation. According to Gen. 1^{28} the very first human beings are the objects of God's blessing. But according to the Old Testament this is known only in Israel. Hence the word of blessing as such can properly be pronounced only in Israel. And it stands always in strange juxtaposition [581] to the curse, i.e., the prophetic word of menace and judgment which, no less than the blessing, accompanies the whole course of Israel's history. Now although God's judgment is perceived and declared only in Israel, it applies to all nations, and the denunciations of the prophets are issued directly or indirectly against them all. Similarly, the greater grace of God, which embraces and includes His judgment, the grace which Israel is privileged to attest to itself in all its members with the blessing of the name of Abraham, is in fact His grace for all nations, and indeed for all creation; and the promise of Israel has implicit but also explicit reference to all men. They are not aware of it as yet, for it is not yet attested to them. They have not yet received it or desired to do so. But as men they are what man is called in Israel. All men come in fact from the place where Israel may seek and find its refuge. For He who was Israel's refuge "from generation to generation," from the inauguration of its particular history, is the same, and in Psalm 90¹ᶠ is rightly attested to be the same, as He who *is* "before the mountains were brought forth, or ever the earth and the world were made," from eternity to eternity. He is their beginning because, turning them to destruction, He is also the end to which they move.

In the New Testament this problem of retrospect, the question of the Whence? of human life and the answer it receives, take on a very different aspect. Of course, the answer given in the Old Testament does not become obsolete. On the contrary, it has a vitality, intensity and concreteness which it probably never had in practice in ancient Israel. For with the appearance of the Saviour of the world to which the community looks back, the general, anthropological significance of the answer first given to Israel is clearly revealed. Yet this Saviour of the world is for the New Testament community indissolubly one with the Messiah of Israel. He is the fulfilment of the promise given to the people of Israel and every individual Israelite from its earliest beginnings. He is the Lord of the covenant from which they too derive. His life is the presence of the kingdom. His death and resurrection are the supreme act and miracle to which they look back. His teaching is the meaning of the commandments handed down and prescribed for ancient Israel. His person is the grace of God in which ancient Israel sought and found its refuge from generation to generation. Hence the community of the New Testament could only regard itself as most intimately connected with that of the Old. As the Church, it should only regard itself as the new Israel now living in the fulfilment of the promise given to the old. The Gentiles who entered it were wild olives grafted into the old tree (Rom. 11²⁴). Believing Jews and Gentiles—the latter raised like the stones of Mt 3⁹, but associated with the former—are together the children, successors and fellows of faithful Abraham, and with him a word of blessing for the whole world (Gal. 3⁶ᶠ, Rom. 4¹ᶠ). Conversely, Abraham, Isaac and Jacob, but also Moses and the people who came out of Egypt and entered Canaan, the Judges, Samuel, David and all the rest were predecessors and partners in their own faith, constituting one great "cloud of witnesses" (Heb. 11⁸ᶠ). Again, according to the Epistle to the Hebrews, the sending of Melchisedec to Abraham, the Sabbath, the tabernacle, the high priest and the sacrifices of the Old Testament were all foreshadowings of the light which had now appeared. Looking back to Jesus as attested in the Gospel narratives, the New Testament community looked with all the generations of Israel to the God who had been for the men of Israel the beginning and meaning of all their ways and works. And conversely, it had only to concern itself with the narratives of the patriarchs, with the prophets and psalms, and therefore with God in these first beginnings, as it did in its early services, to find again the One whom it knew in the Gospel narratives. Quite naturally, therefore, there resulted even formally a certain parallelism and similarity of problems. Again, as time seemed to go on, they had to ask concerning the preceding time and history, concerning the origins and beginnings of the Christian witness, concerning the original Gospel narratives and the first eye-witnesses. Again there were original elements and later additions, direct and dependent witnesses, an original community at Jerusalem, and a Gentile apostolate, the apostles, Paul, and their disciples. Again there was contact and continuity with the "old days," the fidelity of genuine tradition, its preservation but also its renewal as a question and a task. Again the challenge must be heard and accepted to keep to the old, i.e., the

[582]

142

original, i.e., the true, essential and decisive, and to return to it in case of forgetfulness, misunderstanding or even corruption. Again there were in the community, within the framework of the Christian and apostolic character which determined its whole life, πατέρες EN182 and πρεσβύτεροι EN183, with their corresponding privileges and obligations. It is worth noting, however, that while the Old Testament conception of blessing was everywhere maintained as a living reality in the language and thought of the New Testament, the action of giving and receiving the blessing from man to man which is significant in the Old Testament, was not adopted and continued in the New Testament community. The only use of εὐλογεῖν EN184 in this sense occurs in passages which tell Christians to bless their persecutors instead of cursing them (Mt. 5⁴⁴ and *par.*, 1 Cor. 4¹²; Rom. 12¹⁴; 1 Pet. 3⁹). Elisabeth does not bless Mary; she recognises and acknowledges her as an object of blessing (Lk. 1⁴²). With this exception, only Jesus (e.g., Mt. 21⁹) is greeted as the "blessed one," and Himself blesses, e.g., the little children (Mk. 10¹⁶) and His disciples on His final departure (Lk. 24⁵⁰). Beyond this we are merely told that God "hath blessed us with all spiritual blessings in heavenly places in Christ" (Eph. 1³); that "God, having raised up his Servant Jesus, sent him to bless you" (Ac. 3²⁶); that Paul hopes to come to Rome "in the fulness of the blessing of Christ" (Rom. 15²⁹). That is all. And it is very different from the word of blessing passed on from man to man in the Old Testament. We look in vain in the New Testament for a parallel to the Aaronic blessing of Num. 6²²ᶠ, or for the adoption of this blessing, or for any blessing of one Christian by another. The laying on of hands, which was practised only in special situations, may be a partial substitute for the vacuum thus created. But it is probably better to look for the real substitute in a very different direction. The real explanation is probably that the divine word of blessing, as the New Testament sees it, has been uttered once and for all in the incarnation of the Word of God (as contrasted with the call and election of Abraham), and cannot therefore be repeated (as in Israel), just as the whole continuity "from generation to generation," which had as its goal the coming of the Messiah, was suspended with this coming, like circumcision.

For all the similarity of the phenomena, it is impossible to conceal the difference between the Israelite looking back to the beginning of its life in the election and calling of his people and the New Testament Christian looking back upon the beginning of his life in Jesus Christ come as the goal of Israel's history. For what stands behind the Christian in Jesus Christ as the beginning of the Church and his own personal life is not, strictly speaking a second longer or shorter history, "Church history," but the conclusion of Israelite and human history in Jesus Christ, the passing of this aeon, the end of time, whose pendulum is still as it were making its final swing, so that it has still to be seen that it is really over. In face of the fulfilment of the promise given to the Old Testament fathers, what Christians hope for as their successors and associates is the general and comprehensive revelation of what has already been fully accomplished in Jesus Christ—not a second history with further consummations, not Church history as a further extension of salvation history, not a "Christian era." And on the basis of the Gospel narratives and the apostolic message, what they believe in their present is simply that the end of history and the goal of time are already behind them in the death and resurrection of Jesus Christ. It is from this that they come and by this that they live. This is where they seek and find and have their refuge. As they see it, the concrete form in which God is their refuge, their prior history and time, is the man Jesus nailed to the cross and raised from the dead, in whom, before they were, everything took place and is [583] revealed for their present and future, and whom they need to continue and complete their

---

EN182 fathers
EN183 elders
EN184 to bless

own life. What they need for this purpose is simply His Spirit. But this is only to say again that they need Him who was then; His Word and presence to-day as yesterday; the faith, hope and love in which He is one with them. As the One who was before them, who was before they were, He upholds and sustains them. He is the gracious God who has already saved them and will not let them fall, either in the further course of their journey, or at its end.

This has to be realised if it is to be seen that, although the whole problem of the backward context of our existence is the same in the New Testament as the Old, it has to be stated differently. When it is not realised, the centre and therefore the periphery of New Testament faith and life cannot be perceived. In the Old Testament sphere it is not only possible but necessary for the individual to look back to the long history of his people and thus to recall with confidence his own origin and beginning in the grace and election of God. The history and the mediation of the divine promise and command accomplished in it have in this case a fundamental significance. The meaning of every single, human life in Israel is to be found in its participation in this history and in the accompanying mediation of the divine promise and command from generation to generation, until the whole process reaches the goal foreseen and implicit in its beginning with the appearance of the expected salvation, the birth of the Messiah and the inauguration of His kingdom. This fundamental significance of the history which transpires between the election and call of Abraham and any given present is both the completeness and the limit of the completeness with which Old Testament man is comforted in respect of his origin. It is impossible to ascribe any similar basic significance in the New Testament sphere to the history which begins with the foundation of the Church. The establishment of the Church, upon which the individual Christian looks back as the origin and beginning of his own existence, is certainly the work of the same gracious and faithful God with whom the Israelite in earlier days sought, found and possessed his refuge. But "God" now means the salvation which has appeared, the Messiah, born, crucified and resurrected, the kingdom which has now come. This is something far greater than the blessing of the name of Abraham and the succession of blessings which followed under his name. It is the God who elected and called Abraham in a human person. Old Simeon (Lk. $2^{25f.}$) and Anna (Lk. $2^{36f.}$), who waited for the consolation of Israel and the deliverance of Jerusalem, are now dismissed like faithful sentinels whose duty is done: "Lord, now lettest thou thy servant depart in peace, according to thy word; for mine eyes have seen thy salvation" (Lk. $2^{29f.}$). This final word on this side of the turning-point in time becomes with its fulfilment the first and exclusively normative word for the future. "We have found him, of whom Moses in the law, and the prophets, did write, Jesus of Nazareth, the son of Joseph" (Jn. 1^{45}). The apostles can only testify to this search and discovery. It is conclusive and final. Those who would relegate this search and discovery to the same level as the promise and command of Israel, as though the latter had not attained their goal in this search and discovery, would be false apostles. The same applies *a fortiori*[EN185] to those who would supplement and enrich the testimony to this search and discovery with new promises and commands. The Christian man looks back to this search and discovery and nothing else. He lives directly by the beginning made with it. The Gospel story and the apostolic message mediate to him nothing but this beginning. And so the Church, whose life is sustained by the Gospel story and the apostolic message, can only mediate this beginning, testifying to the individual Christian that this beginning, Jesus Christ, is the beginning of his life too. It has, therefore, nothing else to offer to him; nothing of its own, whether old or new. The historical existence of the Church is legitimate only in so far as it refrains from giving specific weight to its own possibilities, developments and achievements, from interesting its members in these things and therefore in itself instead of pointing simply to that beginning in direct and exclusive proclamation of

[584]

[EN185] all the more

Jesus Christ. The Christian Church exists only where it attests to its members and the outside world this beginning and nothing but this beginning. Only as it does this is it the "pillar and ground of the truth." It cannot, therefore, build itself on either its antiquity or its renewals. It cannot consolidate its life around its ministry or dogmas, its cultus or orders. It cannot place its confidence on its ministerial succession or on the religious, intellectual and political lustre of the fathers and saints and doctors and leaders with whom it has been blessed, on the certainty of its doctrinal and constitutional tradition, or on the progressive development of its preaching, institutions or activity. Nor can it insert all these things between that beginning and its contemporary present, between Jesus Christ and the men after His time, as though they had a special and independent value and authority and importance by the side of His. It can understand itself and its history in all its forms only as the context of a service which it has to perform. But in this service it is always pointing beyond itself. With all that it is and has and can do, it is always weighed in the balance. Hence it must always be ready to retire gracefully when the higher interests of the beginning to which it owes its existence demand. Only in this way is it the body, the bride, the people of its Lord. It must never forget what it has to proclaim, that the history of Israel and the history of mankind have attained their goal and end in Jesus Christ, and that this goal and this end are now the *prius*[EN186] for every human life. It has to take seriously the fact that the time in which we live *post Christum*[EN187] is the final time, the time when the pendulum is swinging for the last time, and there is no more room for the rise and perpetuation of independent human kingdoms alongside and in competition with the kingdom of God which has come, but all such kingdoms can only prove to be fleeting shadows. This being so, how can it try to found such a kingdom in the name of Jesus Christ? How can it try to present and preserve itself as such? This attempt can be made only in misunderstanding and error. It can lead only to shipwreck. It must always allow itself to be recalled to order by its beginning, to the true order of its service; and it must be full of joy and gratitude when this happens. It must always become small and humble again, and in so doing find its true greatness and glory. Only when this takes place does it mediate to men that search and discovery, and therefore comfort in respect of the Whence? of their existence—the answer that in life and death they may come from the gracious God. It would be an offence not only against God but also against man for it to insert itself between men and this saving beginning of life, as though it were itself the source of comfort.

But if it is not to fall into this sin, it must never forget that, although it is a people, the new Israel, it is not (like the old Israel) a "nation," a natural society linked by race and blood and the sequence of generations, but a people gathered solely by the preaching of the Word and the free election and calling of the Spirit. The first Israel, constituted on the basis of physical descent from Abraham, has fulfilled its mission now that the Saviour of the world has sprung from it and its Messiah has appeared. Its members can only accept this fact with gratitude, and in confirmation of their own deepest election and calling attach themselves to the people of this Saviour, their own King, whose members the Gentiles are now called to be as well. Its mission as a natural community has now run its course and cannot be continued or repeated. For what begins with the rise of the Christian community is not a natural people, a nexus of blood, a succession of generations, a complex of tribes and families and fathers and sons which are as such the bearers and recipients of the promise. Even the individual Israelite is now confronted with a question which is not answered by the mere fact that he is an Israelite, or is circumcised, or has the blessing of the high-priest. Nor is it answered for the proselyte by the mere fact that he has been given proselyte baptism. Even within Israel there

---

[EN186] presupposition
[EN187] after Christ

is a new election and decision, and the summons to a new calling and personal faith. "He came unto his own, and his own received him not. But as many as received him, to them gave he power to become the sons of God, even to them that believe on his name: which were born, not of blood, nor of the will of the flesh, nor of the will of man, but of God" (Jn. 1¹¹f·). It is in this way that the Church is constituted and gathered. This is the question which is put before all men. The fact that woman acquires an independent part in this event illustrates the new situation. And it is for this reason that the Church does not equate baptism with circumcision, but (as in Col. 2¹¹⁻¹²) draws a radical distinction between them. Of course the individual Christian has a father and mother. He, too, is the member of a family, tribe and nation. And it may well be by this natural mediation that he is led to the Church and pointed to his origin and beginning in the grace of God. But this is obviously not necessary. And the fact that he may live in faith and have assurance of faith in the light of that origin and beginning, that he may become a "son of God," is not created for him by his parents, family or nationality. He does not have this privilege either by birth or descent. Indeed, he does not have it through the Church, but from God Himself through the ministry of the Church. In this matter no man can stand proxy for him. No historical nexus can provide or guarantee it. He owes it directly to Jesus Christ Himself. He owes it to the Holy Spirit. His recognition and assurance that he is a "son of God" he owes to his baptism. For through the Holy Spirit, in whom primarily Jesus Christ is active towards him, he comes to faith. And through baptism, in which primarily Jesus Christ is again active towards him, he is given the confirmation and seal that his faith is not arbitrary, but the gift of God's grace, so that it cannot be shaken by any unbelief, superstition or heresy which may assault him, but he can live by his faith and rejoice, whatever may befall him. We may indeed make bold to suggest that in the New Testament community baptism has actually replaced the Old Testament blessing as regards meaning and content. At any rate, as a human ministration it is related to the work of Jesus Christ in the same way as in the Old Testament the human act of blessing is related to the real word of blessing which has its power only from God, and which can therefore be uttered only by God Himself. However that may be, the birth of the Christian life "of water and of the Spirit" (Jn. 3⁵) signifies a direct relationship of the individual Christian to Jesus. He does not follow father and mother or the line of his ancestors, but, taken out of this succession, or at any rate in independence of it, he follows Jesus. He believes that there is one holy catholic Church, and that he may be a living member of the same. Yet he does not believe in the Church, but in the Holy Spirit, who is consubstantial with the Father and the Son. He does not therefore honour and accept the Church's tradition and order in becoming a Christian and confessing himself to be such, but he places himself behind and confesses the beginning which all ecclesiastical tradition and order can only serve, and which he can now recognise and receive as his own beginning. He believes, thinks, speaks and acts therefore, not as the member of a so-called "Christian nation," but in gratitude to the Lord that even in his—in no sense Christian—country He has His community, by and to whose ministry among this people he himself is called.

But a fateful confusion has continually afflicted the Church from its earliest days. It quickly regarded and conducted itself as a kind of continuation, renewal or repetition of pre-Christian Israel. It so easily ceased to understand itself as the community of the last time inaugurated with the death and resurrection of its Lord. It forgot that it comes from the goal of all history. Instead, it understood Jesus Christ, and consequently its own foundation, as the beginning of a new epoch in history. It thus tried to establish, consolidate, assert and propagate itself as one kingdom with others. It was unable or unwilling to honour its Lord in the simplicity which is content to leave Him to speak and act for it, to renounce all striving for its own honour and authority, and therefore to seek nothing for itself. And so it was unable and unwilling to see men in that immediacy or simply to call them to realise that immediacy: "Ye are Christ's; and Christ is God's" (1 Cor. 3²³). Instead, it began to act as if it were a natural community continuing from generation to generation and bound by ties of kith and kin. It identified itself (on the plea of what was later euphemistically described as "Christianisation") with a whole succession of genuinely natural communities and finally with the whole of the West, which came to be thought of as the "Christian West." The freedom of the Holy Spirit, the freedom of the divine election and calling, the freedom in which Christ awakens faith in Himself and in which the Christian Church alone can be constituted, was no longer respected. Nor was the responsibility of entry into the community, of its desire for baptism as the desire of faith for its divine confirmation and sealing. It was thought to be known in advance who would become Christians, members of the Church and members of the body of Christ, i.e., all children who find themselves within the sphere of the Church and are born of ostensibly "Christian" parents. Were not the male children of the Israelites circumcised on the eighth day and thus separated as participants in the covenant? Are the children of Christians to be deprived of a privilege enjoyed in Israel? So the argument ran, forgetting the tiny detail that now that the covenant has been fulfilled by Jesus Christ, it is no longer possible to foresee and arrange and anticipate the divine separation of participants. With the generous inclusion of girls, all children born in a Christian environment were regarded as potential Christians, as though the Church were a natural and historical entity like Israel. And since they could not be asked about their desire for baptism and required to make a profession of faith, they were baptised without making this question and therefore baptism a matter of personal responsibility commensurate with the freedom of the Holy Spirit. They were made Christians by millions in their sleep and over their heads as it were. These millions of baptised could not and cannot now remember their baptism as an event at which they assisted in the responsibility of the personal faith given by Jesus Christ and now confirmed and sealed. For they did not assist at it in this way. This is the fatal outcome in relation to the present discussion. It certainly sounds rather strange, and demands complicated reflection, if in answer to the question of their Whence? we simply refer men to the fact that they are baptised, and are therefore assured that they have received the gift of the Holy Spirit, and thus come directly from Jesus Christ, from His birth, His baptism in the Jordan, His crucifixion and resurrection, and may therefore live as members of His body in calm and cheerful confidence that while their faith may be assaulted it can never be destroyed. This is what baptism does in fact tell us *post Christum*[EN188]. *Post Christum*[EN189] the only answer to our question is in fact to refer to the fact that baptism tells us this. Hence the embarrassment created by our current practice, which if it does not make this reference impossible at least makes it very difficult, curiously emasculating and obscuring what baptism has to tell us. But this questionable practice of infant baptism is in the last resort the expression of a much more deep-seated ignorance that the Christian community of the last time, as distinct from pre-Christian Israel, can upbuild and fashion and maintain itself only under the law of the Spirit, so that while it is not so visibly and tangibly established as the natural and historical nexus of ancient Israel it is grounded directly in God incarnate, and the consolation which the Christian may receive and have in retrospect of the beginning of his existence indicated in baptism is incomparably greater and deeper and surer than it could ever be for the ancient Israelite, although in effect this was the same. But only under the law of the Spirit does this consolation flourish, whereas under the domination of a supposedly Christian law of history competing with the law of the Spirit it can only be distorted. Because of that deep-seated ignorance, we know the consolation to-day almost exclusively in

---

[EN188] after Christ
[EN189] after Christ

[587] a distorted form. Christian faith in the so-called Christian West is rarely a matter of absolute certainty and triumphant joy. And the only hope of breaking through and destroying that deep-seated ignorance lies in a fuller recognition and appreciation of the power of the New Testament answer to the question of our Whence? than *rebus sic stantibus*[EN190] is generally possible to-day.

5. ENDING TIME

Let us now turn our attention to the other aspect of our problem. Time as we are given it is coming to an end. This is the second point settled with the time given to us. We are proceeding towards a point where we shall be no longer. "I go and know not whither." We have already mentioned one reason why the question of our being or non-being as posed by this end of our set span, the question of our Whither?, is in practice much more disquieting than when seen from the first standpoint. It is because our life runs from beginning to end, and not in the reverse direction. Hence when we look ahead it is our end that we see and contemplate, and indeed our approaching end. Our beginning on the other hand lies behind us, receding ever further into the past. Hence the nearer our end approaches, the less does our beginning seem to claim our attention.

There is, however, a more profound reason, though one connected with the fact that our beginning causes us disquiet, if not inevitably, yet certainly in practice. Life desires life; it hungers and thirsts for it; it strives and calls for further life. Life is terrified at every limitation of life. It would fain overcome these limitations, and that as quickly and as thoroughly as possible. Life would fain assert itself against these limitations and renew itself in defiance of them. It is in flight from the non-existence from which it springs. It is constantly reminded of its origin by the limitations it encounters along its path. It reaches its present point from the non-existence in which it originated. It is in a state of transition. It has its present in this transition, but in no present can it find satisfaction. For the present never stays. It can only be passed through, and offers no abiding. Life must therefore repeatedly demand that transition. And being in time, it continually demands a future. And the real disquiet arising from the fact that our existence in time comes to an end consists in the fact that the point will come when, still alive and therefore still involved in that flight from non-existence, still hungering and thirsting after further life, we shall not be able to live any further. For the time we shall then have will be a time with a present (and with our whole past behind us), but with no more future. We shall then have been, and we shall still be. But the transition will now be out of life as it was formerly into life. It will mean that "all is over." The last of the icefloes on which we placed our feet again and again will no longer support us. Our progress and transition will then be our fall. Though we still

---

[EN190] things thus standing

148

are, we shall be no longer; or more precisely, we shall only have been. We shall [588] again be confronted, though now very differently, after our being and not before, by the absolute edge of our existence. The very same question from which we started will face us again, namely, whether this is the edge of the abyss, the abyss of our negation. From the very beginning our life could never answer this question. And now it will face us again. There will then be no doubt that all through our life it had never been answered, and never could have been. This will be the last grim fact which will stare us in the face. We shall die. This, and nothing else, will be the end awaiting us. Whether it be near or far, it is certainly approaching nearer and nearer. "Time departs and death comes." And since death comes and time departs, our attempted flight, however long it lasts, becomes increasingly hopeless. The chances of life are for ever diminishing, and its limitations loom ever larger. Our hopes, expectations and plans become increasingly relative and limited, and their futility ever more apparent. They hasten and we hasten—whether we are unconscious of it or not makes no difference—towards the point of negation, the same point from which all things, ourselves included, derive. When we die, all things and we ourselves come to an end. This is what makes the finitude of the time given us the more critical and incisive form of its limitation. Because our time is finite, our life in time—irrespective of whether we are conscious of it—is in fact a time fraught with anxiety and care. It is overshadowed by death. There thus arises again and with particular urgency the question of the relation of our existence to our non-existence, i.e., whether our non-existence in time may not mean our negation, or in what sense it has any other meaning.

If we are to hear what Holy Scripture has to say concerning the finitude of human life in time and the nature and reality of our death, our best plan (on the following cf. Christoph Barth, *Die Errettung vom Tode*, 1947) is to start with the most general type of insight which the Bible has to offer us on this subject. When, for example, Deut. 30[19] says: "I have set before you life and death, blessing and cursing," it is clear beyond all doubt that there are certain connexions between blessing and life, cursing and death. But this is no proof that death is intrinsically a curse, nor life a blessing. Death is intrinsically the end and limit of human life. It challenges it remorselessly and in its totality. It confronts man as an incomprehensible, inexplicable and unassailable reality. But this means it has about it something of the character of what the Bible calls "heaven." At any rate it serves as a concrete reminder that this earth and man's life upon it are overshadowed and surrounded by an incomprehensible and intangible reality beyond his control. That is why death in the Bible always appears (to man at least) as a strange and in the most concrete sense of the word "uncanny" reality. If it is not for man an intrinsic evil, the question inevitably arises whether it may not be so in fact for some factual reason, just as life, while it is not intrinsically good, stands generally under the promise and command that it may be so.

The saying in Ps. 90[12] is best translated: "So teach us to number our days, that we may attain a heart of wisdom." To "become clever" (Luther) or to "attain a heart of wisdom," whatever other implications it may have, is connected with the necessity of remembering that our days are limited, not unending. And this is to number our days. Whatever existence [589] in death may mean, it cannot consist in a continuation of life in time. One day we shall have had our life. Not even death can throw any doubt upon this. We shall one day have been.

Death cannot alter this fact either. But then we shall only have had our life in time. What we shall then have and be on the far side of our life in time, is what death calls in question. We shall then only have been. What will then become of our being as such when it is one which has only been? This is the question which presses upon us as we contemplate the fact of death. Man desires continuation. That is why he resists the notion of an untimely death in the noonday of life, which would make his life an uncompleted fragment. That is why he prays that he may escape such a death (Is. 38^{10}; Ps. 102$^{24f.}$). But is not long life in itself merely a fragment which cries out for continuation? Death at any rate means being deprived of all prospects for the future. It means being deprived of the capacity of living any longer. Death therefore overshadows even a long and full life. We must die, and according to 2 Sam. 14^{14} this means that we "are as water spilt on the ground, which cannot be gathered up again." "As the cloud is consumed and vanisheth away: so he that goeth down to Sheol shall come up no more. He shall return no more to his house, neither shall his place know him any more" (Job 7$^{9f.}$). "When a few years are come, then I shall go the way whence I shall not return" (Job 16^{22}). To be dead means to be able to live no longer. To be dead means to be deprived of the freedom for true and meaningful action and movement. The Old Testament never questions the possibility of the dead reappearing to the living, and on occasion (e.g., 1 Sam. 28$^{7f.}$) it is even presupposed. But in no sense does this imply that they are still alive or continue to live. In no sense does it alter the fact that the essential thing about life, i.e., the capacity for movement and action, and the possibility of entering into fellowship with the living, has ceased. It is from this society that the dead is snatched away. He is no longer to be found in the "land of the living" (Job 28^{13}). In the land which is now his, he will "not see the Lord, even the Lord in the land of the living": he will "behold man no more with the inhabitants of the world" (Is. 38^{11}). Yet he is not entirely alone even in this other place. For, in so far as he has died and been buried, in the common phrase of the Old Testament he has been "gathered to his fathers" or "to his people." To this extent he is still in a certain indirect relationship to his descendants who are still alive and who still belong to the same tribe. But there is no living fellowship in which he can bear an active part, no fellowship either of the dead among themselves or between the living and the dead. "For there is no work, nor device, nor knowledge, nor wisdom, in the grave, whither thou goest" (Eccles. 9^{10}). The dead exist in a state of utter weakness and helplessness. They are, so to speak, always dying (Is. 14^{10}). This is what is meant when the dead are called *rephaim* (without power). What the living person had and was is now gone; death has brought it to extinction. Gone is his character as a living person, his being as the soul of his body. For the fact that he is dead means that the spirit, the power of the living breath of God which constituted him an existent subject, has been withdrawn. He exists only as one who has been, who is therefore deprived of the Spirit, who has disintegrated, and who is thus incapable of enjoying the good things of life, wellbeing, fortune, security, prosperity and honour. And at least the fear suggests itself that there he will have the very opposite—misfortune and decay, poverty and deprivation. That death can in any way be conducive to man's well-being is utterly out of the question, death being what it is. Man cannot even take with him anything he has acquired here or retrieve it as it were from the debris. "Naked came I out of my mother's womb, and naked shall I return thither" (Job 1^{21}, cf. Eccles. 5^{14}). The custom of offerings for the dead, although it is known in the Old Testament (e.g., Ez. 32^{27}), is never approved or made the subject of discussion. Because of this state of complete deprivation the dead are sad. And they are so decisively

[590] because they are cut off from the help of Yahweh which is promised and given to the living, namely, to the living people of Israel (Ps. 88^6), to the whole life of Israel which is ruled and blessed by Yahweh, and in particular to its life as a worshipping community. "For in death there is no remembrance of thee: in the grave who shall give thee thanks?" (Ps. 6^5). "Shall the dust praise thee? shall it declare thy truth?" (Ps. 30^{9b}). No, "the dead praise not the Lord,

neither any that go down into silence" (Ps. 115^{17}). "For the grave cannot praise thee, death cannot celebrate thee: they that go down into the pit cannot hope for thy truth. The living, the living, he shall praise thee, as I do this day" (Is. 38$^{18f.}$). And conversely: "Shall thy lovingkindness be declared in the grave? Or thy faithfulness in destruction? Shall thy wonders be known in the dark? And the righteousness in the land of forgetfulness?" (Ps. 88$^{11f.}$). If we are to give due weight to all these questions, we must remember that in the Old Testament the world of the living provides the sphere in which Yahweh speaks to His people and deals with them. It is the land occupied and inhabited by Israel in accordance with the promise and as contrasted with the wilderness, and also with Egypt and Babylon. And in particular it is Jerusalem, and most especially the temple, which is the place where God does all this, and therefore where Israel finds the mainspring of life and may thus live. Death has for him, therefore, something of the wilderness about it, something of Egypt and Babylon. This is what makes it all the more sinister. It removes him from that holy place and cuts him off from that mainspring of life. This is what makes the enigma of death so profound. This is why the greatest of all questions is posed to Israel by the fact of death. How is it possible or tolerable? What will be the result of it, of the fact that even the great assurance: "With thee is the well of life" (Ps. 36^{9a}), is made pointless if not fallacious by it? The worst feature of death, which has to be borne but which makes it so bitter, is that we are absolutely precluded from discovering what will be the result of it.

For death does not merely confront man with the limitations of life which he has experienced all along. It is not a partner which in part at least can be known and handled. The menacing feature of all the preceding limitations of life is that they presage this latent and more potent force, death as the power which man cannot hope to know, but which is wholly superior to him. Death is not only a place where man will be, but also a power which holds him in thrall (Ps. 49^{15}). It is a kingdom (Ps. 89^{49}). It is, of course, defined and described in topographical terms in accordance with the various world views of antiquity. But here it is to be observed—and this seems to apply not only to the Old Testament, but also the similar metaphysical speculations of all other peoples—that it is not the particular cosmological and topographical notions which are important here, but the conception of the reality and nature of death itself. The fact that the place of death is conceived as a kind of city or house which is sealed up (Jonah 2^7), or locked with a key (Rev. 1^{18}, 9^1, 20^1), or as a place where men are bound with cords (Ps. 18^5, 116^3), or again in Ps. 94^{17} and 115^{17} as the land of silence, or in Is. 26^{19} as the house of "dust," or in Ps. 88^6 etc. as the realm of "darkness," shows that these are simply pictures which reflect the actual view of death which is being entertained. This is even more true of its localisations, and especially of the fact that the place of death and the realm of the dead is always sought somewhere in the depths, and that it is described as an "underworld" (*Sheol*). It often appears in a remarkable combination of antithesis and unity with heaven as the comprehensive term for that which is "above." With this it makes up the sphere of God's sovereignty (Amos 9^2; Is. 7^{11}; Job 11^8; Ps. 139^8). Properly and primarily, however, it is not in relation to heaven but to earth as the sphere of terrestrial life, or to the surface of the earth as the abode of the living, that it is called the "underworld." It has all the characteristics of the "pit." Into it the dead "descend" or "go down" never to return. It can be called quite simply the "grave" or "pit" Ps. 28^1; Is. 38^{18}, etc.). "In entering the visible world of the grave the dead also become the denizens of the realm of the dead and are subject to the conditions of life obtaining there" (J. Pedersen). The underworld is in an unqualified sense the grave, the "primal pit" (J. Pedersen), of which every individual grave is a manifestation, just as "Israel" or "Moab" is the archetypical Israelite or Moabite respectively, acquiring concrete form in each individual Israelite or Moabite. The terms "grave" and "underworld" evidently mean the individual and total aspect of the one reality of death. But death has not only the "form" of the grave. As the end and terminus of

[591]

151

life it stands in an ominous relation to chaos. Now in the creation story of Gen. 1 chaos is represented in the world which is created, and therefore separated from its earth by the upper and nether ocean. And since the upper ocean, according to Gen. 1[6ff], is separated from the nether, and therefore also from our whole sphere, so that it does not come into account, the place of death is sought as a locality beneath the nether firmament. Hence the floods, the waves which break in from every side, the fathomless deeps and the muddy slime which make residence in the underworld so unpleasant according to so many passages in the Old Testament. Hence, too, the affinity between death and Egypt, or the sea monster Rahab (Is. 30[7], etc.). But the comfortless prolongation of life, the loneliness, dereliction and impotence of man in its sphere, also caused them to identify its location with the wilderness surrounding Babylon and Egypt as well as Canaan. Grave, ocean and wilderness—it would be impossible to harmonise these three most important descriptions of the place of death and the dead. And there is certainly no need to postulate various stages in the development of the whole conception. They are the "three non-worlds" (Pedersen). They manifest and represent and attest death and thus the place of the dead as that which ultimately borders and concludes man's living space. The grave, ocean and wilderness show that it is painfully remote from this living space of ours, being alien and opposed to it in every way. Because they do this, the living Israelite regards them as the place of death, to enter which spells unqualified danger and defilement and a mortal threat. That is why he is always so cautious about such places.

But the Old Testament knows more about the realm of the dead than is indicated by these localisations. For death has and retains not only its own allotted place, but its own dynamic, in virtue of which it invades the areas which properly belong to the world of life. That death is not only an irresistible force but comes as such is a common biblical view. Its kingdom is on the offensive. It has a "hand" which reaches out (Ps. 89[48]). The same is true of the under-world (Ps. 49[15]). The underworld "hath enlarged her desire, and opened her mouth with-out measure: and their glory, and their multitude, and their pomp, and he that rejoiceth with them, descend into it" (Is. 5[14]). "Death ... cannot be satisfied, but gathereth to (itself) all nations, and heapeth unto (itself) all peoples" (Hab. 2[5], cf. Prov. 27[20]). Just as no country can be sure that it will not some day be flooded by the ocean or become a desert, and nature in its regular course is inevitably exposed to decay, so man, and his house and people, are threatened by the victorious onslaughts of the kingdom of the dead. The darkness of death spreads like a shadow "under the sun" (Eccles. 1[3f.]). Even during his lifetime man may find himself in its clutches. Sick, accursed, imprisoned or lonely, he may find himself on its slip-pery slope and under its sentence—a grim picture of the denizens of the underworld and the next-door neighbour of its real and permanent inhabitants. We do not have merely the exaggerations of poetic fantasy, but depictions of real states, in such descriptions of extreme misery, unsurpassed both in quality and quantity as we find in Lamentations and some of the Psalms and above all the Book of Job, whether in relation to the people visited by divine judgment and therefore exposed to this offensive of the realm of the dead, or by individuals in a similar situation. "In the midst of life we are in death." The various descriptions of the different kinds of distress in which men cry aloud to God (e.g., in Ps. 107), the afflictions of those lost in the desert, of the sick, of prisoners, of those in peril on the sea—all these frequently coincide. They are all reduced to the same denomination and set in the same lurid light. All this shows that in the theme of all serious human lamentation we are finally concerned with the same supreme trials and tribulations which cannot be exaggerated, because they call man in his totality in question. Behind them all is the fact that already here and now man can find himself exposed to the onslaughts of the invading realm of the dead. Left alone, he is powerless to face them. The entire Book of Job is a description of such an attack successfully directed against man, though not without the permission and control of

[592]

152

God. It is really with death itself that living man has to deal. All this death means in terms of weakness, decay, loneliness, in short, loss of life; all this makes the grave, the ocean and the wilderness places of death as present here and now in full actuality for the sick, the outcast, the persecuted, defeated and oppressed, the prisoner in his prison, the wanderer in the wilderness, the storm-tossed sea-farer. For although they are not yet actually dead, they already experience the full reality of death. To this context belongs the mirror of old age and final death—a mirror which cannot be too highly commended for its brutal frankness—held before the face of youth in Eccles. 12^{1-8}: "Remember now thy Creator in the days of thy youth, while the evil days come not, nor the years draw nigh, when thou shalt say, I have no pleasure in them; while the sun, or the light, or the moon, or the stars, be not darkened, nor the clouds return after the rain: in the day when the keepers of the house shall tremble, and the strong men shall bow themselves, and the grinders cease because they are few, and those that look out of the windows be darkened, and the doors shall be shut in the street, when the sound of the grinding is low, and he shall rise up at the voice of a bird, and all the daughters of music shall be brought low; also when they shall be afraid of that which is high, and fear shall be in the way, and the almond tree shall flourish, and the grasshopper shall be a burden, and the caperberry shall fail: because man goeth to his long home, and the mourners go about the streets: or ever the silver cord be loosed, or the golden bowl be broken, or the pitcher be broken at the fountain, or the wheel be broken at the cistern; then shall the dust return to the earth as it was, and the spirit shall return unto God who gave it. Vanity of vanities, saith the preacher; all is vanity." And last but not least, the worst thing about death, the really deadly thing about it, is true already here and now, namely, that man can no longer see God, or worship Him, or praise and adore Him. Man is no longer present before God and for Him. He is forsaken by God. God is no longer his Comforter, Helper, Avenger and Saviour. All he can do is to cry and sob helplessly. Where is he then? What has become of God's promises for him as an individual, or for the whole people of God in this present plight? In this context it hardly seems to make sense to boggle at the so-called imprecatory Psalms of the Old Testament. What is man's enemy but a human witness of death's onslaught upon him? And what can man do under its onslaught but beseech God to smite and destroy this witness of death? In close association with man's enemy there are the friends of Job (surprisingly found in other places as well) who misunderstand and desert and turn against him. The whole bitterness of his complaint against the destruction which overtook him in this form is expressed in Ps. $55^{13f.}$: "It was thou, a man mine equal, my guide and mine acquaintance. We took sweet counsel together, and walked unto the house of God in company." With his eye on such friends as these the same Psalmist says immediately after: "Let death seize upon them, and let them go down quick into hell: for wickedness is in their dwellings, and among them." But will God hear him? "Where is thy God" (Ps. 42^{10}). The relevant Old Testament passages in this vein are not to be taken as a kind of final and supreme human achievement. Occasionally to be sure, sometimes very powerfully and sometimes marginally and very quietly, there can burst forth from the depths praise and adoration of God. But this does not mean that man has gone on thinking, and that after all [593] his laments and complaints he comes to the opposite conclusion, that God is present, that He is faithful and gracious, that He will help man, and that He is actually helping him already. How could he come to this opposite conclusion when he is already in the sphere of death? "*Hope* thou in God: for I shall yet praise him," is the final word which the Psalmist can address to his soul, i.e., to himself, even in Ps. $42^{5\ 11}$, 43^5. What lies beyond is the absolute miracle of salvation out of the midst of death, and the proclamation of this miracle. In death as such man has no ability to speak in this way. He does not have the right and power to say: "Nevertheless I am continually with thee" (Ps. 73^{23}). In itself, to be dead is to be unable to live, even to live with God. And the meaning of the tribulation of the people and individuals described in the Old Testament is that it is the tribulation of death, translating man into a depth from which he can never emerge because the way down to it is a one-way street. To be sure, a miracle may still happen. He can still complain to God and inquire of him. This is what makes him different from those who are already dead. He is still only in the territory which death has annexed by its victorious onslaught. He is still only in the territory adjacent to the kingdom of the dead. It may still be said of him that "a living dog is better than a dead lion" (Eccles. 9⁴). He still stands as it were on the very edge of the abyss. There are still many different kinds and degrees of tribulation, varying in intensity in proportion to their proximity to the abyss. The true and final victory of death has not yet come. A man in this type of tribulation is still only in an indirect sense a dead man. All these reservations must be made. Yet we cannot overlook or dispute the fact that already here and now he is assailed by death itself, and therefore in mortal tribulation. Indirectly, he is already a dead man. For what matters is not that he has not yet definitely succumbed to death. What really determines his situation is that death is already so near to him. For this means that its power has already attacked him, that his foot is set "in slippery places." He is on a slippery slope, and as far as mortal eye can see, he cannot stop. And as he looks to his inevitable end, he is already here and now a lost man. To this extent he is "partially," and in a very real sense, already in the realm of the dead.

This, then, is how the Old Testament sees the nature and reality of death. We shall not quote individual New Testament passages to elaborate the picture. In the New Testament death stands wholly under the sign of the divine judgment of sinful man fulfilled in it, and even more so under the sign of the setting aside of this judgment and therefore the defeat of death. We shall have to speak later of these special standpoints from which death is also to be seen. But so far as concerns its nature and reality, the finitude of our time and the inherent limitation of our life, we may simply assume that the Old Testament picture as outlined is accepted in every respect by the Evangelists and apostolic writers (who after all were Israelites), and may thus be presupposed in whatever else they have to say on the topic.

The extraordinarily difficult question which has to be answered in this connexion is whether and how far we have to understand the finitude of our allotted time, and death as the termination of human life, as a determination of the divinely created and therefore good nature of man. How do we stand at the moment? We began with a comprehensive survey of the limitation of our time as such and as a whole. We saw in general terms how right it is to say that our time is bounded and our life correspondingly limited. We then took up the question afresh, paying special attention to the fact that our time has a [594] beginning. This consideration led us to a confirmation of the general positive result. Shall we again find our position confirmed in respect of the end of time? The question of the beginning of our time was serious enough, but not, as we have seen, so urgent. Consequently, we may also say that it was not so very difficult to give it a positive answer. It is quite different with the question which now concerns us. It may at least be asked whether we shall not be left with a certain disquiet even in respect of the positive answer which we gave to the general and all-embracing question. May it not be that the Yes which we worked out there is not quite right after all? What is there there to cause disquiet? Obviously the fact that our answer embraces the second problem as well as the first, and it perhaps seems to be asking too much that we should give this second question a positive answer. An end is set to our time. One day our life will be no more. Death is a reality. But how is this reality compatible with God? How can God be the good Creator of a human nature good in this respect too? Is not this intolerable and from the standpoint of biblical theology untenable? But if so, we must obviously revise and restrict the general result provisionally attained. We must say that our positive answer applied only to the limitation of our time in a backward direction, only to the fact that our life has a beginning. And perhaps even this aspect of our conclusion is shattered and needs to be replaced by a very different one. Perhaps the whole of our previous investigation and presentation hitherto hinges on whether it is possible and right to push forward to a positive answer at this point too, in respect of the end of our time.

But in fact it cannot be disguised that this is just where the shoe pinches. In our attempt to consider the problem of our destiny we cannot avoid certain emphases which do not arise in respect of that of our origin. We have described our being in time as a flight from our non-being from which we come, a flight which is finally destined to be futile if we must ultimately die and again find ourselves confronted by non-being. Is there any other way of seeing and putting it? Obviously this is the only way we know of. But if our life is a flight, and a futile one at that; if it is a story of fear and failure; if it is therefore a twofold terror, how can it be the good creation of God? When we describe it in these terms, do we not speak of something very different from the good creation of God? Have we not spoken of something which on any positive estimation is intolerable and from the standpoint of biblical theology untenable?

Can we accept the Old Testament's designation and description of the nature and reality of death without realising that, above and beyond what may belong to the nature of man, there speaks in it a view of man and judgment on him which are related to the determination of his existence in which he is still under the will of God, but which is not normal, which is definitely abnormal, which was not there originally but is an intrusion from without, which does not square with God's positive will for man but contradicts it, and only so is subject to Him? How else could death be so sinister? How else could it pose to human life such a threat of complete deprivation, even in its relationship to God? How else could it be an underworld described in purely negative terms? How else could it have such dynamic power and force? How else could its kingdom be so overwhelming and tyrannical, overshadowing the whole of human life? [595]

Is it possible to make a single statement about the finitude of our being in time without bringing to light this negative aspect of the matter? And is not all that the Bible itself has to say about the nature and reality of death determined by this negative aspect, which is something for which we have no cause to praise and thank God?

The question is whether it would not be better simply to stop at this negative aspect of the matter. Is not this all that there is to say about it? Is not the finitude of our time, i.e., death, to be regarded as an evil which for reasons best known to Himself God has suspended over us, and to that extent willed, but which does not spring as such from His good creation or belong to human nature, so that it is quite impossible to give any positive answer at this point, and we must deliberately refrain from doing so? Is not the end of our being in time as such an unequivocal negative pronounced over our creaturely existence? Is not this the only way to understand it? Can we therefore find any real place for it in a doctrine of the creature of God?

That is the question which obtrudes upon us here as it could not do in regard to the beginning of our life. In that respect it could acquire significance only at very most in the light of this end. The fact that at a particular moment, at the beginning of our time, we emerged from non-being to being is not intrinsically negative or necessarily evil. It is, indeed, the very opposite. It signifies something supremely positive if it is the case, as we have seen, that we come from God. It can be negative and evil only if our end means passing not only into non-being but into the negation of being. If this is what is meant by the death which is the end of our time, it follows as a consequence that we have also emerged from negation. We are then forced to conclude that our beginning is also negative and evil. At first sight there seems to be no reason why we should draw this conclusion about our beginning. But here, in respect of our end, the whole picture is obviously quite different.

For if death is indisputably a return to non-being, and if this can mean only a return to the same God who called us out of non-being to being, our future prospect is to be seen in a very different light, or rather in a gloomy shadow as compared with our beginning. For between the two termini, the beginning and end of our life as already lived and still to be lived, there stands our life which in accordance with its determination and the freedom we enjoy in it may be lived in a positive relation to God and an equally positive relation to our fellows, but which we have not lived and do not and shall not live in this [596] way but very differently. Between our beginning and our end, between our emergence from God and our final confrontation with Him, there stands the fact of the abysmal and irreparable guilt which we have incurred from the beginning of our existence, are still incurring and will increasingly continue to do so until the end: guilt in relation to God and also to our divinely appointed fellows; guilt of many kinds, great and trivial, gross and refined, blatant and complicated, but always guilt. Guilt means retrogression. And retrogression consists in a failure to use our God-given freedom; in a failure to be truly human in our relationships with Him and our fellows; in an inconceivable renunciation of our freedom; in our incredible, inexplicable and impossible choice of the imprisonment of a being in renunciation on both sides; in our incomprehensible lapse into a state of ungodliness and inhumanity. That we are guilty in this boundless and quite inexcusable way is what will confront us at the end of our time and stare us in the face when we die. It is in this irreparable state of transgression that we shall be translated from being to non-being and brought face to face with our Creator. With all our life up to this point, with our life as it is now concluded and a thing of the past, we shall meet Him and be wholly dependent upon Him. That we shall be no more will mean concretely that our past will be only one of total guilt and retrogression—one long failure. Can we doubt that for this reason death must inevitably seem to be negative and have only the character of an unqualified evil? What else can its onset mean but the approach and execution of God's judgment upon us? What can this judgment mean but our rejection? And what can its execution mean but the ending and expulsion of our unworthy and degenerate life from before the eyes of the Creator from whom it has already alienated itself by its guilt? What can it mean but its total destruction, dissolution and abolition in confirmation of what it has made of itself? What fate can measure up to life's deserts, and what can its goal be, but absolute negation? Was it not a thing of nought? What has it to expect from its end but the divine subscription to its nothingness? As we approach our end, we approach God. And since we are guilty in relation to Him as our Creator, this excludes any other prospect. Not to be any more is to be powerless to alter the fact. To die is to be caught in the toils of this unalterable fact. It is to be at the point to which we fall. And because even now we are powerless to alter it—and the less so the longer we live—our life is already overshadowed by its end. Hence Holy Scripture is right in describing the realm of death not only as an underworld but as an onslaught to which man's life in time is already exposed.

Death, as it actually encounters us men, is the sign of God's judgment on us. We cannot say less than this, but of course we must not try to say more either.

That this judgment is executed as we die, that when our life comes to its end we shall have to pay what it is worth, or not worth, with the fulfilment of our rejection, our plunge into negation and then, if we may use the phrase, our being in negation, in outer darkness, in the eternal torment of a past and non-recurrent opportunity, this cannot be posited as a general truth. For there is a possibility of our being spared this death because Another has suffered it in His death for us. The New Testament assumes that this is in fact the case. [597]

But it can and must be said generally that death as it actually meets us is the sign of this judgment. In other words, it is its supremely real and full proclamation and representation. Limiting our life and thus belonging to it, it bears all the marks of this judgment. Our life as bounded by it is thus necessarily a life marked for this judgment (like a tree marked for felling). It is devoted and delivered to this judgment, like a bracket with a minus before it which changes every plus in the bracket into a minus. The bracket is still there, but the minus stands in front of it cancelling every other prospect but this fatal change. The inevitability of death means that this threat overshadows and dominates our whole life. It cannot be gainsaid or defied. It might well be, indeed it is necessarily the case, that the ultimate truth about man, which dominates every prior truth, is that he stands under this threat which is not to be gainsaid or defied. Less than this we cannot say. Death, as it meets us, can be understood only as a sign of God's judgment. For when it meets us, as it undoubtedly does, it meets us as sinful and guilty men with whom God cannot finally do anything but whom He can only regret having made. For man has failed as His creature. He has not used the previous freedom in which he was privileged to exist before God. He has squandered it away in the most incredible manner. He can hope for nothing better than to be hewn down and cast into the fire.

Of death as it actually meets us we certainly cannot say that it is an inherent part of human nature as God created it and as it is therefore good. There is no doubt whatever that it is something negative and evil. Yet we have to realise and state that it is an evil ordained by God as a sign of His judgment, and not therefore a fate but an ordinance which proceeds and is to be accepted from God. And because it is our sin and guilt which God encounters with this sign, we have also to realise and state that when we stand under this sign it is our just desert, so that we have no reason to complain or protest. But our standing under this sign is not something intrinsic to our human nature. For God did not create us to exist under this impending threat of being hewn down and cast into the fire. It does not correspond to our determination to have no other prospect but a being in outer darkness and eternal torment.

We cannot talk ourselves out of it, or persuade ourselves that that is not really our plight. It is so, even though we may wish things were different. And we really know this. There has never been a man who was not afraid of death. It
[598] is possible to stifle this fear. But in so doing, we only show that we have it none the less. Man lives in fear for his life. But this fear in all its forms, even that of Stoic resignation, is basically the fear of death which we cannot talk ourselves out of.

Again, we cannot persuade ourselves that death as the sign of divine judgment standing over us, the fear of death and a life spent in fear of death, is natural, normal and good in the sense of being a positive ordinance of God. If there is anything natural about it; if it belongs in any sense to man's divinely appointed creaturely status that his time should have an end; if death is not intrinsically and essentially a curse and a misery, then its intrinsic and essential quality is for us at any rate unfathomably and inaccessibly concealed beneath the unnatural and even anti-natural guise in which it now comes to us. In any case, there is no question of our being able to change the meaning of the judgment symbolised by death into something different. We should have to forget our sin and guilt if we were to persuade ourselves that death is after all not so dangerous as all that, and even a cheerful and welcome prospect. The man who fears death, even though he contrives to put a somewhat better face on it, is at least nearer to the truth than the man who does not fear it, or rather pretends that there is no reason why he should do so. Since it is the sign of the divine judgment on human sin and guilt, it is very much to be feared. There is no truth in the suggestion that death is our "brother," or in some way our friend, or even our deliverer. Such turns of expression simply fail to face up seriously to the grim reality, and will only vanish like bubbles in the air. The natural being of man resists his end—perhaps not necessarily his end as such, but at any rate the kind of end we have before our eyes as we contemplate our sin and guilt. And he is right, even though his resistence is futile and the shears of death show no mercy. It is never the natural being of man, but always man deceived and doubly deluded who speaks of death's reaper as though it were a kindly angel of light. Since death is the sign of divine judgment, man as he naturally is can face it only with sorrow. If we are to tackle honestly the question of the meaning of the finitude of our time, this is the first thing to see and accept. The whole situation is in fact very different from what it is when we ask concerning the meaning of its beginning.

In biblical demonstration of what has been said, we can first point only to the wholly negative character which the Old Testament gives to its picture of the nature and reality of death. In the perspective of the Old Testament, what is natural to man is his endowment with the life-giving breath of God which constitutes him as the soul of his body, not his subsequent loss of it. What is natural to him is the fact that he is and will be, not that he has been. What is natural to him is his being in the land of the living, not his being in the underworld. What is natural to him is life, not death. Death, on the other hand, is the epitome of what is contrary to nature. It is not, therefore, normal. It is always a kind of culpable extravagance to man when he longs for death, like Elijah under the juniper tree (1 K. 19⁴) or Jonah under the gourd (Jonah 4⁸). It is only hypothetically that Job protests to God: "So that my soul chooseth strangling, and death rather than my bones. I loathe my life; I would not live alway" (Job 7¹⁵ᶠ·). In extreme situations a man may curse the day of his birth (Jer. 15¹⁰; 20¹⁴ᶠ·; Job 3³ᶠ·). But he cannot rejoice at his death, or seriously welcome it. It is an exception which proves the rule when Job 3²¹ᶠ speaks of those who "long for death, but it cometh not; and dig for it more than for hid treasures; which rejoice exceedingly, and are glad, when they find the grave," or when reflection about all the injustice that there is under the sun culminates (Eccles. 4²) in the statement: "I praised the dead which are already dead more than the living which are yet alive." Hyperbolic statements of this kind do not mean that death is naturalised or neutralised or made into something heroic. When Saul (1 Sam. 31⁴) falls upon his own sword, or when in later days Judas (Mt. 27⁵) goes and hangs himself, these are deeds of despair which demonstrate their rejection by God and prove that death is the supreme evil of human life.

But it is the New Testament which is most direct and explicit on the point that death is the sign of God's judgment, and therefore the supreme evil. In the Old Testament this interconnexion of sin, guilt and death is asserted only as it were in specific cases, i.e., in relation to the end of particular ungodly men or in prospect of the wholesale destruction threatened against and in large measure fulfilled upon Israel and other nations. There are also particular sins and transgressions whose perpetrators must "die the death" according to the Law or by a special decree. Above all it is worth noting that a direct encounter with Yahweh is regarded as an experience which results in immediate death. "Thou canst not see my face: for there shall no man see me and live" (Ex. 33²⁰; Jud. 13²²). The story of the call of Moses includes the remarkable story of how Yahweh sought to kill him, so that he enters his office only as one who has escaped the ultimate crisis (Ex. 4²⁴ᶠ·). Intercourse with Yahweh's holiness is at the very least a threat to life, and in certain cases can actually bring death. This is taught in 1 Sam. 5–6 by the story of the fortunes of the ark among the Philistines and its subsequent restoration, and in 2 Sam 6¹ᶠ by the account of its removal to Jerusalem. From such passages it would perhaps be possible to draw the general conclusion that death is the immediate result when man is confronted with the holy God before whom he is unclean and unholy and cannot stand upright. This is an encounter which man cannot survive, because the life-giving breath of God can only be taken away from him again now that he has proved

[599]

unworthy of Him. But this truth is never stated in general terms. The only direct statement which suggests that death is to be understood generally as the effect of the divine curse and as a punishment is in the threat uttered in Paradise (Gen. 2^{17}), and its confirmation in Gen. 3^{19} and 6^3. From the rest of the Old Testament the only general conclusion to be drawn is that, not merely when it actually comes, but in its total significance for a man's preceding life, death is a great woe which God suspends over him, and which he can only bear in submission and sadness. Its character as such emerges very clearly. But the Old Testament gives us only occasional hints as to why it is a woe.

We are shown this very vividly when we turn to the New Testament. Here the line is drawn with unequivocal clarity even in the Gospels. For Jesus, at least during His Galilean ministry, was from the very outset engaged in open combat with suffering and sickness in all its forms. Now that the Messiah has come, the immediate and inevitable result is an onslaught against the invasion of the realm of death in the world of life. Note that for Jesus even sickness is not a natural but an unnatural evil. It is an outbreak and effect of the demonic world, which, while it operates with divine permission, functions exclusively in opposition to God. In other words, the divine permission is only provisional. It would therefore be utterly nonsensical to try to translate the relevant statements on this subject into the relatively harmless language of modern medicine. When the Gospels discern the work of demons in sickness, this is not merely the expression of contemporary beliefs, but a fact of theological significance. The Messiah is the Representative of the positive will of God who engages the advance posts of the underworld (i.e., demons) in victorious combat. In His environment the blind necessarily see, the lame walk, the deaf hear, the dead are raised, and the Gospel is preached to the poor, i.e., the oppressed of the Old Testament Psalms. Surely this can only mean that the signs of divine grace and assistance are provisionally set up against the sign of divine judgment. All the miracles of Jesus, including the stilling of the storm (the reader will recall the connexion between the ocean and the underworld!) and the feeding of the multitude (which significantly takes place in the wilderness), are countersigns of this nature. God will not chide for ever. He will not always allow death, which has broken loose, to run its course. This power of death is already unmasked by the countersign of Jesus' miracles as a power which is opposed to God, as God is opposed to it. No wonder it is the demons who first recognise who Jesus is, and address Him as such (Mk. 1^{23}, 5^7).

[600]

In Jerusalem He performed no such healings. For the Galilean healings and those on the way to Jerusalem were only preliminary skirmishes. In Jerusalem He Himself died—paradoxically enough, as those who mocked Him on the cross (Mk. $15^{29f.}$) quite rightly observed. Yet the dying of Jesus is the decisive event, the climax of the whole drama, of which the miracles are only a preliminary announcement. The only point which has now to be stressed about the significance of this event is that by undergoing death in His person Jesus provided a total and conclusive revelation of its character. For He suffered death as the judgment of God. It would be out of place to say here that He did so as the sign of God's judgment. Here, in the person of the Messiah, it is God Himself, His embodied grace and help, who is genuinely and definitively present, both as Judge and Judged. He judges as He created and established between Himself and man the justice which had to fall on man, so that he had to suffer what he had deserved—death as a consuming force, eternal torment and utter darkness. But He is also judged as, knowing neither sin nor guilt, He caused this judgment to fall on Himself in place of the many guilty sinners, so that it availed for them all, and the judgment suffered by Him was fulfilled on them in Him, and their dying no longer has to be this dying, the suffering of punishment which they have deserved, but only its sign. What death is remorselessly as it encounters us is revealed in this act of judgment. At this point we cannot possibly fail to see that it hangs over us like a threat, and what it threatens us with. It is the enemy, the "last enemy" (1 Cor. 15^{36}), of man, whom God, in the death of Jesus, declares to be His enemy as well, and treats as such by placing Himself at the side of man in the verdict there pronounced, and snatching man from its jaws by the death of Jesus for him. It remains for us as a sign of the divine judgment. We have no longer to suffer the judgment itself.

But it is still the case that we have to suffer when we die. We have still to do with this sign, and therefore with the threats of the enemy. The New Testament faces up to this insight at its centre and therefore with full seriousness. Our death is intimately connected with our sin and guilt. This can no longer be disregarded when we remember that man's sin is forgiven, that his guilt is cancelled, that the judgment of God has been executed upon it, and that it has thus been removed from us. As man's eternal corruption, but also as its sign, death is not a part of man's nature as God created it. But it entered into the world through sin as an alien lord (Rom. $5^{12\ 14\ 17}$; 1 Cor. 15^{22}). It is the wages of sin (Rom. 6^{23}), just as sin, conversely, is its "sting, i.e., that which makes the suffering of death so bitter and poisonous, constituting it an evil for man (1 Cor. 15^{56}). According to Heb. 2^{14} the power over it which gives it its might is that of the $\delta\iota\acute{\alpha}\beta o\lambda os$ EN191. It is with his kingdom that we have to reckon in death, and quite directly. Death is the $\phi\rho\acute{o}\nu\eta\mu\alpha\ \tau\hat{\eta}s\ \sigma\alpha\rho\kappa\acute{o}s$ EN192, as Rom. 8^6 says so fittingly. This means that [601] death is really the objective goal of carnal, i.e., sinful and guilty and therefore lost man, not life as he imagines. What this man thinks and does is futile, and can only issue in futility. "Sin ... bringeth forth death" (Jas. 1^{15}). "If ye live after the flesh, ye must die" (Rom. 8^{13}). "He that soweth to his flesh shall of the flesh reap $\phi\theta o\rho\acute{\alpha}$ EN193" (Gal. 6^8). Living according to the deceitful lusts, the old man is *ipso facto* EN194 in decay ($\phi\theta\epsilon\iota\rho\acute{o}\mu\epsilon\nu os$, Eph. 4^{22}). "Sin revived, and I died" (Rom. $7^{9f.}$). "He that loveth not abideth in death" (1 Jn. 3^{14}). When Lk. 1^{79} describes the men of Israel as those who "sit in darkness and in the shadow of death," and Heb. 2^{15} speaks of all men before Christ as those who" through fear of death were all their lifetime subject to bondage, "this is still, as it were, Old Testament language, and falls short of the true New Testament insight, which sees that before and apart from what God has done for him in Jesus Christ man is dead even while he lives (Mt. 8^{22}; Lk. 15^{32}; Eph. 2^1; 1 Tim. 5^6), and that his works are "dead" works (Heb. 9^{14}). In the light of this new insight Rev. 3^1 can even say of a whole Christian congregation: "Thou hast a name that thou livest, and thou art dead." It is also to be understood as a superimposition of Old Testament thought upon the insight and language of the New Testament when in Ac. $1^{17f.}$ (Judas) and $5^{1f.}$ (Ananias and Sapphira) particular sins are specially punished with death, or when in Rom. 1^{32} a catalogue of vices closes with a reference to the divine $\delta\iota\kappa\alpha\acute{\iota}\omega\mu\alpha$ EN195 according to which "they which commit such things are worthy of death," or when in 1 Cor. 11^{30} certain specific fatal instances of sickness and infirmity in the Corinthian Church are linked with the unworthy reception of the Lord's Supper. The general understanding of death as the fruit of sin naturally involves such particular applications and can lead to occasional emphasis on them. Yet according to the insight and language of the New Testament, as Rom. 5^{12} makes particularly clear, the connexion between sin and death is not conditioned by particular sins, but is necessary and general. Every man dies (and lives already) in this involvement. Every man is liable to death and moves towards it. Every man stands under the sign of the merited judgment of God. It is obvious that the estimation of death as a purely natural phenomenon, or as a friendly or at least conceivably neutral fate, is not only conspicuous by its absence, but basically alien. Death is the great mark of the unnatural state in which we exist. And it is this, not because of a chance fate, but because we exist under the thrall of the devil. It is this

---

EN191 devil
EN192 flesh's way of thinking
EN193 corruption
EN194 for that very reason
EN195 judgement

because we are sinners involved in guilt. It is this because our behaviour makes our life *eo ipso*[EN196] a forfeited life given over to death. As we said above, it is the centre of the New Testament perception which makes this particular perspective and language necessary. The centre of the New Testament perception is the cross of Jesus Christ. It is not because the apostles and the earliest Christian Church were for some reason more deeply shocked at death than their Israelite and Hellenistic contemporaries, nor is it because for some reason they took sin more seriously than their contemporaries, that they were so unanimously agreed in seeing death and sin in that strict, general and necessary connexion, and so unequivocal in all that they said on the subject. The reason for their unequivocal unanimity is that they could contemplate it only from the point where they saw man's deliverance accomplished, and life, salvation and felicity offered in ineffable fulness. They were not pessimists, whether in their view of the sinful life of man or in that of the nature and reality of death. But they were realists in their view of what had happened in the crucifixion and death of Jesus Christ and its accompanying revelation in respect of the death of all men. For three decisions were openly declared and given universal validity in this event.

The first is that there is no human greatness and grandeur which is not exceeded, over-shadowed and fundamentally called in question by death: not even that of the promised and manifested Messiah and Son of Man; not even that of the incarnate Son of God and the great Servant of God. When the divine Logos became flesh, this meant that in so doing He deliv-

[602]

ered Himself wholly and utterly to φθορά[EN197]. "Be it far from thee. Lord: this shall never be unto thee" (Mt. 16²²), is Peter's reaction to the first prediction of the passion. And the Evangelist frankly calls this reaction an ἐπιτιμᾶν[EN198]. It was indeed strange that immediately after the first Messianic confession and Jesus' joyful acceptance of it there should follow the prediction that Jesus must go to Jerusalem to be killed. It was strange that He who had done so much to save others from death should face and actually come to the situation of being unable to save Himself from death (Mk. 15³¹). It was strange that death should be permitted to achieve this masterstroke by which all the signs erected against the onslaught of the realm of death, and with them the One who had erected them, were to be wholly called in question again. What was meant by the promised constancy of the Church against the "gates of hell" (Mt. 16¹⁸) if He who gave this promise was Himself obliged to submit to this sphere? The whole terror of this paradox is reflected in the saying of the disciples on the road to Emmaus in Lk. 24²¹: "We trusted that it had been he which should have redeemed Israel; and beside all this, to-day is the third day since these things were done." But it was no use complaining or lamenting. It had to happen, and it was right that it should do so. The life of the man Jesus is included in this bracket. His mission as Messiah and Son of Man is fulfilled along the lines of Is. 53. There is no question of His by-passing death and the grave. He has to tread this road to the bitter end. He is as helpless in face of death as any other man. Nor would he be the Son of God—of a God friendly to man—if he were not "obedient even unto death" (Phil. 2⁸). When Peter rebukes him on this point, he has to endure the shame of being called "Satan" and "offence." He does not think in divine but in human terms (Mt. 16²³). Death must show what it can do on Him supremely, as in a masterpiece. No place must be left for foolish dreams, as though everything were bound to come right in the end. Deliverance from death cannot be deliverance from before it but only deliverance from out of it. Even the power and significance of those countersigns depends on His not refusing to drink this cup (Mt. 26³⁹ᶠ). They would not be countersigns, the preliminary signs of His resurrection and the resurrection of all the dead, but only the unimportant acts of a skilled wonder

---

[EN196] in itself
[EN197] corruption
[EN198] rebuke

worker like many others, if Jesus had refused this course. As the One He is, He must submit to being baptised with a baptism from which He shrinks with fear like any other man, or even more so (for a reason to be indicated in a moment, Lk. 12[50]). For the reality to which He pointed with these countersigns would not be real, that counter-offensive against the onslaught of the realm of death would have been powerless, the fire which He came to kindle on earth would have remained unkindled (Lk. 12[49]), if He had shrunk from this baptism and had not defied death in the realm of the dead by submitting to it as a willing victim. But this seals the fact that it is not merely *de facto*[EN199] but *de jure*[EN200] and therefore necessarily and universally that death has power over man. Even on the shattering view of the Old Testament it has this power only *de facto*[EN201]. Men see and know it only as the grave and underworld which awaits us all. It is the New Testament which tells us that this has to be, and it does so by proclaiming Him who was crucified, dead and buried as the Lord of life.

The second decision is that the death to which we all move implies the threat of eternal corruption. As Jesus suffered it, He suffered *eternal* corruption. This is what distinguishes His death from all others. "He was made a curse for us" (Gal. 3[13]). This cannot be said of every one who is hanged or who dies in any other way. But of Him it must be said. It may surprise us that the ideas of man's being in death are not mitigated or even displaced in the New Testament as compared with the Old. We might have expected this now that the "glad tidings" are proclaimed. But in fact they are accentuated as never before. Instead of the negative picture of a shadowy existence of departed "souls," we now have a picture of human existence in "hell." Hell means punishment of a very positive kind. We can only be disappointed if we foolishly expect the New Testament to be more "human" in this respect than the Old. It is the New Testament which first gives us a picture like that of Dives, who in the realm of the dead is in "anguish in this flame" (Lk. 16[24f.]). It is in the New Testament that we first hear of men being cast out into outer darkness where "there shall be weeping and gnashing of teeth" (Mt. 22[13]). It is here that we first read of the "worm which dieth not, and the fire which is not quenched" (Mk. 9[48]). It is here that we first have threats like those of Rev. 14[11]: "And the smoke of their torment ascended up for ever and ever; and they have no rest day nor night, who worship the beast and his image." Is not all this far worse than the imprecatory Psalms which come in for so much censure? It is true, of course, that partly under Persian influences the speculations of later Judaism about life beyond the grave have intensified this picture. But this does not really answer the question how the Church of Jesus Christ came to appropriate these intensified conceptions. If this surprising procedure meant anything at all, it could only mean that, irrespective of detail, in the sphere of the revelation and experience of the divine kingdom, grace and salvation, they were precluded from understanding man's existence in death merely as an existence in unwelcome but tolerable neutrality. On the contrary, they had to understand it positively as intolerable suffering. And they had to do this because it was only in this way that they could understand the being of Jesus in death. This was the unique cup which made Jesus shrink back in fear. This was the unique baptism of which He was afraid. He did not submit to a blind fate or chance, but to the judgment of God. In dying, He did not merely surrender Himself to that alienation from God which, as we learn from the Old Testament, is the climax of what man has to suffer as one whose life is over. He did this too, of course, as attested by the word on the cross: "My God, my God, why hast thou forsaken me" (Mk. 15[34]). It is no accident that this saying has come down to us in Aramaic and is a direct quotation of Ps. 22[1]. But the last "loud cry" with which Jesus died (Mk. 15[37]), and above all the representative character proper to

[603]

EN199 as a matter of fact
EN200 as a matter of right
EN201 as a matter of fact

this death, His vicarious bearing of the sin of all Israel and indeed the whole world, points beyond the comfortless but tolerable situation of the righteous man of the Old Testament as alienated from God in *Sheol*. In this respect the Old Testament comes close to the New only in those passages which speak of the deadly significance and effect of the direct encounter between man and the living God. Here is the direct encounter there conceived only as a remote possibility. Here we see that it is indeed a fearful thing to fall into the hands of the living God (Heb. 10³¹). Here man—the man who is wholly and unreservedly for God—has God against him. Here God is wholly and unreservedly and in full seriousness against man. Here God metes out to man the kind of treatment he has deserved at His hand. This is how He must deal with him now in His mercy, which is "righteous" to the extent that in it He wills to establish His own right and that of man. Here He treats man as a transgressor with whom He can only deal in His wrath. Here He treats him in accordance with the enmity which man has merited from Him. Here, namely, in this One whom He has destined and appointed the Head of all who are descended from Abraham and indeed from Adam, the realm of the dead loses the last traces of creaturely naturalness which still cling to it in the Old Testament perspective. Here it becomes "hell." Here the alienation from God becomes an annihilatingly painful existence in opposition to Him. Here being in death becomes punishment, torment, outer darkness, the worm, the flame—all eternal as God Himself, as God Himself in this antithesis, and all positively painful because the antithesis in which God here acts cannot be a natural confrontation, but must inevitably consist in the fact that infinite suffering is imposed upon the creature which God created and destined for Himself, when God reacted against this creature as it deserves. It is, of course, true that this man is the Son of God. In Him God Himself suffers what guilty man had to suffer by way of eternal punish-

[604] ment. This alone gives the suffering of this man its representative power. This is what makes it the power by which the world is reconciled to God." God was in Christ reconciling the world unto himself " (2 Cor. 5¹⁹). But it is the Son of God, this man, who in His death as the Representative of all men, as the revelation of what was due to them, endured this suffering, and bore this punishment. And it is this character, this quality of human death as eternal punishment, which the Church of Jesus Christ contemplates in His crucifixion. This is why the New Testament thinks and speaks so much more harshly of man's being in death than does the Old.

The third point is that death is the goal which is the appropriate reward for the life of man as it is actually lived. The warning has already been issued that the New Testament does not speak so harshly about man and his desires, so slightingly about his best possibilities and works, so remorselessly about his relation to God and what he may expect from Him, because the men of the New Testament found reason to abandon an optimistic or at least neutral view of life and to arrive at a pessimistic view. Man's estimate of his life usually oscillates between one extreme and the other when it is measured and evaluated by a norm, standard or law, and then thought to be just or unjust as the case may be. The whole issue at stake in the great struggle of Paul in the apostolic age was that the Old Testament Law must *not* play this part in the Church of Jesus Christ and its preaching. It is, of course, one of the most painful enigmas of Church history that the meaning of this struggle was forgotten as early as the 2nd century, and that only relatively seldom has it been rediscovered and put to profitable use. Yet it should have been obvious that this was not just a special concern of Paul's, but the general concern of the New Testament as a whole. It was the genuine Christian insight on the subject. The New Testament judgment upon the sinfulness of human life and its deserving of death reaches its highest accentuation in the Pauline Epistles: "For all have sinned, and come short of the glory of God" (Rom. 3²³). But this is not because Paul and the other New Testament witnesses viewed man from the standpoint of the Israelite *nomos*[EN202], placing him under that standard and measuring him by it. We are not to imagine that it was the Law which caused Paul when he was still Saul the persecutor to fall to the ground on the road to Damascus, convincing him that he was on the road to ruin. Nor are we to suppose that when he said: "By the law is the knowledge of sin" (Rom. 3^{20}, cf. 4^{15}, 7^7), he was seeking to ascribe to this instrument the inherent capacity to convince man of his perverse and lost condition in the very serious sense in which Paul understood it. Nor are we to suppose that his realisation that Christ is the end of the Law (Rom. 10^4) is irrelevant when we are trying to put man in his place in relation to Christ. Nor are we to imagine that the saying: "God will judge the world in righteousness by that man whom he hath ordained" (Ac. 17^{31}), or the saying that God will judge the hidden things of man by Jesus Christ (Rom. 2^{16}; 1 Cor. 4^5), or the saying: "We must all appear before the judgment seat of Christ" (2 Cor. 5^{10}; cf. Eph. 6^8), or the parables in Mt. 25 (in all of which it is Jesus who is the Judge), apply only to the eschatological end and are not yet in force, so that it is now necessary to pronounce judgment upon man according to very different criteria. The truth is that no law, not even the Law of Moses, can judge a man as the New Testament judges him. No law can say that his life is perverted, so perverted, and so devoid of glory in the sight of God, that death is the only reward it deserves. This is just what even the most zealous Pharisees, and Paul in his Pharisaic stage, could not learn from the Law. But in the light of the crucifixion of Jesus Christ this is just what can be learnt, so radical an expression is it, both in intensity and extent, of the New Testament judgment upon man. The crucifixion of Jesus Christ is the revelation of what it cost to restore the right of God and man which man had disrupted. It shows what that disruption implied. It shows how great was the remissness, and what was its inevitable consequence. This restoration, man's salvation, cost no more and no less than the self-oblation of the incarnate Son of God. It cost His death under the wrath of God, with its quality of eternal punishment. Its cost was that the man Jesus, He, the Son of God, He and no other, He who had not deserved it, should die under this determination as the enemy of God. God was merciful in Him in the fact that He assumed this self-oblation and did not shrink from eternal death. This is the standard by which the New Testament judgment on man is made. This is only norm by which we can know what to think about man, namely, about what he does and fails to do, what he is and is not in disruption of the right of God and man, and therefore as the one who can be helped only by the judgment executed in this self-oblation. The New Testament sees man from a standpoint from which he is helped. That is why the New Testament thinks and speaks of his guilt and punishment in such a radical way. It does not see man in the abstract, in the light of some norm which he ought to have satisfied. It sees him in the person of One who championed his cause and died for him. And in this One it sees both the sin of man which Jesus took upon Himself and for the sake of which He endured the wrath of God, and the death of man which He suffered in his place as the eternal punishment which is the just lot of the enemies of God. It is just because the New Testament sees and understands man in this light that it cannot oscillate between optimistic, neutral and pessimistic opinions about him. It is for this reason that it sees and understands his way and destiny in the severe, remorseless, uncompromising and unsentimental objectivity with which alone it can be seen and understood with mercy. No judgment pronounced in the light of the Law can be merciful. Such judgments give him no real help, whether severe or lenient. On the contrary, such judgments usually harden him, leaving him indifferent or defiant as he was before. Since the New Testament judgment on man derives from the mercy and help already given to him, it is itself *eo ipso*[EN203] merciful and helpful. It measures man by

[605]

EN202 law
EN203 in itself

what God has done for him, by what Jesus Christ has accomplished in his place for his justification and deliverance from this burden, for his peace and salvation. On the basis of the accomplished restoration of the right of God and his own right it tells him that he is in the wrong and therefore under threat of perdition. It accuses him by showing him that all the charges against him have been dropped. It threatens him by showing him that he is out of danger. No Pharisee or moralist can accuse him as soberly and straightforwardly and totally and comprehensively as this. No existentialist with his teaching about the fallenness of human existence, no imaginative poet singing of the temporal and eternal inferno which he deserves, can terrify him as much as this. All such preaching of repentance and judgment lacks the profound Yes of God which underlies the No and which gives it strength and makes it the really powerful No which man must hear in respect of his way and final destiny. The No uttered by preachers of the Law, including Heidegger and Sartre, is always too human a No. The No of the New Testament, which declares that human life deserves death and meets in death its due, is distinguished from every human No which superficially may look very similar, and perhaps even stronger, by the fact that there is no escaping it once it is pronounced and really apprehended.

This, then, is how the New Testament sees human death in the light of its centre. The centre of this insight is God's judgment accomplished in the crucifixion of Jesus Christ. No other man stands at this centre, and therefore no other really stands under the judgment of God. Other men, Christians consciously and the rest unconsciously, find themselves somewhere on the periphery around this centre, and therefore—for we must now take up this concept—under the sign of this judgment. The threat posed by death, the infinite peril which confronts man through death as the wages of his sin, the assault of the undeniable fact that his way is one which can lead only to eternal punishment—all this is the inevitable lot of those who stand on the periphery around this centre. It is to be noted that the Evangelists and apostles spoke not only of the unbelieving Jews and Gentiles, but also to the Christian communities and all their members, under the unvarying assumption that the threat, peril and assault which proceed from the judgment of God are the lot of all men. On the contrary, those who in the New Testament are always exhorted, warned, reproved and challenged with such urgency to remember this sign, to fear death as the judgment of God, are those who have heard and recognised and apprehended the fact that this judgment made at the centre, in Jesus Christ, has already been accomplished for them, and that they are therefore graciously preserved from the execution of that threat, from the actual irruption of that danger, from succumbing to that assault. Those who know that they are preserved cannot forget, but genuinely to be preserved must always keep before their eyes what it is they have been preserved from. But faith in the free grace of God in Jesus Christ consists in holding fast to Him as our Representative, as the Son of God who has given Himself for us (Gal. 2[20]). This faith is obviously not the end but the beginning of the fear of God. It does not mean going to sleep on comfortable cushions, but always waking and rising up anew. To wake and rise up in the fear of God, however, is to be constantly aware that the man who finds himself on that periphery is freed from the judgment of God only to the extent that the circle has that centre; only to the extent that in Jesus Christ there has been accomplished for him his necessary justification and remission. If this were not so; if he could not hold fast to this; if he could not live as a man sustained by that centre, to what then could he hold? And what could hold him? The judgment of God would have to be executed upon him. In himself man is after all a sinner who has deserved wrath, and he will never be anything else. The crucifixion of Christ teaches him that so far as he himself is concerned there is no height to which he can climb or depth to which he can sink where he will not be found by death as eternal and merited punishment. In himself he is not freed at all from the judgment of God. He never can and never will escape it. In himself, according to the New Testament insight, he is irre-

[606]

trievably fallen. But in Jesus Christ and Him alone, not in any depth of being or height of achievement, he is preserved from this execution of judgment on him with the severity with which it was executed at the cross. This is the only refuge to which he can flee to escape this judgment. Otherwise it awaits him in death, and in his life as it moves inexorably to death. And to flee to this, to flee to Calvary, or, as Rom. 6³ᶠ· entitles us to say without qualification, to baptism, is the meaning of this waking and rising in the fear of God. This is what differentiates Christian faith from a dangerous self-complacency. This is what differentiates it decisively from the mask of a trust in God which does not deserve the name.

In the light of these considerations we can understand the peculiar impetus of the mission to Jews and Gentiles which is so characteristic of New Testament Christianity, and particularly of the apostle Paul, and which makes it so different from later versions of Christianity. Just as the New Testament Christians understood and saw that in themselves they were condemned, but justified and released in the crucifixion of Jesus Christ, that in themselves they stood wholly under its threat but were preserved from its execution in Him, that in themselves they were in the storm of irresistible assault—"In the midst of life we are in death; of whom may we seek for succour, but of thee, O Lord?"—they naturally applied this all the more to their Jewish and Gentile neighbours who were still blissfully unaware of their plight. They knew all about that centre, and therefore that they stood on its periphery. They knew about the judgment of God executed there, and therefore that they stood under its sign. They knew of the infinite danger and assault in which man lives, and therefore that it is where this danger and assault is acute and manifest that there is also deliverance and preservation. But the others, the foolish and the blind, with or without the Law, did not know this. They saw neither the danger nor the succour. They felt neither the assault nor the comfort. Instead, they went on dreaming dreams, which could only be disappointed, of a kingdom of Israel which they supposed they could bring about by observing the Sabbath and other laws, or of the gods, ideas, or cosmic principles of old and new religions and philosophies. They had no notion that the Judge had already appeared and delivered the verdict against them all, or that this verdict was primarily and supremely pronounced *for* them. They little dreamt that the capital sentence in which it was a matter of their life and death had already been executed once and for all. This contrast between the Church's awareness and the world's terrible ignorance is the motive, and the bridging of the gap between them the problem, of the early Christian mission. The moralist or philosopher may well be a propagator of his theoretical or practical idea, but he does not have to be. He may end up by keeping it to himself and hiding it in his own heart. The apostle of Jesus Christ not only can but must be a missionary. To him this is not a καύχημα EN204 but an ἀνάγκη EN205: "Woe is unto me, if I preach not the gospel" (1 Cor. 9¹⁶). It is not merely the formal necessity of proclaiming the Word of God, nor the humanitarian love which would rather not withhold this Word from others, that forces him to do this. The determining factor is the concrete content of the Word itself. The truth which he knows about Jesus Christ and human life compels him almost as it were automatically to speak wherever it is not yet known. It is like air rushing into a vacuum, or water downhill, or a fire to more fuel. Man and his life stand under the sign of God's judgment. This is not just a religious opinion. It is a universal truth. It applies to all of us. It decides concerning every man as such. It leaps all frontiers. It is more urgent and binding than any human insight, however clear and compelling, or any convictions, however enthusiastically embraced. This truth is the driving power behind the Christian mission. Apart from it, there would be no indication where it should be pursued or not pursued. Where it is recognised it bursts all barriers. The sign of God's judgment seeks recognition. It

[607]

EN204 matter of boasting
EN205 necessity

is objectively given to all men by the fact that they must all die. All attempts to overlook or reinterpret this fact are doomed to failure. No one can persuade himself that he does not live in fear of death or that this life is normal and natural. But this is after all only the indication, the sign of the sign, so to speak. The sign as such is now set up and revealed, and it demands recognition. According to the New Testament, its power rests exclusively upon the fact that the judgment of God is not only indicated but executed in Jesus Christ, and that humanity is thus made the periphery on which, whether it knows it or not, it is placed under this sign, and its dying, whether it knows it or not, is established as this sign.

We have seen that the finitude of human life stands in fact in the shadow of its guilt. What else can death be for sinful man but the sign of God's judgment, and therefore—if man is indeed not created to be a sinner or to suffer God's judgment—not a divinely willed and created determination natural to his being, but an alien intrusion? Yet this cannot be our ultimate or even penultimate word.

What is the justification for this negative aspect of our being? What is the basis of the profound necessity of human fear in face of death? It is obviously to be found in the fact that death is an enemy with its own destructive purpose and power to which we have rightly fallen a prey in virtue of God's right against us, and the wrong which we have done Him. This means, of course, that we are threatened on this frontier of our being by the negation which corresponds to the power and purpose of this enemy. But it also means that in death we are confronted not only with death itself but also with God; with the very God who [608] is in the right against us and against whom we have done wrong. In death He demands that which we still owe Him. He threatens us with the payment which we have deserved. It is not any negation which threatens us in death. It is not a harmless, neutral and finally welcome negation as imagined by Buddha and his kindred. It is the very dangerous and painful negation of our nothingness before God. If this were not so, if death were a tyrant in its own right, we could await it with secret equanimity or even open defiance. But it is not a tyrant in its own right. It rules only but precisely at the point where God is in the right against His creature and His creature is in the wrong against Him. It reigns in the no man's land where God is in conflict with man and man with God. It rules with the authority and power of the Law of God obtaining even in this no man's land. In the rule of death we have to do with the rule of God. It is really our nothingness in His sight which is revealed in the destructive work of death. This is what makes this work so ineluctable, so bitter and so terrible. Our end is not a tolerable evil, but the great and serious and intolerable evil, to the extent that in our opposition to God we draw upon ourselves God's opposition to us. In its perhaps concealed but very real basis our fear of death is the well-grounded fear that we must have of God.

But this is to say that at the point where we shall be at our end, it is not merely death but God Himself who awaits us. Basically and properly it is not that enemy but God who is to be feared. In death we are not to fear death itself but God. That this makes our plight worse is only one of the things to be noted

168

in this connexion. The second is that we have to do here not merely with death but with God, with the God who is angry with us, who punishes us in death. And God and death are not two equal partners of like dignity and power. What is death compared with God? Its power is simply the power to convince the creature which strives against God, sinful and guilty man, of his nothingness before God. And it cannot do this of itself but only as a servant commissioned by God. It belongs to chaos, to the world which God has neither willed nor created. It stands under God's No. It exists only to the extent that it is denied by God, just as the world which He willed and created exists only to the extent that it is affirmed by Him. If it must acquire form, power and effect in the no man's land of the conflict between God and man; if we have to do here with an irruption of chaos, occasioned by man's sin and guilt, into the world willed and created by God, this does not alter in the slightest the fact that death is as much under God as any of His creatures, and therefore stands no less under His power and at His disposal. Though it is our last enemy, it cannot do what it likes with us. God has appointed it to its office, but He can also dismiss it. He has armed it, but He can also disarm it. He has given it power, but He can also take this power away again. Thus in death we are not in the company of death alone, nor are we in the kingdom of a second god. For with death the Lord of [609] death is also present. To be sure, He will be present as the Judge and Avenger, as the One who causes us in death to reap what we have sown, as the One whom we must fear even now, and then still more. But He is also the Lord of death. If death has such terrors for us, it is because in death we shall finally fall into the hands of the living God. But we shall fall into *His* hands and not the hands of another. Death will not be the lord in this happening, but a servant and slave. And the will of the One who alone will be the Lord will always be a free will in face of death. Death will be bound to Him, not He to death. Without Him death will not be able to do us the slightest harm. If God wills otherwise, the purpose of death for us will be frustrated. His whole power over us will become impotence. In the midst of death we shall be shielded from death. In the midst of it we shall find happiness. But what if God does not will otherwise? What if it be His intention to damn us as we have deserved? If so, it is He who will do so and not death. It is from Him and not death that we shall have to receive the eternal pains of death. Therefore even in hell we shall be in His hands. Even in its torments we shall be shielded with Him. We shall not be alone in death. We shall be with God who is the Lord of death. And this is not in any sense an unimportant factor.

But the God who awaits us in death and as the Lord of death is the gracious God. He is the God who is for man. Other gods who are not gracious and not for man are idols. They are not the true and living God, the One who speaks to us in His eternal Word incarnate in Jesus Christ and crucified and put to death for us. We do not deprive ourselves of anything when we hold fast to this. In so doing, we simply accept Him as He has given Himself to us. We do not make any arrogant attempt to alleviate our own situation. We simply adjust ourselves to the situation which He Himself has created and in which He himself has set us. He is the gracious God, and for us men, even when He places us in death under the sign of His judgment, and in this sign, but only in this sign, is undoubtedly against us. Indeed, it is just as the One who is so palpably against us that He is so much the more mightily for us. If the fire of His wrath scorches us, it is because it is the fire of His wrathful love and not His wrathful hate. Man has always stood up to the hatred of the gods. But God is not one of these gods of hatred. Man cannot stand up to His wrath because it is the wrath of His love. The reason why His curse falls so hard upon us is that it is surrounded by the rainbow of His covenant. It is the dark side of the blessing with which He has blessed us and wills to bless us. Those whom He loves He chastens. Those whom He will find and have for Himself He pursues to the remotest corner where their backs are to the wall and they can no longer escape Him. From those to whom He wills to be all in all, he strips everything else. This is what we

[610] must experience in death, under the sign of His judgment. We do not know what and how we shall be when we are no more and have no more time for being in virtue of our death. But it is certain that we shall be convicted of our most secret sin and guilt; that we shall thus be convicted of our secret nothingness before God; that we shall look quite foolish, stripped of all our glory, and standing helpless and naked before Him. It is equally certain that we shall not then be able to press even the slightest claim upon God, not even by appealing to His righteousness, which would be to condemn ourselves, nor by appealing to His grace, which would obviously not be grace if we could appeal and have a claim to it. Again, it is certain that God would be no less God, nor less worthy of our praise, but only meting out to us what we deserve, if He allowed death, His servant, to do its worst with us, bringing us to that perilous and wholly painful state of negation to which we hasten in our life. Again, it is certain that even in our death He will in some way be the gracious God and for us. We cannot see or say how or how far He will be gracious to us and therefore for us. We cannot dictate to Him. We can make no dispositions concerning our future when we shall have no more future. We can only cling to the fact, but we can really do so, that even in our death and as its Lord He will be our gracious God, the God who is for us, and that this is the ineffable sum of all goodness, so that everything that happens to us in death will in some way necessarily work together for good. We shall fail to see this only if we take God for an idol instead of our gracious God, and do not see that as such He guarantees with His own existence that no evil can come our way but only good, however unexpected or hidden its form. Is He not the God who has elected Himself for us and us for Him? Is He not the God who has entered into solidarity with us and made Himself responsible for us? We hold fast to this existence revealed to us in His word and effective for us in the act of His Son, when in the last resort we do not fear death because we fear God so much. Since God is the Lord of death. He is the One whom we really ought to fear, and how can we fear the gracious God without finding comfort in Him, and the more powerfully the more clearly we

170

realise that apart from His existence we have no other comfort? But if we find comfort in the One who is the Lord of death, how can we fear that which is only His slave?

It is really true that we need not fear death, but only God. But we cannot fear God without finding in Him the radical comfort which we cannot have in any other. But this simply means that it is God who is our Helper and Deliverer in the midst of death. If He, the Lord of death, our gracious God, the ineffable sum of all goodness, is present with us even in death, then obviously in the midst of death we are not only in death but already out of its clutches and victorious over it, not of ourselves but of God. We die, but He lives for us. Even in death we are not lost to Him, and therefore we are not really lost.

One day we shall cease to be, but even then He will be for us. Hence our [611] future non-existence cannot be our complete negation. The ineluctable, remorseless and terrible work of death will be executed on us. But whatever else may happen, we cannot cease to be under His sovereignty, His property, the objects of His love. Death's power and work are not so great as to alter that in any way. We are subject to change and decay. We are mortal and transitory. And death is the seal which shows that this is really so. But God is unchangeable. He is not subject to decay. He is not transitory. And this is true of Him as the gracious God, and therefore as the One whom we have to fear and in whom we may find full and radical comfort even in death. For when we die He is still the One He is. Death is subject to His power and control. Even our last enemy can do nothing more to us than it is ordered to do. Death can be dismissed by the One who has appointed it. It can be disarmed by the One who has armed it. It can be deprived of power by the One who has empowered it. Death is our frontier. But our God is the frontier even of our death. For He does not perish with us. He does not die or decay. As our God He is always the same. Even in death He is still our Helper and Deliverer. But if so, we ourselves derive from Him. As He is our hope, even in death we are already out of its clutches and victorious over it. Even as we suffer it, it is already behind and beneath us. We do not boast of an immortality which is ours when we say this. We do not glory in anything of our own. With our death as the sign of God's judgment it is decided that nothing at all belongs to us, not even grace, let alone a righteousness which can only mean our condemnation. We cannot boast of anything before God, not even of His existence as the Lord of death who is our gracious God. Yet we cannot refrain from saying, without any boasting, that according to His own Word He is this, and that as such He is our Helper and Deliverer and therefore our hope. We cannot refrain from speaking of God Himself. And therefore we must see ourselves as those who in the midst of death are already out of its clutches and victorious over it. Imprisoned by it, we are already freed. Enduring its mighty onslaught, we are already victorious. As those who must die, we shall nevertheless live. Death may still be the tyrant, but it is no longer an omnipotent tyrant. We may not be able to escape it, but a limit is set to it. It is a bitter foe, but not a deadly one. It is terrible, but cannot destroy us. It is our frontier, but one which has its own frontier. It can take away from us everything we have. It puts an end to our existence. But it cannot make God cease to be God, our God, our Helper and Deliverer, and therefore our hope. It cannot do this. And since it cannot, we may seriously ask: What can it do? What is all that it can do compared with what it cannot do? What is the power of its prison, its assault, its bitterness and its terror? What is the meaning of what it can and does do to us? Is not its great darkness into which we enter already outshone by a dazzling light? This light, however, is not our own, or under our control. It belongs to God alone. It may seem but a tiny ray, almost imperceptible. And yet it is far brighter than all the lights of immortality which we may have under our own control. For it is the one great and true light, the light of our life in and over death. In this light is not death weak and small instead of great and strong? Is it not behind and under instead of before and above us. The hushed funeral rites, the coffins and urns and last remembrances of the departed with which we mark the end of human being in time, are not the last word on the subject. Can we not already hear the joy of resurrection over all the coffins and urns and hushed memories when the Word from which this light streams, the Word of our God, is proclaimed and received?

[612]

Was not Paul Gerhardt right in his paraphrase of the 73rd Psalm?

> If Thou alone, O Hero strong,
> Art with me in my woe,
> I need not fear though all the world
> Be shattered at a blow.
> Thou art my heaven, Thy keeping power,
> Shall ever be my strength and tower,
> When I must leave this earth below,

And in the more familiar hymn:

> Mists give way to sun and light,
> Sorrow to joy and sweet delight,
> Surest grief and bitter pain
> To comfort and to strength again.
> Now my soul which heretofore
> Sank right down to hell's dark door,
> To the gate of heaven doth soar.

> He whose terror fills the earth
> Gives my soul a second birth;
> His all-powerful, saving hand
> Frees me from perdition's band.
> All His love and mercy kind
> Overflows my heart and mind;
> Sweet refreshment there I find.

I will go through pain and tears,
I will go through mortal fears,
I will go, and not be sad,
All my days I shall be glad
When the Lord of Hosts is nigh,
When He lifts me up on high,
I cannot perish finally,

Can we really see or express it in any other way?

But perhaps to ask this question is already to have said too much and too little. Too much, because it involves treating as a certainty a hope whose cer- [613] tainty is strictly to be sought and found only in the existence of God as such, so that in respect of its fulfilment all inferences, even in the form of questions, may seem to be only rash anticipations of what is really intended for us. And too little, because we perhaps do not treat seriously enough the certainty of this hope as orientated on God and genuinely grounded, so that in respect of its fulfilment our inferences even in the form of questions fall far short of the reality. There are good grounds for this "too much" and "too little" to the extent that we have so far been moving on biblical but formally on Old Testament ground. The God of whom we do not say too much when we view our lives wholly and utterly in the light of His existence as our Helper and Deliverer, and therefore wholly and utterly on the other side of death, and conversely the God of whom we do not say too little when we seek and find our own being out of and above death wholly and utterly and exclusively in Him, is the God of the New Testament revelation and perception. But this God is the same as that of the Old Testament. Hence there is no need to retract or correct anything we have said. But as the same God, as the Lord of death and our gracious God, and therefore as the infinitely saving but exclusive frontier beyond death, He is revealed and perceptible to us according to the New Testament in such a way that all inquiry concerning Him necessarily carries a positive answer, and the positive answer which we grasp in Him necessarily leads us to genuine inquiry concerning Him.

We learn nothing materially new when we formally enter New Testament ground. We are again concerned with our God as the limit of our death: with the One who is the Lord of death and therefore alone is to be feared in death; with our gracious God and consolation, our Helper and Deliverer in the midst of death, so that in hope in Him death is already behind and under us. But when we take our stand upon the New Testament revelation and perception, the first thing to strike us is that this is undoubtedly not just a question but a strong positive answer given by God Himself. According to the witness of the New Testament it is enacted in the union of God with the man Jesus of Nazareth. It is in Him that He is our gracious God. For in His union with this one man He has shown His love to all and His solidarity with all. In this One He has taken upon Himself the sin and guilt of all, and therefore rescued them all by higher right from the judgment which they had rightly incurred, so that He is really the true consolation of all. In Him He is our Helper and Deliverer in the midst of death. For in the death of this One it has taken place that all we who had incurred death by our sin and guilt have been released from death as He became a Sinner and Debtor in our place, accepting the penalty and paying the debt. In Him God has already acted in this sense as the Lord of our death, as the One who can dethrone and disarm it and strip it of its power. In Him [614] God has made use of this freedom in our favour. In Him God, the Lord of death, has already put death behind and beneath us. For He did not merely give this One to suffer in our stead and on our behalf. He caused Him, again in our stead and on our behalf, to triumph over death, not merely dying, but also rising again for us, so that we can now contemplate the prospect of death as something which is really behind and beneath us. In Him, in this One, God is therefore in very truth the boundary of the death that bounds us. What is death? What meaning can it still have? Certainly not our condemnation, perdition and negation. What have we to fear from it now that God has suffered and overcome it for us all in this One, thus creating order in the no man's land of conflict between Him and man, and thus setting a limit to the irruption of chaos? In Him, in this One, God Himself has made our death the mere sign of His judgment. In Him God has decided that our own hope in Him who alone is immortal, our hope of our own life out of and over death as grounded on Him, is not only possible and legitimate but necessary and imperative. In relation to this one man Jesus Christ we cannot set our hopes too high in death and beyond it. Nothing is too bold or lofty or all-embracing. We are no longer in the sphere of inference or hypothesis. In Him the eternal God Himself has really turned to us, and acted for us, and indeed become our own. In Him the promise of eternal life—not just an extension of this life in a continuation of time, but a life in communion with the eternal life of God Himself—is really given. In Him the fulness of this life is already poured out upon us. This One, in whom all this is introduced in a concrete, tangible and unmistakeable form, is the new factor in the New Testament revelation and perception of God in His relation to death. From the Old Testament standpoint we cannot really do more than ask concerning all this. But from the New Testament standpoint we cannot ask concerning it without realising that the answer is given us in such a way that it is quite obviously not the solution to a riddle of our own, and may thus be accepted with true and final assurance.

But on the ground of the New Testament revelation and perception it is also the case that the positive answer which God Himself has given in power is necessarily an object of genuine, meaningful and legitimate inquiry. It is not just a general truth that God is the frontier of our death, that He is the Lord of death, that in death He and He alone is to be feared, that He and He alone is our consolation, that He is our gracious God and therefore our Helper and Deliverer in death, that He is our hope that through death we shall pass into life. This cannot be abstracted from the union of God with the man Jesus of

Nazareth as this has taken place according to the witness of the New Testament. We cannot suppose that it is true and valid in itself. The Old Testament certainly does not think so, and the New Testament makes it abundantly clear that it is all true in Him, in this One, and in Him alone. The Old Testament insight remains, and is even strengthened, that in death God alone is to be feared and He alone is our consolation. The concentration is now more concrete than ever, viz. the concentration of all help and deliverance in and from death in the person of God Himself. The necessity remains, and is now perhaps for the first time really compelling, to look right away from ourselves in order to see that death is already dismissed, disarmed and rendered impotent, that it is already behind and beneath us. The material unity of the Old and New Testament revelation and perception is clear and convincing at this point. God is always the One concerning whom we must ask exclusively when it is a matter of our preservation from death and victory over it. It is the fact that this exclusiveness is now made concrete that the suggestion concerning Him becomes meaningful and relevant. The one God, who is alone our Helper and Deliverer, is now revealed and perceptible in His unity with this one man. If He is not sought in Him, He is not sought at all. If He is not found in Him, He is not found at all. That we are still threatened by death and still stand under the sign of God's judgment, is thus given a new significance. For it summons us to gather around Jesus Christ, to believe in Him alone and resolutely to refuse all other offers. Without Him we should not only be under the sign of God's judgment in death. We should be under the judgment itself and irretrievably lost. In Him alone God is our gracious God. If our sin and guilt were not laid upon Him, they would still rest upon us, and it could be no real consolation to us to meet our God in our death. In Him alone is God our Helper and Deliverer. For in His death alone our deliverance from sin and guilt and therefore our liberation from death is accomplished. In Him alone death has not merely been endured but overcome. In Him alone it is really for us a defeated foe. In Him alone we may and must seriously reckon with the fact that God is the boundary of the death which bounds us. In Him alone that menacing no man's land is stripped of its menace, and invading chaos repulsed. In Him alone rests our hope, namely, that we may expect everything from God even in and beyond our death when we shall be no more. If we cannot fix our hopes too high when they are set on Him, we cannot be too reserved or cautious or critical in respect of all expectations which are not directed to Him and Him alone. It cannot and should not be too small a thing for us that He and He only is our hope, our future, our victory, our resurrection and our life. Nor should we regret that we have to gather around Him, concentrate wholly upon Him, wholly and utterly believe on Him as God's positive answer to us, allow God's Word of help and deliverance to be spoken to us wholly and exclusively in His person, in His death and resurrection. It is not really too small a thing which remains for us. We have not really anything to regret or lose. This gathering

[615]

[616]   and concentration is not a restriction, but a liberation; it is not an impoverishment but an enrichment. What conflicts and restrictions would entangle us if we had to seek our help and deliverance anywhere else but in Jesus Christ! And in the attempt to seek it elsewhere, how much we should miss of the consolation which is not merely to be sought but found at once in Him! This, then, is the way in which the New Testament gives clarity and precision to the one biblical revelation and perception.

    We may sum up by saying that in the light of the New Testament it is not too much to say that God's existence is our full consolation, assurance and hope in death. For God's existence is visibly and concretely actualised in Jesus Christ as this fulness which excludes any lack. But we may also say that in the light of the New Testament it is not too little to say that our consolation, assurance and hope in death are restricted to the existence of God. For this is all actual and visible in fulness in its restriction to God's concrete existence in Jesus Christ, whereas outside this restriction there can only be lack.

    The biblical material underlying this further step on our way has already emerged in outline in our dogmatic presentation. But we must now give it independent treatment.

    The fundamental Old Testament insight at this point is Yahweh's decisive superiority over death and the underworld. In the Old Testament death may be a powerful menace to man. But it is not an independent god of death confronting Yahweh. God does not have to contend with it for the mastery. "I form the light, and create darkness; I make peace and create evil; I the Lord do all these things" (Is. 45^7). "I kill, and I make alive" (Deut. 32^{39}; cf. 1 Sam. 2^6; 2 K. 5^7). The power of death, in all its salient features, is certainly one of chaos. It is the perverse power of Satan which is radically separated from the powers created by God, which is alien to His creation, which in His creation is denied and excluded and to that extent opposed to His creative will. But as it erupts in the world created by God, it cannot put forward an absolute claim any more than Satan himself. Death has come (Rom. 5^{12}) into the world. It has become a tyrant over man. But so far as God is concerned it is not a sovereign power. For as soon as it entered the world it came under His dominion. Like all the other forces of chaos, it is radically called in question. Even that which is intrinsically negated by God, i.e., in its purely negated being, derives from God. Hence it does not exist side by side with Him or above Him, but under Him. It cannot, then, be a true and effective freebooter. It is God who sends the angel of death Ex. 12^{23}; 2 Sam. 24^{16}; Job 33^{22}) according to His wisdom and good-pleasure, just as Satan begins and continues his dark course only by God's will and permission. According to Amos 9^2, Ps. 95^4 and 139^8, Yahweh rules the underworld as He rules heaven and the earthly land of the living. It is to be noted that the threat in Hosea 13^{14} has the form of a command: "Away, O death, with thy plagues! Away, O grave, with thy destrution!" Above and beyond this command, the recipient of it has no power. Its capacity and achievement in relation to man stand under Yahweh's perpetual and absolute oversight, control and disposing. Yahweh is really the boundary of death, as death is the boundary of man. But this has a further implication. It rules out the view that in the matter of life and death Yahweh wears a Janus head, as though in mysterious ambivalence and neutrality He were both the God of life and the God of death. He is the Lord of death, but this does not mean that He affirms it. As the Creator He afirms life and only life. Similarly, as

[617]   Lord of the covenant with Israel, He affirms its life and preservation and salvation, not its destruction. His control over death is exercised for the sake of life and not for the sake of death. "Have I any pleasure at all that the wicked should die? saith the Lord God: and not

that he should return from his ways, and live?" (Ez. 18²³, cf. 33¹¹). More than this, "He will swallow up death in victory" (Is. 25⁸). These are voices from the later strata of the Old Testament revelation and perception. But they are representative of its whole trend. For it is an explicit or implicit attestation not merely of Yahweh's superiority, but of His definite position in relation to death and the underworld. As He is for Israel, for His covenant with it, for its salvation both corporate and individual, He is not for death but against it. He may have to "kill" as well as "make alive," but painful and necessary though this may be, it is only a stage in the way and work in which it is obviously His purpose not to kill—but to make alive.

It is on the God of this superiority and definite position that Old Testament man relies as he faces death and the underworld and their offensive upon his life. He sees clearly that even in this offensive it is God who is first and last to be feared. He sees that the power deployed and the suffering inflicted by this enemy come first and finally from Him. God punishes man in His wrath and chastens him in His anger (Ps. 6¹). He crushes man's bones (Ps. 51⁸). When he rends him asunder, there is no deliverance (Ps. 50²²). "If he will contend with him, he cannot answer him one of a thousand" (Job 9³). It is worth noting how much more frequent are the passages in which the threat and agony of death are directly attributed to God than those in which they are designated and described as the work of that alien power subordinated to God. Job's persistent complaints are directed against God and not that alien power. It is not death but God who is so terrible in the dominion and work of death. Death is such a thing of terror because God can turn away from man, hide His countenance from him, cast him away in His wrath, desert, reject and forget him (Ps. 27⁹, etc.). It is only in the vacuum created by this attack on God's part, only as man is betrayed into this hopeless *cul-de-sac*[EN206], that that alien power can establish its menacing dominion and do its dangerous work upon him.

From God alone, therefore, are consolation, help and deliverance to be expected under the assault of that alien power. None can give new confidence or be man's assurance but He who first and last shattered it. What does man expect from God as the Helper and Deliverer from this ruin, from this vacuum where death has laid hold of him and he is so completely in its power, if God does not help and deliver him? What is meant by help and deliverance in this connexion?

It corresponds to the picture of a vacuum in which death is threatening and dangerous that the Old Testament speaks of man's being brought or drawn or fetched out from it, and therefore of the possibility and opportunity of escaping and finding a hiding-place and refuge from it. The dimension from which man hopes to escape is, of course, the world of death and the realm of the dead depicted as a sea or wilderness. And the idea is that Yahweh somehow penetrates this desolate waste to fetch man out of it. But where does He take him? To the land of the living, of course, if there is still time for it; to the place where men are healthy and free and have still the capacity to use and enjoy life. But supremely to the place where God's own countenance shines again on man; to the sphere of His grace and favour. For he can be delivered only as Yahweh Himself is again present to Him and takes his part.

Help and deliverance, however, can also have the sense of "redemption" (Ps. 26¹¹, etc.), i.e., of the rescue and restoration of man by means of a ransom. This notion shows clearly that human death is brought about by human guilt. Redemption means that when guilt is atoned for death loses its hold (cf. Johann Jakob Stamm, *Erlösen und Vergeben im Alten Testament*, 1940). The idea cannot be wholly clear in the context of the Old Testament. Who pays what to whom? Can anyone else pay but Yahweh Himself? Can He pay anything else but His own person? Can He pay anyone else but Himself? In the last resort no other answer can be

[618]

EN206 dead-end

177

given to these three questions. The process of redemption, of man's redemption from death, is obviously only hinted at in the Old Testament. It is not yet displayed as a real historical process. And the same applies to those passages where deliverance is described as the helping and upholding of man (as in Ps. 54^4), as his healing (Ps. 6^2), or as his restoration to life (Ps. 71^{20}). Indeed the same is basically true of our deliverance in the primary and most important sense, as our being snatched from death, to the extent that this is to be understood as our deliverance from the final and not merely the initial onslaught of death and the underworld. There are good reasons why man's deliverance from death should not be visible in the sphere of Old Testament revelation and perception, and therefore in its attestation, and therefore in the Old Testament witness to hope in God.

Yet it has a good deal to teach us on the subject. Indeed, rightly understood it can teach us everything. There can be no doubt that Old Testament man, not merely in his complaints and prayers, but also in his thanksgivings and praises, can know and confess the same God whom he has so much cause to fear as the Lord of death as the God who is his radical Helper in and out of death. He knows that he is not left to face death and the underworld alone. He knows further that when he gets there he will find himself face to face with the God who punishes him according to his deserts and thus delivers him up to death. He knows that if there is a Helper and Deliverer it can only be God. God must intervene miraculously to snatch him from that realm which is as such so inaccessible and impenetrable. He must come in might to snatch and free him from it. He must redeem man from his guilt as the root cause of his death. He must perform His sovereign work of restoring His right over man, and thus restoring the right of man before Him. It is seen that this is something that only God can do. Apart from Him there is none to help, whether man, creature or angel. Least of all can the prisoner help himself. For he is wholly and utterly called in question by death. Yet Old Testament man knows God as the One who has done this for him. He asks why He does not show Himself as such. He prays that He may do so. He thanks Him and praises Him that He is this One, and as such his one but certain hope. "I shall not die, but live, and declare the works of the Lord" (Ps. 118^{17}).

The witness of the Old Testament never rises above this level. It speaks of the existence and faithfulness of God which await him even in death. That God exists, and is true to Himself, is Israel's help and consolation in death, its deliverance from death, and its hope. The Old Testament knows nothing of a renewal of man in a time after his death, of a continuation of his life, of resurrection in this sense, and therefore of an eternal life granted to him. Even the few passages which are sometimes quoted to prove the opposite do not actually speak of this. The saying in Ps. 16^{10} ("Thou wilt not leave my soul in hell; neither wilt thou suffer thine Holy One to see corruption") is regarded even in Ac. 2^{29} and 13^{36} as a statement that the final thing to be said of David, in contrast to Jesus Christ, is that "his sepulchre is still with us"; and in its original context it obviously refers to a deliverance from the danger of death rather than from its true and final onslaught. The case is similar with Ps. 17^{15}: "As for me, I shall behold thy face in righteousness: I shall be satisfied, when I awake, with thy likeness." The same is true of Ps. 27^{13}: "I had fainted, unless I had believed to see the goodness of the Lord in the land of the living." At first sight Ps. 49^{15} looks stronger: "But God will redeem my soul from the power of hell: for he shall receive me." But this does not seem to mean any more than that the man who trusts in God, in contrast to those who put their trust in power and riches, has no need to fear these two enemies and the consequent threat of death. Similarly Ps. 73^{26} is a very beautiful expression of the decisive positive content of the Old Testament hope: "My flesh and my heart faileth: but God is the strength of my heart, and my portion for ever." Yet once again it says nothing of an unconditional reversal of this failure to the extent that this is the final disappearance of life in death. We should, of course, include among these passages Job 19^{25}. This verse may be obscure in detail, but its general

[619]

178

import and true significance are clear: "For I know that my redeemer liveth, and that he shall stand at the latter day upon the earth: and though after my skin worms destroy this body, yet out of my flesh shall I see God: whom I shall see for myself, and mine eyes shall behold him, and not as an enemy." This passage says no more than that God is the Advocate and Representative of man "upon the earth." For even the vision of God of which it speaks is confined, as the context suggests, to this life which hastens towards death. It does not look to a continuation of life after death. It is in the moment of dying that Job expects to see God, not as his enemy but "for him" as his Advocate and Representative, as his "witness in heaven" (Job 16^{19}) and as the champion who enters the lists for him (Job 17^3). But even this famous passage does not seem to go further than that. Finally, in Is. 26^{19} and the great vision of Ez. 37$^{1-14}$ we obviously have pictures of the promised renewal of Israel in history. The fact that these images are selected is not insignificant, but they cannot be regarded as evidence of Israel's concrete hopes for the solution of the problem of death. And the same is perhaps true of the most explicit of all the Old Testament passages on this subject, namely, Dan. 12^2: "Many of them that sleep in the dust of the earth shall awake, some to everlasting life, and some to shame and everlasting contempt." For even this passage refers specifically to the people of Israel as such, and possibly has no more general implication. Otherwise we can only say that here on the fringe of the Old Testament Canon we have the exception which proves the rule.

This rule is to accept a rigid contrast between man's temporally limited being in death on the one side and the temporally unlimited being of God on the other as the Lord not only of life but also of death and the underworld. No attempt is made to resolve this sharp contrast, or to prove it to be a salutary one. Of the dead only two things may be said, and they are so unlike as to sound almost contradictory. First, they were once alive and therefore have not simply become nothing but are as those who used to be. Second, even in this state of having been they are still in the divine power and hand of which Israel knows that there is no limit to the miracles which it can do in evocation of the praise of its creatures, in demonstration of its grace and faithfulness, in salvation and self-revelation. "He fainteth not, neither is weary" (Is. 40^{28}) when, men become *rephaim*[EN207]. Even for those whose life is now past He is not past. Even for them He is present to help as the One He was both when they were and before they were. He is not merely the God and the Lord of the covenant for each successive gener-ation of His people, even though the departed generations no longer have any share in the ongoing fulfilment of His covenant with Israel, and clearly cannot accompany it any further even as spectators. For the fact that in their day they had a share in it, and heard His Word and were the objects of His action, is still true even when they pass. To be sure, it is only their relation to God which still remains. Only to this extent have they themselves not passed for Him and before Him. Yet to the extent that God Himself has not ceased to be their God, even after their being in time has come to an end, they have not really passed. To this extent they are still partners of the covenant, and God is still their hope. But what does this mean for them? What is the radical hope and deliverance of which they are assured in the fact that God is for them and they are still there for Him? This question is never answered in the Old Testament. Yet it is not a vain or hopeless question. It is not the question of an eternal unsatisfied hunger and thirst. It is a question full of hope and confidence, bearing its non-answer within it. For it is not flung into an empty void but addressed to God. We may tacitly assume that the New Testament explanation of the saying: "He is not the God of the dead, but of the living" (Mk. 12^{27}), and the Lukan addition: "For all live unto him" (Lk. 20^{38}), [620] represent good Old Testament doctrine to the extent that they express the positive content

---

[EN207] powerless

of the Old Testament question, its secret consolation. Yet it is still a question, and a resurrection and continuation of life after death is definitely not its positive content. This simply consists in the fact that those who have been in their own day are as such before God, who is not a God of the dead, but of the living. All man's deliverance, redemption, preservation, and salvation in and out of death is enclosed in God, in His existence in faithfulness. That it is all enclosed in Him and to be expected from Him, is the hope of the Old Testament in relation to death.

The hope of the New Testament is not materially different. But it has now attained a concrete basis and form in which the positive content of the Old Testament question is so illuminated that the answer which it undoubtedly encloses as a question is unmistakeably and compellingly revealed as such. Yet it is to be noted that even in important passages in Paul its character as a question is still or again indisputable: "O wretched man that I am! who shall deliver me from the body of this death?" (Rom. 7^{24}). The same is true even of such triumphant passages as Rom. $8^{31f.}$: "If God be for us, who can be against us? ... Who shall lay anything to the charge of God's elect? ... who is he that condemneth? ... Who shall separate us from the love of Christ?" and 1 Cor. 15^{55}: "O death, where is thy sting? O death, where is thy victory?" But everywhere the question is immediately confronted by the answer, in the light of which alone it is properly asked: "I thank God through Jesus Christ our Lord" (Rom. 7^{25}). "He that spared not his own Son, but delivered him up for us all, how shall he not with him also freely give us all things? ... It is Christ that died, yea rather, that is raised again, who is even at the right hand of God, who also maketh intercession for us ... Nay, in all these things we are more than conquerors through him that loved us. For I am persuaded, that neither death, nor life ... shall be able to separate us from the love of God, which is in Christ Jesus our Lord" (Rom. $8^{32\ 34\ 37f.}$). "Thanks be to God, which giveth us the victory through our Lord Jesus Christ" (1 Cor. 15^{57}). At the same time there are Old Testament overtones in passages like 2 Cor. $1^{8f.}$, where Paul, looking back on his tribulations in Asia Minor, writes: "We were pressed out of measure, above strength, insomuch that we despaired even of life: but we had the sentence of death in ourselves, that we should not trust in ourselves, but in God which raiseth the dead: who delivered us out of so great a death, and doth deliver: in whom we trust that he will yet deliver." But this hope has now a solid basis. It is a hope triumphant in the midst of all the serious threats of death and all the doubts and uncertainties to which they give rise. Even the sentence of death which seems to have been already pronounced serves only to drive the Christian as never before to trust and hope in God as the One who raises the dead. The question now is not where God is, but what has become of the victory and power of death (1 Cor. 15^{55}). Man can now look back and down, not upon a past life overcome by death, but upon defeated death itself. Hence these two elements, life (incessantly hastening to its end) and death (1 Cor. 3^{22}; Rom. 8^{38}) are no longer contrasted as in the Old Testament. They are placed alongside one another as two neutral possibilities and surveyed from a higher standpoint (Rom. 8^{38}). They are thus classified with other possibilities like angels, principalities, things present, things to come, powers, height and depth, which all have it in common with life and death that they cannot separate us from the love of God. It is to be noted how death is thus subjected to a certain relativisation. "For whether we live, we live unto the Lord; and whether we die, we die unto the Lord: whether we live therefore, or die, we are the Lord's" (Rom. 14^8).

It is not pious optimism, nor a lack of sensitiveness to the problem of death, but the radical change of view brought about with the giving of a solid basis to the Old Testament hope, which is what makes the apostles think and speak in this way, allowing and commanding them to see and express from above, from the divine standpoint, the hope in which the Old Testament righteous lived but saw and expressed only as it were from below, from the human standpoint. Paul does not think or speak from his own standpoint. When he does, he does so

[621]

(Rom. 7²⁴) as an Old Testament Psalmist might have done, but he then goes on to make an immediate correction. For "in Christ Jesus" it is he himself who is first behind and under him. He lives (Gal. 2²⁰) by the faith of the Son of God. He thus thinks and speaks from His standpoint. To do so is both his privilege and his responsibility. The Fourth Gospel gives us the decisive commentary on this point; "He that heareth my word, and believeth on him that sent me, hath everlasting life, and shall not come into condemnation, but is passed from death unto life" (Jn. 5²⁴). "If a man keep my saying, he shall never see death" (Jn. 8⁵¹, cf. 11²⁶). And in brief and summary form: "He that believeth on me hath everlasting life" (Jn. 6⁴⁷). Hence also 1 Jn. 3¹⁴: "We know that we have passed from death unto life." Paul does not put it in this way, but it is from this level that he speaks. He has not attained to it of himself. In himself he stands at exactly the same point as Job and the Psalmists stood, but "Christ Jesus hath abolished death, and hath brought life and incorruption to light through the gospel" (2 Tim. 1¹⁰). And the strong statements of the Fourth Gospel are not general truths, nor mere affirmations transcending the wisdom of the Old Testament in relation to death, but sayings of the man Jesus: "Verily, verily, *I* say unto you." And they do not transcend the wisdom of the Old Testament. Nor do they refute it. On the contrary, they reveal and confirm that in all its severity this is wisdom because it bases man's hope in death so wholly and exclusively on the existence and faithfulness of God. What else does the New Testament attest but the existence and faithfulness of God as they have now become concrete and historical, and therefore are not merely constant but triumphant on our behalf? In the man Jesus Christ they were made flesh, and where they are seen and believed in Him there takes place the change of view in virtue of which man can now look back and down upon the death which threatens him and therefore go to meet it victoriously from this new place of his. Jesus is the Victor. Because He is this for man, man may and must be victorious too. As he knows Him, follows Him, believes in Him and sets his hope on Him, man is with Him as surely as He, his Fellow and Brother, is not without him but for him and the Victor with him. The reality of this victory is the death of Jesus, for God Himself has entered the lists for man in this Fellow and Brother of every man, taking his sin and guilt, making death irrelevant as its consequence and thus snatching man from its jaws and accomplishing that redemption. And the token and pledge of this victory is God's self-manifestation during the absolutely unique forty days in which Jesus was present again to His disciples after His death in demonstration of His glory and His victory. The New Testament hope derives from this reality and revelation.

Those who believe in Jesus can no longer look at their death as though it were in front of them. It is behind them. For as they believe in Jesus they belong to Him and are elected to κοινωνία EN208, i.e., to a share in His being (1 Cor. 1⁹). And as they belong to Him they have their death actually behind them. There, in the reality of His death, He has suffered for them, and abolished it, making it irrelevant as the consequence of their sin and guilt. There, too, they are with Him. Their old man which had gone so hopelessly astray, has been crucified (Gal. 2²⁰; Rom. 6⁶)—the same word which is used of the two thieves in Mk. 15³²—and has died with him (Rom. 6⁸, Col. 2²⁰, 2 Tim. 2¹¹). With Him? Yes, with Him. For the fact that they belong to Him is ratified and confirmed in baptism as the correspondence to the burial which sealed the death of Jesus, and in their baptism they have Jesus' burial, or Jesus' burial as the original of their baptism, behind them (Rom. 6⁴, Col. 2¹²). It is quite fitting that those who believe in Jesus should as it were be marked by His death, bearing the στίγματα EN209 of Jesus on their bodies as Paul puts it in Gal. 6¹⁷, or the νέκρωσις EN210 of Jesus in the even

---

EN208 fellowship
EN209 marks
EN210 dying

stronger expression of 2 Cor. 4¹⁰, which is followed at once by the statement that they "arc alway delivered unto death for Jesus' sake" even while they live (2 Cor. 4¹¹). In Phil. 3¹⁰ Paul can say that he is "conformed" to the death of Jesus, being set in the κοινωνία EN211 of His suffering. In Col. 1²⁴ he can use the bold expression that with his suffering he is "filling" up that which is lacking of the afflictions of Christ, namely, their correspondence in the life of His body, the ἐκκλησία EN212. Those who have been crucified and are dead and therefore live with Him (Gal. 2²⁰) cannot help bearing the traces of this event, suffering the aftermath of His woes and living in His shadow. This correspondence does not in any way diminish the uniqueness of Christ's death. On the contrary, it confirms it. For the remarkable point about these passages is Paul's insistence that his sufferings are not his own but Jesus'. They are the marks stamped upon him to show that he belongs to this Lord.

And this event, the redemption and reconciliation there accomplished, the overcoming and destroying of death which there took place, and now form the starting-point for those who believe in Jesus, is for the New Testament no more and no less than the end of time, the last day, or to be more precise, the midnight hour of the last night when the last day has dawned for each individual and all humanity. "Old things are passed away; behold, all things are become new" (παρῆλθεν, 2 Cor. 5¹⁷). This is the case because in this event time is fulfilled. What is to happen in time and as the meaning of the cosmos existing in time has happened in this event. Those who believe in Jesus know that they—and not they only but all other men as well, though they are still unaware of the fact—live in this last day, and no longer have before them any other time but the time of this last day. Its dawning after the midnight hour is the resurrection of Jesus and the appearance of the forty days as an indication that this event has happened, that death has been deprived of its power and that time is at an end. What can follow this indication is simply the running out of this last day, and then its end in accordance with its beginning: the conclusive, general and definitive revelation of this event; the manifestation of the Saviour and Victor of Calvary as the One He is, as the Head not only of His community but of all creation (Eph. 1¹⁰). The sole purpose for the extension of time after this decisive event is to allow space before the kingdom comes to repent and believe the Gospel (Mk. 1¹⁵) on the basis of this event and its indication. And there can be no other task for those who believe in Jesus (and who are thus aware that this is the last day, and what it means) than to make known this event and its indication as quickly and widely as possible. Unwitting men, and indeed all creatures, must know that the hour has struck. They themselves, those who believe in Jesus, continue to live in the only possible way, namely, in the light of this indication and the resurrection of Jesus. And they do not do this arbitrarily or in their own strength but as those who were not only with Him in that night but also in the morning, being raised and quickened with Him (2 Cor. 4¹⁴; Col. 3¹; Eph. 2⁵) "through the operation of God who hath raised him from the dead" (Col. 2¹²), "begotten again unto a lively hope by the resurrection of Jesus Christ from the dead" (1 Pet. 1³). And as they provisionally live in the power of this indication of the resurrection of Jesus, their life in provisional correspondence to His resurrection life is necessarily orientated on the definitive point of that revelation, the coining of Jesus Christ again in glory. They, too, must still wait expectantly, as the whole universe is engaged in waiting, for this last event. The last day which has already dawned is still running its course. To be sure, they are already called the "sons of God." But it has not yet appeared what they shall be, so that the world which does not yet know Jesus cannot recognise them for what they are (1 Jn. 3¹ᶠ·). Their life is still hid with Christ in God (Col. 3³). And it is not they who can usher in or even foresee the end of this last day and therefore the revelation of what was indicated in its beginning, and there-

---

EN211 fellowship
EN212 church

fore the goal which they expectantly await, and not they alone but the whole cosmos (Rom. 8$^{19f.}$). The last event of this revelation, like the first, will be wholly and utterly the work of [623] Jesus. All they can then do is to be "with Him" (1 Thess. 4^{17}; Phil. 1^{23}). When He is revealed, when they see Him as He is, they too will be revealed with Him (Col. 3^4; 1 Jn. 3^2), though this will also mean that they will "appear before the judgment seat of Christ" (2 Cor. 5^{10}). It is His life which will then be revealed to them (2 Cor. 4^{10}), though this will mean their subjection to the *krisis*^{EN213} described in 1 Cor. 3$^{12f.}$, when they will be tested by fire, and what is built on the foundation of Christ will be disclosed, whether gold, silver and precious stones, or wood, hay and stubble. They will then live with Him His own revealed life (1 Thess. 5^{10}; 2 Cor. 7^3; 13^4; Rom. 6^8 and 2 Tim. 2^{11}). They will then be glorified with Him (Rom. 8^{17}). They will then be conformed to the image of His glory (Phil. 3^{21}). They will then reign with Him (2 Tim. 2^{12}). As Jas. 1^{18} says, they are "the first fruits" of God's creation. Surrounded, as Rom. 8$^{19f.}$ says, by the whole creation groaning and travailing together, they have death behind them and this prospect before them. Their faces will reflect the glory of the Lord. They will be transformed into His image (2 Cor. 3^{18}), ἀπὸ δόξης εἰς δόξαν^{EN214}, from the lower glory of faith to the higher glory of the vision of the Son, who will then lay down the kingdom of creation, and Himself as its King, at the feet of the Father.

This, then, is the New Testament hope. To understand it, we must fix our eyes firmly on three points:

1. the relationship between the crucifixion of Jesus as the event in which man's sin and guilt and consequent death are abolished and time is fulfilled, and His resurrection as the preliminary indication of this event establishing faith in Jesus as the Deliverer from death;

2. the relationship between the resurrection of Jesus as the preliminary indication inaugurating the last time and establishing the Church, and its mission, and His return in glory as the conclusive, general and definitive revelation of this event;

3. and above all, the being of man with Him which is promised to and actualised in faith in Jesus, and in virtue of which he has his own death and the dawn of the last time behind him in the death of Jesus, is born again in His resurrection to a life in God concealed throughout the last time, and will be revealed in glory as one who has this life when Jesus returns in glory as the goal of the last time.

Points 1 and 2 give us the specific form of the hope of deliverance from death in the New Testament. The name of Yahweh, the only source of consolation and salvation in the Old Testament, is now filled out concretely by the saving event whose Subject is the man Jesus, His death, resurrection and coming again. This is why the Old Testament question concerning deliverance from death is secretly pregnant with a positive answer. For it is Israel's God who acts in the man Jesus, confirming in Him His covenant with the fathers. The saints of the Old Testament were not mistaken or disappointed in believing that the God of Israel was the Lord of the living and the dead, and in regarding Him even in death as their rock and refuge. This filling out of the name of Yahweh by the revelation, perception and attestation of this saving event is the new element in the New Testament.

Yet point 3 shows the New Testament form of this hope is not only not alien to the Old Testament form but indirectly identical with it. The rigorous one-sidedness of the Old Testament, which sees all hope solely in the contrast between the omnipotence of God and the impotence of man, and all help and deliverance in the person of God Himself, does not disappear in the New Testament, but is concretely disclosed and shown to be meaningful as never before now that the man Jesus has come as the filling out of the name of Yahweh and the Subject of that saving event. The salvation in this event, and the whole hope of the New

---

^{EN213} judgement
^{EN214} from glory to glory

[624]

Testament, are exclusively dependent on Him as this Subject. It is only with Him that man has a share in it. There is not a single eschatological statement even in the New Testament which allows us to ignore this One. His death, resurrection and coming again are the basis of absolutely everything that is to be said about man and his future, end and goal in God. If this gives way, everything collapses with it.

But the question seriously arises whether the New Testament form is really distinguished from that of the Old by the fact that its content and contents are to be understood as new beginnings, developments and continuations of human life in the time after death. For in the crucifixion of Jesus is not the end of time, both for the individual and all time, accomplished? Does not His resurrection usher in the last day, when even the believer in Jesus can only live a life hidden with God in Christ? Do not His coming again in glory and the consequent revelation of this hidden life mark the end of this last day and time, the handing over of the kingdom of the Son to the Father? Even in the chapter he devoted so expressly to the resurrection of the dead in its connexion with the resurrection of Jesus, Paul can see beyond this end only one further prospect: ὁ θεὸς πάντα ἐν πᾶσιν[EN215] (1 Cor. 15²⁸). It is clear enough that the end of the last time is a historical and therefore a temporal event. But as the event of creation took place in a present without a past, so this event is that of a present without a future, in which, as ἐν ἀτόμῳ, ἐν ῥιπῇ ὀφθαλμοῦ[EN216], there does not follow any further information or promise of further occurrence but only the sounding of the "last trump" (1 Cor. 15⁵²). In this unique moment of time, when the secret of Calvary will be revealed as indicated in the forty days, there will be raised up in incorruption, glory and power, as this last temporal event, that which was sown in corruption, dishonour and weakness (1 Cor. 15⁴³). At this moment it will be necessary (δεῖ) for this corruptible to put on incorruption and this mortal to put on immortality (1 Cor. 15⁵³). But nothing further will follow this happening, for then "there shall be time no longer" (Rev. 10⁶). There is no question of the continuation into an indefinite future of a somewhat altered life. The New Testament hope for the other side of death is very different from that. What it looks forward to is the "eternalising" of this ending life. This corruptible and mortal life will be divested of its character as "flesh and blood," of the veil of φθορά[EN217] (1 Cor. 15⁵⁰). It will put on incorruption and immortality. This earthly tabernacle, which is doomed to destruction, will be "clothed upon" with the building prepared by God, with the house in heaven not made with hands. This mortal will be swallowed up in life (2 Cor. 5¹ᶠ·). Our past and limited life, which did not begin before time and does not continue beyond it, our real but only life, will then fully, definitively and manifestly participate in that καινότης ζωῆς[EN218] (Rom. 6⁴). It will then be eternal life in God and in fellowship with Him. To be sure, the past life of every man in its limited time has a place in this fellowship with God, the Eternal who was and is and is to come. It can only be a matter, therefore, of this past life in its limited time undergoing a transition and transformation (1 Cor. 15⁵¹) and participating in the eternal life of God. This transition and transformation is the unveiling and glorifying of the life which in his time man has already had in Christ. It is the resurrection of the dead, which according to the indication given after the resurrection of Jesus is our participation in His future revelation. This is our hope in the time which we still have.

The Old Testament never said this explicitly, nor could it do so *ante Christum*[EN219]. It simply refers transitory man to the abiding existence and faithfulness of God. And it does this so

---

EN215 God being all in all
EN216 in a moment, in the twinkling of an eye
EN217 corruption
EN218 newness of life
EN219 before Christ

emphatically that there can be no doubt as to the positive implication of the reference. But it never makes it openly. It never actually says that transitory man with his temporal life will one day have a share in the eternal life of God. It never says anything about resurrection, about that transition and transformation, about that manifestation of this life of ours in the glory of God. The New Testament speaks of this as and because it speaks of the saving event whose Subject is the man Jesus. Yet it also confirms what the Old Testament says. For it places transitory man as such, his life in his time, his being with its beginning and end, in the light of the promise vouchsafed in the death, the resurrection and the second coming of the man [625] Jesus. It has not abandoned the sober realism of the Old Testament. On the contrary, it has shown how sound it is, and given it its real force. For as it takes the majesty of God not less but more seriously, because concretely, than the Old Testament, so too it takes the littleness of man in his creatureliness and finitude more seriously. It agrees with the Old Testament that this lowly and finite creature, man, in his time is affirmed by the Most High God and that the power of this affirmation is the secret of his beginning and end, his true help and deliverance in and from death. If we wish the New Testament had more to say about this than the Old, it may well be that we are pursuing pagan dreams of a good time after death, and not letting the New Testament say the radically good thing which it has to say with the realism which it has in common with the Old Testament.

We have now reached the point where we can answer the real question facing us in this connexion, namely, whether in the finitude of our time, in the fact that man's being has an allotted span, we really have to do with its nature as willed and created by God, and therefore with His good and immutable determination. This question has been with us at every step, and the answer has surely been given in the biblical quotations adduced in the last *excursus*. But the question must now be emphasised as such, and a direct answer given.

We saw that finitude means mortality. We tried to show clearly that if we have an end this means that we have to die. And from the very outset we have found it hard to see in this any good determination of our being, or even one in whose immutability we can acquiesce. Even when we considered the biblical view of death, we saw no reason to pretend that black was white. On the contrary, the biblical view compelled us to face up to realities without beating about the bush. Mortality means subjection to death, and death means the radical negation of life and therefore of human existence. Death is not only non-existence. It is the seal and fulfilment of man's negation. Death means that our existence as human beings is really and finally a negation. The necessity of death means, therefore, that our life is one which is bounded by the menace of this negation. We are obliged to live in fear of death. This fear is necessary and justified, and cannot be evaded. How can we help fearing the end of our life when it consists in death? What good can it do, and what reason is there, to acquiesce in this fact which we are powerless to alter? What is there to give us courage to face this prospect? That our existence is finite; that there is a boundary ahead of the time given to us; and that on the other side of this boundary we shall be no more, is something which we can regard only as an evil, as an abnormal determination of our being, and therefore as unnatural.

All this was only confirmed when we brought our life and death into connexion with God: our life into connexion with Him as the One to whom we are engaged and responsible; and our death into connexion with Him as the One [626] who summons us to account and judges our life according to its deserts. When we set it in this light, we saw how far our life is really negative in character and therefore can only hasten towards negation. For in this light we saw that its fatal mortality, its bondage to death, is not just a blind fate which we might perhaps accept as a brute fact and make the best of it, reconciling ourselves to the prospect. For when our life is confronted by God, it is shown to be that of a debtor who absolutely fails to satisfy and even contradicts the claim which his existence entails. It is shown to be a sinful achievement which can only lead to destruction. And if at the end of life man is finally and conclusively confronted with God, this means that the negation in which it has been spent will be confirmed by the negation which he has chosen for himself and which God for His part can only justly affirm. In death we receive the final evil which our actions deserve. We saw why the Bible does not hold out any prospect of relief at this juncture. We saw why the New Testament verdict is even sterner in this respect than that of the Old. We have to fear death because it is God whom we have to fear in death. It is our relation of our life and death to God which explains why death is an evil. This relation explains death as the sign of the divine judgment under which we are placed. But this does not mean that death is explained as a natural or normal determination of human existence. On the contrary, what could be more unnatural than that the end of human life should consist in the fact that God will say No to us, allowing us to fall into the negation which we ourselves have chosen?

We saw, of course, that this was not the end of the story. In bringing our life and death into relationship with God, we were not working with an abstract concept of deity which might have allowed us to stop at the idea of death as a merited judgment or even as an overhanging destiny. We had before us the fact that God is the gracious Creator of man and the Lord of the covenant which He concluded with man in creating him and to which He is faithful even though man is unfaithful. We had before us the fact that He is the God who is merciful even in His righteousness, whose mercy is indeed the true meaning and work of His righteousness. We had before us the fact that He is God in the flesh, God in the man Jesus Christ, and that this means that death is only the sign of God's judgment which can threaten us in our death because God has graciously undertaken to suffer the judgment of death in the death of this man and thus to release us from it. We had before us the fact that God has wiped out men's sin and guilt, and therefore abolished their death, by taking the place of all others in this one man, so that He has become their Deliverer from death in this One. We had before us the fact that He who is to be feared in death is also man's hope in death, and in his life as it hastens towards death. He is the hope in which man, as he moves towards death and inevitably succumbs to it, has death behind him as an enemy already vanquished, not by [627] himself, but by the merciful and righteous omnipotence of God. That is exactly the case. But even on this view death has not become a friend, a normal and natural phenomenon. What the man Jesus, the Son of God, suffered for us at Calvary is not what God planned for man in creating him. It is not life, nor is it a characteristic or determination of life, but death in its irreducible terror— the death which if He had not suffered it would still have to be feared, and which is thus intrinsically fearful and nothing else. In what He has suffered for us death is clearly revealed as the radical negation of human life, its condemnation to hell. It is in the New Testament that this is indisputably attested. The New Testament has to give this witness. We should not know the God who is our Deliverer from death and as such our hope, and who is attested in the concrete reality of His biblical form as such to be also the God of death, the mighty phenomenon of divine wrath and punishment, if we did not know death as an alien intruder, contrary to human nature as God created it.

The conclusion is everywhere suggested that in the finitude of human life, in the fact that a term is set to it, we have to do with the great curse laid upon man, with an alien and inimical threat to human nature. We have not concealed from ourselves the extraordinary difficulty of understanding aright the temporal character of human nature. If we really had to come to that conclusion, we should find it necessary to revise everything that we said about the fact that man's time is limited. Grave doubts would even be thrown on our affirmations concerning the beginning of this time. Such a revision might well lead us to the further conclusion that the limitation of the time given to man can be understood only as an unmitigated evil and overhanging curse, that unlimited time without beginning or end would be more appropriate to man's true nature, and that man's redemption and deliverance from death ought to consist in the renewed possibility of a temporally infinite life on the other side of death. Is such an idea of redemption too absurd to be true? Is there no real redemption from death at all? Was it in His wrath that God created man for only a short span of life? Is our life as such an unmitigated evil? If we take up the position which is suggested on all sides, the consequences which seem to be unavoidable are by no means negligible.

In spite of everything, however, it would be ill-considered to jump to this conclusion without thorough investigation. And this will show that even what we have said does not constitute a final objection to the fact that the finitude of our being belongs to our God-given nature.

To clarify this question, and give it a legitimate answer, we have to realise that in our whole exposition thus far, and similarly in the brief recapitulation which we have just given, we have made and continually presupposed an equation whose limitation will emerge once we seek to establish it. We have only to see that it is a legitimate but relative truth, and the way is opened for an answer [628] which will turn out to be very different from that which seems to be forced on us from every side. The equation which we have constantly made is that of the temporal end of human life with death, or of death as the boundary of human life with death in the harsher sense which it usually bears in the Bible, i.e., as the negation of human existence, as the curse lying upon man, as the radical threat of negation, as the sign of the divine judgment, and in relation to Jesus Christ even as this judgment itself, as the execution of the punishment which we deserve as guilty sinners. And it is in the light of this equation that we cannot understand the end of human existence, dying or death, as a normal and natural phenomenon, but only as a determination alien to the creaturely nature of human existence, as an unmitigated evil, as the enemy of man. It is not arbitrarily but for good reason that we have made this equation and assumed it to be self-evident. This identity is a simple fact. In the judgment of God man is in fact a sinner and debtor, and therefore by divine sentence subject to death, i.e., to death in the harsher sense, the "second death." And Jesus Christ has actually gone in our place to death, to death in this second sense, in this absolutely negative sense of the term. It is actually the case that we cannot see or describe in any other way but as the second death the end of human existence and what death means for man. In making and constantly presupposing this equation, we have kept to this fact revealed in God's act of judgment and unequivocally in His act of salvation in the death of Christ. We know the end of our temporal existence, our death, only as it overshadowed by His death. Even those who face death with their hope fixed on God, and in the triumphant retrospect of faith know that death is vanquished in virtue of the death which Jesus Christ suffered in our place, know it only in this form. The death which is behind them is an evil, an enemy of man. In the light of this fact there can be no doubt as to the unnatural and discordant character of death.

Yet this fact itself calls for explanation. Impressive though it is, it does not have in itself the character of a final word.

It is both possible and necessary to see this clearly when we see it in the light of its centre, namely, the death of Jesus on the cross. What was it that happened there? It was that Jesus suffered the end of His life in death as an atonement, not for His own sin and guilt, but for that of others. In His end, therefore, dying actually coincided with death in this negative sense. But in His case at least death in this negative sense is obviously not the inevitable but the freely accepted end of His human existence. It was an alien burden which did not belong originally to His life. As a man like ourselves, He had not deserved this end. His human life was not one of negation. It was not, therefore, subject to death as the seal of its negation. If in His end He took death upon Himself as God's judgment, He did so as the First-born among His brethren and the Head and Deliverer of a world of sinners who were in bondage to death but to whom God willed to be faithful in spite of their unfaithfulness. In this way there was proved the free grace of God operative and revealed in His person. It did not take place, therefore, out of biological necessity. Even if His end had not been the suffering of this judgment, He would not have been any the less true and natural man. Since He was neither sinful nor guilty, the finitude of

[629]

His life did not stand in advance and as such under this shadow. His human life might have ended in quite a different way. And it is a most difficult paradox that His life did not end in any other way. In His human person there is manifested a human existence whose finitude is not intrinsically identical with bondage to that other death. Therefore in His person, in which there is revealed with incomparable urgency the fact of this simple identity, we obviously have to do with a limitation and relativisation of this fact.

In the light of this centre, again, it is possible and necessary to ask what was and is the objective range of that event. It obviously meant and still means that we for whom Jesus took to Himself the judgment of God in death have been freed from our sin and guilt and therefore released from that sentence of death and delivered from having to suffer that second death. The end of Jesus Christ has made our end simply the *sign* of God's judgment. As we consider this end and move towards it, we are free to look back upon the end of Jesus, upon the death which He suffered on our behalf and which rescues us from death itself, as a terror which can no longer terrify us. But this can mean only that our end and our death in that second and negative sense are obviously identical only in an empirical way and not as a matter of necessity, as though our end could not have any other character. A strict identity of dying and judgment in death is possible only if we ignore the fact that God has acted for us at Calvary. By what He did for us there, by the action of His free grace, death has been relativised at least to the extent that our death, as suffered by Jesus for us, is set at a certain distance from our end and can only be its sign, reminding us of the judgment and at the same time of His mighty act of salvation. We cannot say that that fact has been simply removed. For we still stand under this sign. We must still submit to God's judgment and sentence. As concerns ourselves, we can only say that we are sinful and guilty, and will be to the end, and could only expect that terrifying end, the second death, if it all depended on us. But the fact that we belong to Jesus Christ implies a limitation and relativisation of this fact. We have received the grace of God in Jesus Christ. We have been delivered and redeemed in Him. Therefore our end does not have to be the judgment of death. There can be no question of an anthropological identity between the two even in our case. Even without it we should be none the less true and natural men. It is still a fact—and indeed the only one which we can   [630] see and conceive in this matter—but it is no more than this. The finitude of our temporal existence obviously does not necessarily imply that we stand under the wrath of God.

And now it is both possible and necessary, primarily again in relation to the man Jesus, to ask the further question, whether it was not the case that, to be the First-born among many brethren, the Head and Saviour of a sinful world in bondage to death, He had to share our human nature under the determination of finitude. He did not have to stand under the judgment of God or suffer the death of a reprobate. His life did not have to have this end. It was God's free grace, the great love of this man who was His Son for us, that He

took upon Himself this end for us. But He had to be able to die. His being in
time had to have this finitude in order that He might take this end upon Himself. Infinitude and immortality would obviously have disqualified Him from
doing this for us. His life as God's Son had to have an end in its human form. It
had to be able to be given over to death, the point at which the life of all men
meets its temporal boundary. Only so could He overstep this boundary. Only
so could He surrender His divine-human life and thus accomplish that which
brought terror to Him but salvation to us. Only so could the brute fact of
identity between man's end and his judgment be achieved and our deliverance
from this judgment be accomplished. But the finitude of human existence in
time has in His person this indispensable function; if it seems to be for Him an
anthropological necessity, the determination of His true and natural being as
man, how can we maintain that all this has nothing to do with the nature of
man as created good by God? And if His dying—in virtue of what it was as
His—is the sum total of the good which God has shown to the world, how can
we dare to understand man's mortality as something intrinsically negative and
evil?

But let us now turn our attention again to ourselves, to the man who in the
end of Jesus, by the capital sentence suffered in His end, is delivered from this
sentence. There is here an exact correspondence. Is it not the case that our
human existence, if it is to be the object, recipient and vessel of the free grace
of God which has been at work for us in Jesus, must stand equally under the
determination of His finitude? Must we not also be able to die, to go towards
death, if what God has done for us in Jesus is not to have been done in vain? It
is only as a boundary is set for us to which we can move, which we shall one day
pass and beyond which we shall be no longer, that we are in a position to throw
ourselves conclusively and definitively and exclusively on God and therefore
concretely on Jesus Christ as our Deliverer from the wrathful judgment of the
second death? What would become of us if in an endless life we had the
constant opportunity to achieve a provisional ordering of our relationship
[631] with God and our fellows in the way we know so well, or rather to postpone the
ordering of this relationship, accomplishing it at best only in that daily drown-
ing of the old Adam which is always so doubtful a matter because he can unfortunately swim? This could only mean in fact that we should be able to sin
infinitely and even quantitatively multiply our guilt on an infinite scale. What
sense would it then make to say that Jesus Christ has reconciled us to God and
spared us suffering our merited punishment? And in what strange light would
the merciful righteousness of God be set if our reconciliation with Him were
never to take effect? We have to be finite, to be able to die, for the ἐφ᾽
ἅπαξ[EN220] of the redemption accomplished in Christ to take effect for us. As
we are finite and mortal, we find ourselves on the same ground as He, and can
thus allow Him to be our Deliverer in the form in which He became and is our

---

[EN220] once for all

Deliverer. To belong to Him we must be finite and not infinite. Finitude, then, is not intrinsically negative and evil. There is no reason why it should not be an anthropological necessity, a determination of true and natural man, that we shall one day have to die, and therefore merely have been. It belongs to the revelation of His glory in us, to the final proclamation of our justification in the judgment, to the removal of the overhanging sign of divine judgment, to the settled and incontestable factuality of our participation in God's eternal life, that one day we should merely and definitively have been.

We have argued in purely Christological and soteriological terms to prove what has to be proved, namely, that in the fact of the identity between our end and our judgment we do not have to do with an absolute but a relative necessity. This particular argument is essential. There are, of course, many lines of approach which seem more obvious. It might be asked whether it does not belong to the nature of every living process, including the human, to be exhausted and end as it once began. It might be asked whether dying as the natural end of human existence is not to be understood as an intrinsic evil but not a punishment. It might be pointed out that death is a relative evil, but in the last resort no more, which all available experience shows to belong to the nature of all living creatures. These considerations are all true, but they are only secondary. They simply illustrate the point, and have no intrinsic significance. The fact that man, standing under the sentence and judgment of God, is shown in his end to be a damned and lost being, is too massive a truth to be accepted merely on the basis of the correct observation that every innocent fly must perish when it reaches the evening of its day. For man is not just an innocent fly, and the fact that he is mortal like a fly is in itself no proof that it is right and proper for him to be mortal. He may console himself with the recollection that he shares his fate with all living creatures. This is what he does in Ecclesiastes 3$^{19-21}$, though clearly not without some degree of irritation. But he can do this only when he learns from the fact itself, from the place where [632] death can only confront him in the first instance as something negative and evil, that it is right and necessary for him to have to die. It is not for nothing that we have taken this as our starting-point. We have caused the fact itself even on its own basis to speak of its limitation and relativity.

On the same basis we have seen that a distinction between end and curse, dying and punishment, death and execution, is not only possible and permissible but necessary and imperative. The fact of their identity is indisputable in the sphere of what we can see and conceive. But it is no less incontestable that nature and unnature, good and evil, God's creation and the answer of divine wrath to man's sin and guilt, are identical in this fact. Nature as well as unnature, good as well as evil, God's creation as well as the disastrous collision between the holy God and fallible man, are all present in man's end, in his dying and death. It would be quite perverse to maintain the presence of the latter without the former. It is thus legitimate and imperative for us to insist on the former, although it is only in Christological and soteriological terms that

191

we can see the fact of the identity of the two. When the former are actually seen in this light, however, there can be no doubt that we do really have to reckon with them.

This means that it also belongs to human nature, and is determined and ordered by God's good creation and to that extent right and good, that man's being in time should be finite and man himself mortal. The fact that one day we shall have been answers to a law which does not inevitably mean that we are imprisoned, fettered and condemned to negation by its validity. Death is not in itself the judgment. It is not in itself and as such the sign of God's judgment. It is so only *de facto*[EN221]. Hence it is not to be feared in itself or necessarily, but only *de facto*[EN222]. Death is secretly the very serious and sinister but not intrinsically dark and menacing form of the frontier where for good or evil man must finally meet his God. And this hidden form is the true and proper form of this frontier, and in this form it belongs to human nature, dying being no less a part of life, as the end which corresponds neutrally to its beginning, than conception and birth. Death is man's step from existence into non-existence, as birth is his step from non-existence into existence. In itself, therefore, it is not unnatural but natural for human life to run its course to this *terminus ad quem*[EN223], to ebb and fade, and therefore to have this forward limit.

Man as such, therefore, has no beyond. Nor does he need one, for God is his beyond. Man's beyond is that God as his Creator, Covenant-partner, Judge and Saviour, was and is and will be his true Counterpart in life, and finally and exclusive and totally in death. Man as such, however, belongs to this world. He is thus finite and mortal. One day he will only have been, as once he was not. His divinely given promise and hope and confidence in this confrontation with God is that even as this one who has been he will share the eternal life of God Himself. Its content is not, therefore, his liberation from his this-sidedness, from his end and dying, but positively the glorification by the eternal God of his natural and lawful this-sided, finite and mortal being. He does not look and move towards the fact that this being of his in his time will one day be forgotten and extinguished and left behind, and in some degree replaced by a new, other-sided, infinite and immortal being after his time. More positively, he looks and moves towards the fact that this being of his in his time, and there-with its beginning and end before the eyes of the gracious God, and therefore before his own eyes and those of others, will be revealed in all its merited shame but also its unmerited glory, and may thus be eternal life from and in God. He does not hope for redemption from the this-sidedness, finitude and mortality of His existence. He hopes positively for the revelation of its redemption as completed in Jesus Christ, namely, the redemption of his this-sided, finite and mortal existence. This psycho-physical being in its time is

[633]

[EN221] as a matter of fact
[EN222] of the fact
[EN223] ending point

he himself. He himself as this being makes himself guilty of judgment and the curse. He himself as this being is freed by the crucifixion of Jesus from his guilt and thus released from the judgment and curse of death. He himself is here and now concealed and imperceptible and inconceivable in this freedom, and waits for its revelation. But again he himself as this being clings here and now to God as the One who as the Creator has set him these limits and given him this allotted span, and who now in the concrete form of the appearance and work of Jesus Christ is his only full and perfect hope. And he himself as this being knows that already in the totality of his own this-sided existence, above and beyond which there is no other, he is claimed by and belongs and is committed and thankful here and now to the God who as his gracious Judge and therefore his Saviour from death is his true beyond.

This view of human nature, with its frank recognition of the fact that it ends as well as begins, will be most important for our understanding of the divine command and the bearing of Christian ethics, giving to human life an importance as something which will one day be completed and not be continued indefinitely, and therefore to that which is required of it an urgency which would obviously be lacking if we set our hopes on deliverance from the limitation of our time, and therefore on a beyond, instead of on the eternal God Himself.

It lies in the nature of the subject that at this final turn in our presentation we shall have to be content with a narrower compass of biblical demonstration. When the Bible speaks of the end of human life, it generally means the fact of the end of the sinful being of man in conflict with God and apostasy from Him. Because man stands in a perverted relationship with God, he awaits death as an enemy, as an overwhelming judgment, as the threat of negation. To him death is the punishment of apostasy already announced in Paradise (Gen. 2[17]; 3[4f.]). And since it is God who suspends it over him and executes it by taking away the breath of life which He gave him, it is God Himself who encounters him in death as his enemy. "I [634] was at ease, but he hath broken me asunder; he hath also taken me by my neck, and shaken me to pieces, and set me up for his mark. His archers compass me round about, he cleaveth my reins asunder, and doth not spare; he poureth out my gall upon the ground. He breaketh me with breach upon breach; he runneth upon me like a giant" (Job 16[12f.]). The death of the ungodly means that his name is "come to an end for ever" (Ps. 9[5]; cf. 41[5], 109[13f.]). His death is the $\delta\epsilon\acute{u}\tau\epsilon\rho\sigma\varsigma$ $\theta\acute{a}\nu\alpha\tau\sigma\varsigma$[EN224] of which we read in Rev. 20[14] that it and the realm of the dead are thrown into the lake of fire. This cannot mean the same thing as the triumphant saying in Rev. 21[4] that "death shall be no more," or what is described in 1 Cor. 15[26] as the $\kappa\alpha\tau\alpha\rho\gamma\epsilon\acute{i}\sigma\theta\alpha\iota$[EN225] of death as the "last enemy." It denotes rather the act of judgment in which death and the whole realm of the dead will only then acquire this character of the "last enemy." For it is into the lake of fire that those are thrown whose names are not written in the book of life (Rev. 20[15]; cf. 21[8]). Death in this sense is clearly unnatural. It is, so to speak, the death in death. We see it in Is. 14[4f.] in the particular curse of death which seems to be laid on the king of Babylon as distinct from the general fate of death affecting all the other inhabitants of *Sheol*, so that when he comes this whole realm breaks out into an uproar and the shades are dispersed and burst into a terrible cry of justified triumph. "The seed of evil

---

[EN224] second death
[EN225] destruction

doers shall not be named for ever" (Is. 14²⁰). The fact that he must die can mean for man unmitigated woe. It is for liberation from this evil, hostile, threatening, judging, annihilating death and its woes, that biblical man cries out. And it is just this liberation which is promised and assured him by the existence of his God. In both the Old Testament and the New the Bible sees man as one who is corrupt and ungodly, and therefore it usually views death in this second form. This is the form which is absolutely normative for human observation and apprehension. Wherever death assumes a different guise, it always indicates a remarkable change of standpoint connected with a particular and extraordinary intervention on the part of God.

Yet we cannot ignore the fact that this change of standpoint does actually take place. Another form of death is actually to be seen in the Bible. In the biblical presentation, it is not the case that the unnatural aspect of death has simply crowded out or veiled the naturalness of man's end in itself and as such. There is no compelling necessity why death should be for man an unqualified evil. At the very outset we pointed out that even in the Old Testament blessing and life, curse and death, are not identical even though they stand in a clear relation to one another. According to Ps. 90¹² men acquire wisdom of heart by numbering their days, thus reminding themselves that no matter what happens they must die. "I go the way of all flesh," says David to Solomon on his death-bed (1 K. 2²). He obviously has no idea that death is a curse, or that things ought to be different. It may be that the dead—the reference is to the kings of the nation—"all of them lie in glory, every one in his own house" (Is. 14¹⁸). The memory of the departed may perhaps be perpetually blessed in contrast to the way in which the name of the ungodly shall perish (Prov. 10⁷). Indeed, "his name shall endure for ever, and be continued as long as the sun" (Ps. 72¹⁷). His gray hairs may come in peace into the realm of the dead (1 K. 2⁶; cf. Lk. 2²⁹). Balaam's wish can make perfectly good sense: "Let me die the death of the righteous, and let my last end be like his!" (Num. 23¹⁰). Even an Abraham (Gen. 25⁸) or an Isaac (Gen. 35²⁹) can "die an old man, and full of years." There is no suggestion here of morose resignation. It is merely accepted that when life has run its course it is fit and proper than a man should die. For the same reason and in the same sense as Jacob he can die gladly (Gen. 46³⁰). On certain assumptions the awful guest may come in quite a different guise from that of the second death, hardly indeed as a friend, but with a neutral and even natural aspect. It never fails to come. And it always retains its awful character. But its enmity and menace can disappear. Hence we read in Rev. 2¹¹ and 20⁶ that there

[635] are some over whom the "second death" has no power. It can do them no harm, although death is still for them a serious matter. It can be that in all their finitude and mortality, and in spite of everything, men are so in the hands of God and under His protection, and stand and walk and continue in such fellowship with Him, that their transition from existence into non-existence, and their final state of having been, does not mean their defeat by the "last enemy," but its overthrow and their perfect and final encounter with God, their eternal confrontation and supremely positive co-existence with Him. It can be that the life of the Creator and Lord secures and brings to perfection what they would otherwise forfeit as His creatures by reason of their finitude and mortality. It can be that it is no longer a cause of doubt that they have no future because God makes Himself their future, the future of their whole life that is past. It can be that human nature, the finitude of human being in the time of the unnature which conceals it, is actually put off by the grace of God. And it can be that it is thus seen to be an act, not of God's wrath and even less of His envy, but of His goodness and preservation, that man was kept by the cherubim with flaming swords from enjoying the fruit of the "tree of life" which was never meant for him, and thus prevented from "living for ever" (Gen. 3²²). It can be that the boundary thus drawn becomes the place where God frees man from the curse which would otherwise have destroyed him on this boundary.

That there is here a positive element as well as the evil of death is recognised in one or two

5. Ending Time

Old Testament passages in which the end and dying of certain men is wrapped in a remarkable obscurity, or set in a supremely distinctive light, and thus totally and unequivocally distinguished from the fate of others in death, from their bondage to death as an evil.

It is expressly stated in Deut. 34^{5f} that Moses, the servant of the Lord, died in the land of Moab according to the sentence passed upon him (Deut. 32^{50}). We are told, however, that God Himself buried him opposite Baal-peor, and that no one knows his grave until this day. We also read that "his eye was not dim, nor his natural force abated" (Deut. 34^7). The boundary of his life is thus exposed, and at this boundary the judgment of God, the grave and the underworld. Even Moses died. But he died as a man in the fulness of life, and when he overstepped that boundary and ceased to be, God Himself undertook to bury him. In this way, He showed that this boundary was wholly natural. And the grave, which is the most obvious and easily conceived aspect of the whole matter, could not be found. By the act of God peace between this man and his fate was assured by God Himself in a way which could be seen by all Israel.

It is rather different with the death of Enoch briefly described in Gen. 5^{24}. Enoch walked with God, "and he was not, for God took him." The comment of Heb. 11^5 is as follows: "By faith Enoch was translated ($\mu\epsilon\tau\epsilon\tau\epsilon\theta\eta$ EN226) that he should not see death; and was not found, because God had translated him: for before his translation he had this testimony, that he pleased God." In this case the penal character of death seems to have wholly disappeared. As the New Testament explains, Enoch did not "see death." He stepped over that boundary almost, as it were, unawares. Even more fully than in the case of Moses, $\mu\epsilon\tau\acute{\alpha}\theta\epsilon\sigma\iota\varsigma$ EN227 obviously signifies an exit from life directly effected by God Himself and known only to Him. Because Enoch "walked with God," the problematic character of this exit was concealed from himself as well as from others. He himself did not see the crisis of death, and therefore no one else saw him in its throes. In a moment he was no longer there. He was not even at the place where all other men are found at the end of their life. He was not wrestling with the question of the after-life which this end poses and which man is quite unable to answer. This question was directly answered by God's presence and intervention. It was not death which removed him from this life, but God. To be sure, he was no longer there. He ceased to belong to the society of the living. His being in time was at an end. And therefore we are told in fact, though indirectly, that he died as Moses died. In both cases we learn that this death [636] took place in complete concealment. But it is not denied that his life was over and that he had had only an allotted span of time like others. Enoch is seen and described as an instance in which there is no doubt whatever of the salvation which awaits man on the other side of the frontier of his time.

Another special case is presented by the story of the disappearance of Elijah in 2 K. 2$^{1-18}$. This is the most explicit of all the hints in this direction in the Old Testament. It is also the most difficult. And yet with proper elucidation it could be the most illuminating one. It undoubtedly refers to the temporal end and natural frontier beyond which he ceases to be. The question is what this means and does not mean for his relation as the older prophet to Elisha as the younger. It is the relation of master and pupil, not unlike that between Moses and Joshua. Was the end of Elijah the extinction of his life? This question is answered in the text by a record which completely obscures the fact that Elijah actually died and takes the form of a revelation to Elisha of the divine mission, authority and power of his master. This means that the life which Elijah the prophet lived before and with God was not extinguished when his end came, but that he now lives it before and with God as never before. For his office, commission, authority and power, now revealed to Elisha, are transferred to this one

---

EN226 translation
EN227 translation, change

195

who is left. Elijah's departure consists in the swallowing up of his mortality in life before the eyes of Elisha. This positive meaning of his end is indicated by the question which the sons of the prophets of Bethel and Jericho put to Elisha: "Knowest thou not that the Lord will take away thy master from thy head to-day?" But they did not need to tell him this: "Yea, I know it; hold ye your peace." What will happen is not, of course, in any sense self-evident. The two-fold summons that Elisha should remain behind makes this clear. It is also shown by the necessity of Elisha's prayer for a double portion of his master's spirit, i.e., the share of the first-born. It is shown again by Elijah's answer: "Thou hast asked a hard thing: nevertheless, if thou see me when I am taken from thee, it shall be so unto thee; but if not, it shall not be so." All these retarding elements in the narrative show that it could all have turned out very differently. It is far easier to suppose that it would have done. For it is not in the least self-evident that at the end of human life death should not be seen, but only a life undoubtedly past. It is not at all self-evident that even and particularly a prophet should depart and yet not merely depart. But the sons of the prophets and Elisha were right. It could not be other-wise in the end of the prophet Elijah. Even his last miracle shows this. For Elijah divides the waters of Jordan—the type of death—with his mantle. Master and pupil, predecessor and successor, pass through together dry-shod. Here is a repetition in reverse of the crossing of the people of Israel over the same Jordan into the promised land. And now, prefigured by the miracle, comes the revelation itself: "And it came to pass, as they (i.e., the one who was leaving and the one who was staying behind) went on, and talked (and therefore *ceteris imparibus*[EN228] like Moses in the action of their interrelation), there appeared a chariot of fire, and horses of fire, and parted them both asunder; and Elijah went up by a whirlwind into heaven. And Elisha saw it, and he cried, My father, my father, the chariots of Israel and the horsemen thereof .... And he then took hold of his own clothes, and rent them in two pieces." The fact that he did this (the well-known sign of mourning), and that the sons of the prophets curiously forgot their own prophecy and engaged in a futile search for the departed prophet with fifty men, is a clear indication that we have to do here with the final departure of Elijah, with his temporal end, with what is usually called death. But this is just the point. What is usually called death, even the very last trace of a judgment connected with the temporal end of man, is in this case completely veiled, concealed, and indeed annulled by the revelation of the true nature of the life here concluded, i.e., of "the chariots of Israel and the horsemen thereof," of Israel's invincible power, of the gracious God of Israel, with all the force which He has wielded in the human life now completed. If Elijah met his end, and left the "land of the living," he did so without the gloom usually associated with death. For he was fetched in a chariot and horses of fire. Instead of journeying to the underworld, he proceeded heavenwards in a cloud. Yahweh Himself had intervened as the content, goal and end of Elijah's life. Moreover, Elisha shared in this revelation. As the sign of the spirit which had descended on him, of the divine mission, authority and power entrusted to him, he had only to pick up the mantle of Elijah. Elijah no longer needed this. His life in time was over, his work in history done. But Elisha still had to live his life. He was about to begin his real work. And so he came under this sign. Nor was it an empty one, as shown at his return to Jordan. For here, like Elijah, Elisha smote the water with the mantle which was now his own. He still asked: "Where is the Lord God of Elijah?" But he was answered by what happened: "And when he also had smitten the waters, they parted hither and thither: and Elisha went over." The man Elijah was no longer there. But God had revealed Himself to Elisha as the God of Elijah. Elijah himself had been revealed in his fetching home by God. He was alive to him as the man he had been. For his spirit, office and commission had come upon him by means of this revelation.

[637]

[EN228] all other things being unequal

5. Ending Time

Enoch, Moses and Elijah are exceptional cases. All these passages speak of an extraordinary intervention of God without which these men could never have been set in the obscurity or light experienced. And all the other cases in the Old Testament in which men are privileged to die a peaceful death, or the death of the righteous, or to die "full of years" and "gladly," must be understood in close connexion with an extraordinary intervention of God. The fact that these men were naturally capable of dying in this way does not mean that this is a general privilege granted to man. They themselves have no capacity to choose such an end. They are all God's debtors and enemies. Of themselves they can only die an evil death. If they depart in peace and joy, this can only be because God has awakened in them the capacity which they all have by nature but which is as it were suspended and sterilised in the ungodly. It is by God's free grace and the healing of nature that it is possible in any given case. If there is a natural end of existence, which is a real end yet not judgment but communion with God, this may be known by God's extraordinary intervention, by what is recorded in the end of Enoch, Moses and Elijah as deliverance from death. The fact that the gracious God makes Himself the end of man, and that this is not therefore gloom but glory, plainly and definitively confirms that this end as such is not a question of disorder but of order, and that in it we do not have to do with the sphere of chaos but with the good creation of God.

As regards the situation in the New Testament, we have already called attention to the idea of the "second death" which figures so prominently in the Apocalypse. The assumption is that there is a "first" death without the evil, corruptive and unnatural character of the "second." In Heb. 9^{27} the sacrifice of Christ, offered once for all to take away the sins of many, is both formally and materially brought into relation with this notion. We are told in this sense that "it is appointed ($\dot{a}\pi\delta\kappa\epsilon\iota\tau\alpha\iota$ EN229) unto men once to die, but after this the judgment." From this it would seem that the phrase $\ddot{a}\pi a\xi\ \dot{a}\pi o\theta a\nu\epsilon\hat{\imath}\nu$ EN230 does not of itself signify judgment, but an event which is general and neutral even though in contrast with the sacrificial death of Christ and its uniqueness it also seems to have a higher necessity. Again, the phrase $\ddot{a}\chi\rho\iota\ \theta a\nu\dot{a}\tau o\nu$ EN231 in Rev. 2^{10}: "Be thou faithful unto death," and Rev. 12^{11}: "They loved not their lives unto the death," cannot imply that death is the last enemy, but only the *terminus ad quem* EN232 of their faithfulness and unselfish devotion coinciding with the boundary of their life. Again it is no less clear that when in I Thess. 5^{10}, 1 Cor. 3^{22}, Rom. 8^{38} and $14^{7f.}$ and Phil. 1^{20} life and death are associated under the superior dominion of Christ, death does not signify an armed and powerful foe but the approaching end of human life contrasted with the possibility of its further continuation. There is a dying which throws no doubt on man's participation in the resurrection and life of Jesus Christ. Death in this sense is not ruled out by man's hope in a resurrection. This is expressly shown by Jn. 11^{25}: "I am the resurrection, and the life; he that believeth on me, though he die, yet shall he live." In the New Testament, too, the "death" in death can be abolished. It is never supposed, of course, that this possibility lies in human control. When it happens, it is always the result of God's extraordinary intervention. The concrete form of this is the appearance, death and resurrection of Jesus Christ: "He that heareth my word, and believeth him that sent me, hath everlasting life, and shall not come into condemnation, but is passed from death unto life" (Jn. 5^{24}). In these circumstances the "second death" is abolished and man is freed from unnatural death. But this obviously means that, as he is freed for eternal life, he is also freed for natural death. The New Testament, like the Old, speaks of this natural death.

[638]

EN229 it is appointed
EN230 unto death
EN231 to die once
EN232 ending point

It is worth noting that the New Testament fully matches the sober realism of the Old in this matter. It is striking, indeed, that it offers no parallels to such hints as we have in the stories of the end of Enoch and Moses or the disappearance of Elijah. The New Testament authors are content to refer to these occasionally without adding similar occurrences from their own historical sphere. These remarkable exceptions were obviously regarded in the New Testament age as types which, once fulfilled in the end of Jesus Christ, in His resurrection and ascension, did not need and were not capable of further multiplication. The Roman Catholic Church definition of the assumption of Mary as a dogma of the faith, quite apart from anything else, is an additional proof of its profound lack of understanding of the basic difference between the situation and order of the New Testament and that of the Old. In the New Testament order the exaltation of the one man Jesus Christ, in which the exaltation of His own is already latently accomplished, is followed by only one assumption of which nothing can be said because it has not yet happened, namely, the assumption of the community to meet its Lord when He comes again at the final revelation in which the exaltation which has already occurred in Jesus Christ will be made manifest. In this assumption the dead will share no less than the living (1 Thess. $4^{16f.}$) There now are and may be those who have fallen asleep "in Christ" (1 Cor. 15^{18}) or "in Jesus" (1 Thess. 4^{14}), or who are even "dead in Christ" (1 Thess. 4^{16}). They are not lost (1 Thess. 4^{15}) even though they have not yet been assumed. And no one, not even Mary, can anticipate their assumption with a private one of his own. Death now wears a guise in which we can look it in the face. We can now face it as a natural prospect.

"To fall asleep" ($κοιμᾶσθαι$) is the characteristic New Testament term for the death which is freed from the "second" death by the death of Jesus Christ and is therefore a wholly natural thing for the Christian. "Our friend Lazarus sleepeth" (Jn. 11^{11}). Some of the witnesses of the resurrection of Jesus "are fallen asleep" (1 Cor. 15^6). "The fathers (i.e., those who belonged to the first Christian generation) have fallen asleep," say the false teachers in 2 Pet. 3^4. Similarly, the Corinthian church can look back on not a few of its members who have fallen asleep (1 Cor. 11^{30}). It is noticeable that even David is now said to have fallen asleep (Ac. 13^{36}). Indeed, a violent death like that of Stephen (Ac. 7^{60}) is described almost euphemistically in these mild terms. What does this imply? It relates to the process of dying, or rather to the impression, designated, defined and shaped by faith and love, which the survivors have of what is finally perceptible in the death of a brother or sister. They see him falling asleep. What lies beyond they cannot see. For the Christians of the New Testament Jesus Christ Himself intervenes at once and absolutely on the far side of this event. His death and resurrection avail for those who have now "fallen asleep," as well as for those who survive. The hope in Him is a hope for the former too. The final thing to be said of them (apart from Jesus Christ Himself) is that they have fallen asleep. The expression is deliberately

[639]

mild. It may be euphemistic, but it conveys an impression of peace. It is a striking expression of the freedom of New Testament Christians—the freedom of their faith and love. As they contemplate the dead they are able to use this peaceful term and keep their memory before their eyes in the form of this peaceful process. The decisive thing is not that they suffered or endured the agony of death. The real conflict with death was fought out long ago. All they had to do was to fall asleep. Even Stephen could simply fall asleep under the hail of stones. The term thus signifies the genuine reality visible in the light of Christian faith and love, of what is finally perceptible to those who remain in the dying of their friends. Their recollection of the dead is rivetted to this term. The deduction that the dead are in a state of sleep is an ancient exaggeration. $Κοιμᾶσθαι$ does not mean to be asleep but to *fall* asleep. Those who have fallen asleep means those whom we saw fall asleep, and whom we now recollect as those who then fell asleep and were therefore delivered from death even in dying. Looking back on them, we really look back on Jesus Christ who, as "the first fruits of them that slept"

198

(1 Cor. 15²⁰), robbed their death of its sting and brought life and immortality to light even when they were *in extremis*ᴱᴺ²³³, so that this death could not be anything but a falling asleep. The deduction that they are now actually asleep may seem to be logical, but it has no material basis. What special revelation did the New Testament Christians enjoy to persuade them that when the departed had fallen asleep their being was one of sleep? This inference was first drawn when Christians again began to derive their knowledge (in this as in other matters) from sources other than their knowledge of Jesus Christ. The term "fall asleep" shows that the New Testament Christians never asked independently concerning the being or state of man in death, or tried to find an answer in the postulate of an intermediate state. They simply held fast to the confession: "I am the resurrection and the life," and in the light of this hope they came to see in the visible process of dying the last conclusive symptom of a life surrounded by the peace of God.

If hope in Christ is a real liberation for natural death, this rests on the fact that by divine appointment death as such belongs to the life of the creature and is thus necessary to it. Adamic man was created a ψυχὴ ζῶσα ᴱᴺ²³⁴ (1 Cor. 15⁴⁵), and therefore a being which has only its own span of time. His definitive relationship to God as the end and goal of human life demands that this life itself should be defined and therefore limited. On this limit there is made in its favour the divine decision which is the substance of the New Testament message of salvation. On this limit it was made in the life of the man Jesus. He had to die, to submit to the judgment of God and thus restore the right of God and that of man. "Except a corn of wheat fall into the ground and die, it abideth alone; but if it die, it bringeth forth much fruit" (Jn. 12²⁴). We cannot try to love and maintain finally and absolutely our life in this time; otherwise we shall lose it. We must give it up in order to save it (Mt. 16²⁵). In the harsh terms of Jn. 12²⁵ we must actually "hate" our "life in the world" in order to preserve it to eternal life. That is why Paul can also say: "Thou fool, that which thou sowest is not quickened, except it die" (1 Cor. 15³⁶). If we did not have to do with the definitive end of human life, we should not have to do with its resurrection and definitive co-existence with that of God. Anxious defiance of one's end could only mean the forfeiture of one's destiny. Since Jesus did not love His life and thus rescued our life from destruction, we are invited to accept the limit of the life which He has rescued, and therefore to acquiesce in the fact that we must have an end, and to set our hope wholly and utterly in Him.

In conclusion, however, it is worth noting that, while the New Testament reminds us of the necessity of death and exhorts us not to love our life or seek to save it, it never suggests that we ought to yearn for death or rejoice in it, even in the case of martyrdom, as often happened later. Death is never idealised or made into something heroic. That he should lose his life for Christ's sake is a possibility for which the New Testament Christian is always doubly prepared, but which he never desires or seeks, merely accepting it as a reality when it comes, [640] as Stephen did. Like life itself, the loss of it is in itself a possibility qualified only by the fact that it takes place "in the Lord." In 2 Cor. 5¹⁻¹⁰ Paul contrasts our present life in a perishable tent with the divinely prepared and eternal house with which we shall be clothed; our pilgrimage in time with our being at home in the Lord. He makes no attempt to conceal his longing and sighing for the latter. Yet he finds only a relative and not an absolute place for this desire. And from this train of thought he draws the conclusion: "Wherefore we labour, that, whether present or absent, we may be accepted of him. For we must all appear before the judgment seat of Christ; that every one may receive the things done in his body, according to that he hath done, whether it be good or bad." Again, what he says in Philippians 1²⁰ᶠ· is similar. That Christ should be glorified in his body, whether by life or death, is the prospect

---

ᴱᴺ²³³ in desperate straits
ᴱᴺ²³⁴ living soul

which elates him (παρρησία). He again makes no secret of the fact that it is better for him to die. He has "a desire to depart, and to be with Christ." This is preferable. But he again qualifies his desire. For him to live is Christ. And this, as he puts it bluntly in v. 22, is "fruit" (καρπὸς ἔργου) in His service. Though dissolution would be preferable, his "abiding in the flesh" is thus more necessary for the sake of his communities (v. 24). Faced by this dilemma, with pressing arguments on both sides, he decides in this most important passage for life rather than death. The New Testament Christian does not fear death. But he never hopes for it. He hopes for the One who has delivered him from death. It is because he hopes for Him, and expects to be with Him when he dies, that he is willing to die "gladly" like Jacob. Death is the preferable alternative. But he does not will it. He wills the life bounded by it as the sphere of the decisions in which he moves towards Christ as his Judge. He wills it as the opportunity to serve the One who will be his only hope in his end. And it is because he can already serve in his life the One who even in death will be his Lord that he rejoices in this perfect form of His lordship, in the prospect of being definitely with Him. He does not rejoice in the prospect of being freed from His service, of having his time behind him. On the contrary, the definitive prospect in which he rejoices is for him an authorisation and command to serve God in his allotted span with all the preliminary joy without which his joy in his end and new beginning with Him would be purely imaginary. He affirms Jesus Christ as his beyond. And it is for this reason that he understands his life here and now as one which is affirmed by his beyond.

INDEX OF SCRIPTURE REFERENCES

INDEX OF SUBJECTS

INDEX OF NAMES